An OPUS book

# PHILOSOPHERS AND PAMPHLETEERS

OPUS General Editors
Keith Thomas
Alan Ryan
Walter Bodmer

OPUS books provide concise, original, and authoritative introductions to a wide range of subjects in the humanities and sciences. They are written by experts for the general reader as well as for students.

# Philosophers and Pamphleteers

## *Political Theorists of the Enlightenment*

MAURICE CRANSTON

Oxford   New York
OXFORD UNIVERSITY PRESS
1986

Oxford University Press, Walton Street, Oxford OX2 6DP

Oxford New York Toronto
Delhi Bombay Calcutta Madras Karachi
Petaling Jaya Singapore Hong Kong Tokyo
Nairobi Dar es Salaam Cape Town
Melbourne Auckland

and associated companies in
Beirut Berlin Ibadan Nicosia

Oxford is a trade mark of Oxford University Press

British Library Cataloguing in Publication Data

Cranston, Maurice
Philosophers and pamphleteers: political
theorists of the Enlightenment. —— (OPUS)
1. Philosophy, French —— 18th century
I. Title  II. Series
194   B1911

ISBN 0-19-219208-6
ISBN 0-19-289189-8 Pbk

Library of Congress Cataloging in Publication Data

Cranston, Maurice William, 1920-
Philosophers and pamphleteers.
(An OPUS book)
"Based on the Carlyle lectures . . . delivered at the Univeristy of Oxford in
Trinity Term, 1984"—Pref.
Bibliography p.  Includes index.
Contents: Montesquieu—Voltaire—Rousseau—[etc].
1. Political science—France—History—18th century. 2. France—Politics and
government—18th century.
I. Title.  II. Series: OPUS.
JA84.F8C73 1986   320.5'0944   86-2517

ISBN 0-19-219208-6
ISBN 0-19-289189-8 (pbk.)

Set by Colset Private Ltd.
Printed in Great Britain by
Richard Clay (The Chaucer Press) Ltd.
Bungay, Suffolk

# Preface

This book is based on the Carlyle Lectures which I delivered at the University of Oxford in Trinity Term, 1984. I am grateful to the University for inviting me to give the series and to Nevil Johnson for making all the necessary arrangements. I am also indebted to the Warden and Fellows of Nuffield College for the hospitality extended to me for the whole of that term. My thanks are also due to the Suntory-Toyota International Centre for Research in Economics and Related Disciplines and to the Central Research Fund of the University of London for financial support towards the research on which this book is based. I owe further debts of gratitude to my research assistant, Miss Calliope Farsides, and to my secretary Mrs Paula da Gama Pinto, for their help in preparing the published text.

MAURICE CRANSTON

*London School of Economics and Political Science*

*December 1985*

# Contents

# Introduction

It is widely believed that the philosophers of the French Enlightenment were all more or less in agreement in their support of 'enlightened despotism' as the form of government that would most readily further their programme of salvation through science. Undoubtedly several eighteenth-century despots who thought of themselves as enlightened—Frederick II of Prussia, for example, and Catherine II of Russia and Joseph II of Austria—cultivated the *philosophes*, and took up some of their proposals. But very few if any of those *philosophes* themselves were champions of 'enlightened despotism'. On the contrary, the one thing they all had in common was a sincere attachment to freedom. At the same time they had very different conceptions of what 'freedom' meant, and sharply conflicting ideas about how freedom could best be instituted and preserved.

In this book I have tried to explore some of the more interesting political theories which emerged in the debate. They seem to arrange themselves into three main competing groups, the parliamentary, the royalist, and the republican, Montesquieu being the outstanding exponent of the first, Voltaire of the second, and Rousseau of the third.

Both the parliamentary and the royalist schools were inspired by English philosophy, and both regarded the English system of government as a 'mirror of liberty'. They looked, however, to different English philosophers, and they understood English government in different ways. Montesquieu and his followers drew their inspiration from Locke, and what they admired in England was the constitution established by the Revolutionary settlement of 1689. Voltaire and his friends looked rather to Francis Bacon, and what they admired in England was less its method of parliamentary government than its system of civil freedom and religious toleration. Montesquieu proposed the adaptation to the situation of France of Whiggish policies for sharing sovereignty between the executive, legislative, and judicial authorities. Voltaire aspired to realize in France the Baconian dream of the sovereignty of reason, assured by the progress of science and technology, the centralization of government, and the elimination of superstition.

Up to a point, the disagreement between Montesquieu and Voltaire reflected in eighteenth-century thought earlier, and deep-rooted, political antagonisms. Montesquieu's theory could be seen as a restatement in modern terms of the old *thèse nobiliaire*, according to which the ancient constitution of France established the king as nothing other than the first peer of the realm, subject to the law as defined by the noble magistrates of the *parlements*. Voltaire could equally be thought to be restating the old *thèse royale*, according to which the king was the author of the law, and stood above all the other estates in order to rule for the good of his kingdom as a whole.

And yet while the ideological content of Montesquieu's and Voltaire's theories was to this extent continuous with two seventeenth-century *thèses*, both philosophers developed arguments in support of their ideas which were new in themselves, and were called forth by a new situation. The seventeenth-century had witnessed the continuous expansion in France of royal absolutism at the expense of the nobility and all other intermediate estates, so that the champions of the *thèse nobiliaire* could only appeal to fading memories and a dying tradition. An event in the early eighteenth-century gave the *noblesse de robe* a totally new lease of life: the Duc d'Orléans as Regent found it necessary to convoke the *parlements* to invalidate the will of Louis XIV which would rob him of the powers he sought. Thus unexpectedly reanimated, the parliamentary estate struggled throughout the decades that followed for more and more power. In Montesquieu it produced a theorist of genius to justify such claims.

Part of the novelty of Montesquieu is that he did not argue legalistically. He introduced what came to be known to later generations as 'political sociology'. He looked for general laws of social organization which would enable an enquiring mind to ascertain what constitutional forms and political institutions would best suit a given society, and which arrangements would produce predictable effects. On the basis of these investigations, Montesquieu concluded that freedom could be most effectively preserved in a state where no organ of government could monopolize power and so become despotic. Hence his formulae for divided sovereignty, for checks and balances and the separation of the powers. The relevance of these conclusions to the situation of France was obvious.

The royalism of Voltaire and his friends was presented in no less modern terms. Voltaire, self-consciously and proudly bourgeois, did not dissimulate his personal antagonism towards aristocrats of all orders, but as a 'scientific' thinker giving the lead to the contributors to the *Encyclopédie*, he placed his emphasis on the rational case for absolutism. Bacon, invoked by both Diderot and d'Alembert, the editors of the *Encyclopédie*, as the prophet of their enterprise, had provided them with a double message—first the inauguration of scientific programmes for the improvement of men's life on earth, and then the introduction of a centralized government to put those programmes into effect, a government such as only a powerful monarch, unencumbered by churchmen and law courts and parliaments, could be expected to provide. As a rule, the Enlightenment stood for reason; and while other, more 'old-fashioned' champions of absolutism appealed to tradition, the *encyclopédistes* were eager to put reason on the side of the monarch's claim to a monopoly of power.

'Enlightened despotism' is an unfair name for what Voltaire and his followers had in mind when they called for enlightened absolutism; for they combined with their adherence to the Baconian political design a liberal or Lockian belief in the natural rights of the individual to life, liberty, and property. Montesquieu wrote for the *Encyclopédie*, and he was acknowledged by the younger *philosophes* as Voltaire's equal as a patriarchal theorist of the Enlightenment; but in the 1750s, when the first volumes of the *Encyclopédie* were published, few of its contributors had any sympathy for the claims of the parliamentary estate which Montesquieu represented. When Louis XV banished the Paris *parlement* in 1753 to make way for a royal court, the *encyclopédistes* made no protest. They were more concerned just then to reform the Paris theatre and French music, a revolution in taste being seen as a step towards a revolution in thought.

It was about this time that there emerged the third main strand in Enlightenment political thought, a *thèse républicaine*, so to speak, as an alternative to the modernized forms both of the *thèse royale* and of the *thèse nobiliaire*. Its most important exponent,

Rousseau, was at the time an intimate friend of Diderot and an active contributor to the pages of the *Encyclopédie*. His republicanism was as rationalistic in its formulation as was the parliamentarianism of Montesquieu and the royalism of the *Voltairiens*. To a certain extent, moreover, it had been anticipated in the early writings of Montesquieu himself. But Montesquieu's vision of republican virtue had been derived from reading about the republics of Antiquity; it did not stand the test of experience, on which, as a scientifically minded man, he knew he must rely.

Rousseau, on the other hand, drew his republican inspiration from the modern world, from the city-state of Geneva where he had been born and bred. Until he was well over 40, he did not look below the surface of the liberal Genevan constitution to discern the ruthless domination of a hereditary patriciate. His model republic was Geneva as Calvin had designed it in the sixteenth century, not as it had become in Rousseau's lifetime, but he based his argument on the experience of an actual city, he adopted the stance of a political scientist, and he depicted his model with such eloquence that a republican state became a living and potent ideal in the eighteenth-century imagination.

Montesquieu's Whiggish theory, temporarily out of fashion when he died in 1755, re-emerged a few years later, when the King's ministers at Versailles took more drastic action against the *parlements*. The *encyclopédistes* then split into somewhat bitterly opposing camps; some, such as Holbach and Diderot, restated Montesquieu's arguments for divided sovereignty as the only defence against despotism, while others, led by Voltaire, urged the King to resist the claims of the reactionary *parlements* and clergy and exercise his authority alone.

The success of the American Revolution in the 1770s prompted a new excitement around the idea of republican government. Condorcet, the youngest of the great *encyclopédistes*, corresponded with several American intellectuals, developing ideas about the kind of constitution which a republic the size of the United States could best adopt. Republican government need no longer be exclusively associated in the European mind with the Greek city-states or the cantons of the Swiss confederation. Rousseau's claim that no large state could be genuinely republican was being refuted by events. Republicanism could, after what had happened in America, be contemplated as an option for France.

The French Enlightenment exalted the noble savage; Rousseau was not the first or the only *philosophe* to suggest that the half-naked inhabitants of the North American forests or the South Pacific islands were as intelligent as, and indeed morally superior to the sophisticated denizens of European cities. The explorer Bougainville had suggested it—and dozens of fashionable writers besides Rousseau asserted it; Diderot and Raynal went even further and proposed that the European rulers should leave the 'noble savages' in undisturbed possession of their homelands, neither invading them with armies like the Spanish nor corrupting them with commerce like the Dutch.

Other voices in the Enlightenment adhered to the strict Baconian ideology of progress. The spread of trade, industry, and modern medicine into the continents beyond Europe was welcomed and encouraged as part of the conquest of nature, the triumph of science over ignorance. In place of missionaries carrying bibles, such *philosophes* envisaged technologists carrying the benefits of European civilization to savages whose very nobility would preserve them from the evils of European corruption.

Faith in the innocence of the exotic savage did not go together with any confidence in the simple people of the lower classes at home. Rousseau and Voltaire extolled the democratic elements in the Genevan constitution, but that was only because a system of universal public instruction had made the working class of Geneva an educated class. As a general rule, Rousseau favoured popular participation in legislation, but not in government; and Voltaire did not wish even universal education, let alone democracy, to be extended to France. If there was an exponent of democracy among the *encyclopédistes* it was Condorcet, but even he proposed the limiting of the people's role in politics to voting for representatives, who in turn would ensure that the making of laws and policies was confined to persons of superior intellect. The expert was an ever-present figure in Enlightenment political thought, a simplified version of Plato's philosopher-magistrate; and in Condorcet's writings the conception of democracy is fused with the idea of a cultured and public-spirited civil service running the state for the good of everyone, an ideal which, if Tocqueville's analysis of the *ancien régime* is correct, was not far removed from the self-image of the bourgeois bureaucracy which served the Bourbon kings.

Voltaire, in his celebrated novel *Candide*, mocked optimism, but the Enlightenment itself was an age of optimism. Although the Lisbon earthquake of 1755 shattered belief in a benevolent Deity, nothing seemed able to modify the *encyclopédistes'* faith in progress, their belief in the future being better than the past. Even Helvétius, who conceived of man as a sort of machine built to a standard pattern, looked forward to continued improvement; and Condorcet himself, awaiting arrest by agents of the Terror in 1794, proclaimed the inevitable approach of human perfection.

Yet none of the *philosophes* offered much in the way of rational grounds for their optimism. Predictions of improvement in the future might be expected to find among empiricists a basis in evidence of improvements in the past. But much of the literature of the Enlightenment depicts the past history of man as a history of decay. Rousseau declared that man was naturally good, only to add that man's long experience since he had left the state of nature was one of increasing corruption. Condorcet said the human race was moving stage by stage upwards towards perfection, yet he depicted the achievements of Classical Antiquity being succeeded by a thousand years of darkness and retrogression.

At odds with one another in their theories of politics, the *philosophes* were no less divided in their views on economics. Again, they often looked to English theorists for their inspiration, but some followed the mercantilist teaching of Locke, others the doctrine of free trade. François Quesnay, founder of the physiocratic school, was the most important of the latter. He argued that each man was motivated by self-interest, but that the natural law of harmony enabled unfettered private activity to generate the public good. Paradoxically, most of the physiocrats favoured at the same time the Voltairean policy of enlightened absolutism; they wanted *laissez-faire* in economics, but *dirigisme* in politics, if only as a means of abolishing traditional entrenched restraints on commerce. The failure in practice of the free-trade policies adopted by the government of Louis XV in the 1760s to serve the interest of anyone except rapacious dealers prompted several philosophers of the Enlightenment—notably Galiani, Diderot, and Holbach—to argue for state control of the economy; while others—Turgot, Morellet, and Mercier de la Rivière among them—reaffirmed the physiocratic case for economic freedom.

Luxury was a subject much discussed in the course of this debate, and once more the *philosophes* disagreed among themselves. The champions of luxury argued that it was a motor of industrial progress, increasing both consumption and the quality of goods produced. The opponents held that it diverted industry from the production of things needed by everyone to the production of useless objects for the amusement of the favoured few. Some tried to separate their economic theory from considerations of morality; some suggested that moral considerations need cause no concern. Greed, avarice, envy were even welcomed on the grounds that they stimulated the economy by spurring men to action.

Rousseau was the most eloquent of those who attacked luxury, but he was by no means alone. Diderot added a certain bitterness to his moral indignation at the rich being encouraged in their self-indulgence while the poor were left to starve. Even Holbach, who lived in luxury, denounced the doctrine of luxury. Some critics carried the attack to the point of challenging private property itself; one was the Abbé Mably in a critique of the physiocrats published in 1768, *Doutes proposés aux philosophes économistes*; another was the author of the *Code de la nature*, commonly ascribed, on slender evidence, to the Abbé Morelly. These books were of small importance in the context of the Enlightenment, but they were later recognized as forerunners of the distinctively nineteenth-century theory of socialism.

One tendency conspicuously absent from the political theory of the French Enlightenment is conservatism. One might have expected, as Holbach feared, that scepticism in the fields of religion and philosophy would lead to scepticism in matters of political and social reform and so encourage a conservative outlook. But there was in fact no systematic conservative thought in the French Enlightenment like that of David Hume in the Scottish Enlightenment or that of Alexander Hamilton in the American Enlightenment. This is an indication of the universality of discontent in France. Hume and Hamilton were, after all, post-revolutionary theorists—Hume in the situation established in the British Isles by the settlement of 1689 and Hamilton in that established in America by the War of Independence; both could be conservatives because both had something—namely liberty—to conserve. The theorists of the French Enlightenment had no such motive; if they differed among themselves in their understanding of liberty, they agreed in thinking that liberty was something they did not yet have. Even the enemies of the Enlightenment, the Jesuits and other intellectual equals of the *encyclopédistes*, did not want to keep existing institutions as they were; they wished either to recover what had been lost or to go forward to a different future from that envisaged by the *philosophes*. Moreover this dissatisfaction with the present that was expressed by theorists of all kinds and persuasions reflected something felt by the less articulate members of all ranks and estates in society. And yet if reform was universally desired, the lack of any shared purpose or ideas or any agreed programme for positive change only made reform the more unlikely to succeed and a revolution, if it happened, unlikely to endure.

# 1
# Montesquieu

The Enlightenment as a moment in history could perhaps be said to date from the publication in 1721 of Montesquieu's *Les Lettres persanes*. The style of this work is characteristic of the new spirit as is the content: satirical, witty, urbane, irreverent, expressing deeply held beliefs in an amusing, frivolous, even a flippant way. The central themes of the Enlightenment are registered: condemnation of persecution and cruelty, mockery of religion, praise of liberty, and a barely concealed assertion that France is in dire need of salvation from despotism, superstition, and decay.

The argument is presented in the guise of a series of letters sent from France by two Persian visitors, Usbek and Rica. The device enabled Montesquieu to circumvent the censorship, pretending to be a foreigner feigning surprise at things with which the French were only too familiar. His Persians begin by remarking on such strange customs of the French as cutting off their natural hair and putting on wigs, and reversing the oriental habit of giving trousers to women and skirts to men. They go on to express delicate amazement at more serious things. They describe Louis XIV as a 'magician' who 'made people kill one another, even when they had no quarrel', a king who had 'a minister of eighteen and a mistress of eighty', a pious monarch who contrived 'to increase the proportion of the faithful by diminishing the number of his subjects'. Usbek and Rica write also of another 'conjurer' called the Pope, 'who makes people believe that three are only one; that wine is not wine and bread not bread', a gentle Christian 'who has people tortured and burned to death if they disagree with him on matters of the utmost triviality'.

*Les Lettres persanes* was published in Amsterdam, and became an immediate and enormous success in France. The author was aged 32 and it was his first book to be printed; there was no name on the title-page, but his identity was soon discovered, and he was lionized in society. The only penalty he suffered was to have his election to the Académie Française delayed by Cardinal Fleury.

Like Montaigne,[1] with whom he had much else in common, Montesquieu was a native of Guyenne. He was born Charles-Louis Secondat in 1689—a fitting date for a man who was to become a great champion in France of the English idea of constitutional monarchy, the nearest French equivalent to a Whig; for while most of the other French philosophers of the Enlightenment praised the English constitution, Montesquieu was the only one who made anything like a serious study of it, and drew from it inspiration for his political ideas.

In *Les Lettres persanes* his thoughts on politics are suggested, adumbrated rather than systematically expressed; where he does speak categorically and plainly is where he describes the *parlements* of France as the image of public liberty. For Montesquieu was a *parlementaire* himself, born into the legal aristocracy or *noblesse de robe*, although he also claimed descent from the ancient landed aristocracy, or *noblesse de race*.[2] After receiving the relatively progressive education provided by the Oratorians at Juilly, and pursuing studies in law in Bordeaux and Paris, he became a *conseiller* of the *parlement* of Guyenne at Bordeaux at the age of 25. He had already inherited, on the death of his father, the moated and battlemented château of La Brède together with a modest income. But as Montesquieu was not a man to be content with a modest income, he quickly married a bride with a handsome dowry, undeterred by the fact that she was a Protestant and very plain. It was a *mariage de raison*, and, in the event, not altogether rational; for a few months afterwards, he became rich on his own account. In April 1716, an uncle died, bequeathing him not only all his property but with it, as was possible under French law, the title of Baron de Montesquieu and the office of *président à mortier*[3]—or executive president—of the same *parlement* at Bordeaux where he was already a *conseiller*.

The *parlements* of France had nothing in common with Parliament as known in England. They were 'sovereign courts of law' with the duty—and the right—of approving and registering legislation enacted by the king's government at Versailles; they were not legislative chambers, but, as the Estates-General of France had not been allowed to meet for more than a century, they had assumed a distinct political significance as the one institution which mitigated the absolute power of the Crown. Montesquieu's

Persians in *Les Lettres persanes* note that the *parlements* had allowed their authority to languish under Louis XIV, but had been brought to life in 1715 by the Regent. As Usbek puts it: 'the Regent wanted the *parlements* to be regarded as the support of the monarchy and the foundation of all legitimate authority'.[4] One may doubt that the Regent did want this; but it was what Montesquieu, the advocate of the rights of *parlements*, thought the Regent ought to want.

The prestige of his office in the *parlement* at Bordeaux gave Montesquieu as much pleasure as did the income, and he was known for the rest of his life as 'le Président' rather than by the more commonplace title of 'le Baron'. But the job bored him. He took more interest in writing for the Academy of Bordeaux papers on scientific subjects such as 'The causes of the echo', 'The diseases of the renal glands', and 'The ebb and flow of tides'.[5] In court he grew restless. Realizing that he had not the temperament of a magistrate, he turned from law to jurisprudence, then to a kind of political science in which legal philosophy and political philosophy were merged, and added to it what is nowadays called 'political sociology'. The successor to Aristotle was also the forerunner of Auguste Comte and Durkheim, with the rather puzzling way of being empirical in philosophy and speculative in sociology when one might expect it to be the other way round.

A charge levelled by critics in a long line from Voltaire to Louis Althusser[6] and Dean Franklin Ford[7] is that Montesquieu's political science is really ideology—an elaboration of the claims of the French aristocracy, and specifically the *noblesse de robe*, to be the legislators of the kingdom. This does not diminish Montesquieu's right to be considered a philosopher. If he turned to political theory because he was troubled by the political events of his time and by the direction in which he saw his country moving, similar concerns could be said to have prompted the excursions into political theory of Bodin, Hobbes, Locke, Hegel, or Mill, and indeed of all the best political philosophers.

Once Montesquieu had found his true *métier* as a writer,[8] he decided to move to Paris, the only place in France where a man could lead the literary life. At La Brède he had a fine library, and he might easily have devoted his life to scholarship without leaving home. But Montesquieu was too much the empiricist to do that; knowledge of the world was to be discovered in the world rather than in books. So he left his château and his vineyards, to which he was deeply attached, and his wife, whom he loved perhaps less intensely, to improve his mind and enjoy his fame in Paris as the author of *Les Lettres persanes*.

He soon made himself popular in the places where reputations were made, in the *salons* of Paris, as a favourite of fashionable hostesses. Although there are no recorded examples of his wit, he was always said to shine in conversation. Perhaps the secret of his success is to be found in one of the Persian letters: the way to earn the reputation of a good conversationalist, Usbek suggests, is to listen silently to what other people say and laugh heartily at their jokes.[9]

Montesquieu was not too fastidious to sample the dissipated pleasures afforded by Madame de Prie, the Messalina of the age,[10] but a more serious centre of friendship and conversation for him was the Club de l'Entresol, organized by the Abbé Alary. Its leading figure was the Abbé de Saint-Pierre,[11] who has some claim to importance as a political theorist in his own right, and was certainly one of the most forceful critics of royal absolutism in late seventeenth- and early eighteenth-century France; he had been expelled from the Académie Française for some ungracious words about Louis XIV in one of his books.[12] The Club de l'Entresol was eventually closed down by Cardinal Fleury, but while it lasted it did much to nourish Montesquieu's interest in political theory and to stimulate what one may call, however anachronistically, his liberalism.

By this time Montesquieu had overcome Cardinal Fleury's opposition and secured election at the age of 38 to the Académie Française, largely on the strength of the literary merits of a book which made fun of the Académie Française together with much else that was supposed to be held in respect in France. He was saved by his amusing style, even as the Abbé de Saint-Pierre had been ruined by his earnestness. Montesquieu had taken care in *Les Lettres persanes* to mock his own profession of law and the legal system at the same time as the other French institutions. 'How extraordinary', says the Persian visitor about France's adherence to Roman law, 'that the oldest and most powerful kingdom in Europe should be governed for ten centuries by laws made by others. You would think the French were a conquered people.'[13] He shows no more respect for the Church: 'Religion, which one would assume to be intended to please God, is here simply a matter of quarrels between men, and the more absurd the subject the more violent their passions. Religion draws its fire from the triviality of the material.'[14] As for the morals of the French, Montesquieu's Usbek observes that a husband who wants to monopolize the favours of his wife is regarded as ridiculous in Paris, 'a disturber of the public pleasure, a selfish fellow who wants to enjoy the sun to the exclusion of all other men'.[15] Even Louis XIV is mocked: 'Is it not amazing to find in France a monarch completely dominated by women at an age where you would think he had the least use for women?'[16]

And yet *Les Lettres persanes* is not all epigrams. A story Montesquieu tells, as a fable, in the early chapters of the book offers us an entry into his political thought. This is the Myth of the Troglodytes as related by Usbek. The Troglodytes, we are told, were a community of primitive men so wicked and cruel that they had no principles whatever of equity or justice. At one time they had a stern foreign king who tried to discipline them, but they killed him, and appointed magistrates from their own race as rulers, only to massacre them in turn. Finally the Troglodytes decided to do without any ruler at all, and live in total anarchy, each man looking after his own interests and taking no care of anyone else. Then misfortune came. Half the land was afflicted with drought, and since those who had crops refused to share them with those who had none, half the population died of hunger. Next the other part of the land was submerged by floods, and the victims looked in vain to their neighbours for help. The survivors stole each other's women and possessions; revenge was exacted; and in the end almost everyone 'perished through their very wickedness, victims of their own injustice'.[17]

However, the story continues, two virtuous Troglodytes survived, and with their families they started a new community. Since all its members were just, always putting the common good before private interest, and filled with love for their neighbours, their society prospered. Children who were brought up in the principles of justice grew to be as virtuous as their fathers. They honoured the gods. They lived simple rustic lives; cupidity was unknown among them; they defended their country gladly because it was their own.

'The time came', Usbek continues, 'when because their numbers were increasing daily, the Troglodytes thought it proper to choose a king.'[18] They offered the throne to the wisest of their number, who accepted it, weeping. They asked the reason for his tears. Once the people had a king, he explained, they would no longer need to be virtuous, because the community would no longer depend for its existence on its citizens being altruistic, frugal and totally devoted to the public good. All they would need to be was law-abiding subjects of their king. 'Providing you avoid crimes, you will not need virtue.'[19]

The interest of the Myth of the Troglodytes is that it introduces us to Montesquieu the republican; for the moral of the tale is plain—a republic is morally superior to a kingdom, because it needs virtue in its citizens, whereas a kingdom needs only obedience in its subjects.[20] Other early writings of Montesquieu have the same ideological tendency. He says that the best government is 'that which is most conformable to reason' or 'that which leads men in a way which best suits their disposition',[21] but his praise is reserved for states with republican constitutions. For example, on the subject of population he writes:

Moderation in government contributes wonderfully to the propagation of the species. All republics are a constant proof of this, above all, Switzerland and Holland, which are the two poorest countries in Europe in terms of habitable land, but are the most populous . . . Equality between citizens, which usually generates equality of fortunes, brings abundance and life into all parts of the body politic and spreads everywhere.[22]

Freedom is also associated with republican government. In *Les Lettres persanes* the English are described as being less submissive to their kings than are the subjects of other European monarchs, but this is simply ascribed to their 'impatient temperament', an early instance of Montesquieu writing as a political sociologist. There is nothing in this book or elsewhere to suggest that Montesquieu was disposed at this period of his life to admire the political system of the English.

His admiration for republics seems to have originated in the study of history and to have been in large part an admiration for the abstract concept of republican government. When he wrote in praise of Switzerland and Holland in his early works he had not actually visited either of those countries; he had only read about them. He had, however, been educated in a way which disposed him to idealize any republic. It is one of the paradoxes of the *ancien régime* in France that its best schools and colleges, in teaching the history, literature, and philosophy of the ancient world, exalted the values of the city-states and republics of Greece and Rome at the expense of those of modern kingdoms. The priests who ran those schools might be suspected of seeking to thwart the encroachments of modern kings on the Church by deliberately promoting nostalgia for ancient republics; although by doing so, the priests also encouraged an admiration for ancient religion, a revival of paganism, which was to prove ruinous to their own hold on people's minds and to the authority of the Church.

Montesquieu's friends in the Club de l'Entresol, even those who were *abbés*, had no more tenderness for the Church than they had for the Crown, and their praise for ancient republics was chiefly intended to communicate denigration of both these modern institutions. And yet Montesquieu himself undoubtedly had as a young man a sincere belief in the inherent merits of the republican ideal, and he began his investigation into the political systems of modern Europe by setting out to see for himself how republican governments worked in practice.

Once he had secured his election to the Académie Française—which had entailed fixed residence in Paris—he felt free to travel. In the year 1728, while Voltaire was meditating on the nature of civil liberty in exile in England, Montesquieu left France to study the politics of republican states in Italy.[23] He was soon disillusioned. The 'virtue' which he had described in *Les Lettres persanes* as being essential to any republic was nowhere to be found.

Venice, he conceded, was a handsome city, but he was appalled by both its politics and its morals. The people, he discovered, were 'patient, submissive and down-trodden'.[24] The senators thought only of their private interests, and the power of the Jesuits was everywhere in evidence. Pleasure was the people's consolation for the want of a genuinely republican government. As for liberty, he wrote:

In Venice you enjoy only the kind of freedom that decent people would not want to have—freedom to go in broad daylight to visit prostitutes, or even to marry one of them; to be excused Easter communion; freedom to be entirely anonymous and independent in your actions—*voilà la liberté que l'on y a.*[25]

In short, Montesquieu judged the government of Venice to be thoroughly corrupt. The republic of Lucca shocked him less, but even there he found a population in decline, and a system of government by a patrician class, membership of which was secured by purchase; among 22,000 inhabitants, four or five hundred families belonged to the ruling nobility. He concluded, as he wrote in his *Pensées*, that 'No republic too small can be free.'[26] One thing Montesquieu noted with respect in Lucca was that its citizens, for all their poverty, contributed liberally to the public treasury. In the republic of Genoa, he found the reverse situation: rich individuals and an impoverished state—in fact a republic without any civic spirit whatever. 'The Genoans', he wrote, 'are completely unsocial—and this character comes less from their uncultured nature than from their supreme avarice.'[27] Montesquieu, who always disapproved of the aristocracy engaging in commerce, was scandalized to find that the noblemen of Genoa were so dedicated to trade that in their marble palaces—marble only because marble was cheap in the neighbourhood—the first three floors were put to use as shops and warehouses. 'The Doge is the first merchant of the city.'[28] Money was everything in Genoa, and 'all of this produces the most ignoble souls in the world in spite of their being the most vain'.[29]

Often accused of parsimony himself, Montesquieu was extremely sensitive to the meanness of others. When he left Italy to visit the greatest republic of northern Europe, the Netherlands, he was to meet avarice on a scale that stunned him; here, he protested, if someone in the street tells you how to find your way he will ask to be paid.[30]

Montesquieu liked the look of the Dutch cities, and even considered Amsterdam more beautiful than Venice, but he found nothing to admire in the Dutch people; he called them stingy, grasping, and dishonest,[31] corrupt in their hearts,[32] and stupid in their heads.[33] Their political system reflected their moral character: 'Holland is a republic with two kings—the mayors, who hand out all the patronage . . . and the common people, who constitute the most insolent tyrant you could possibly have.'[34]

Montesquieu had not one good word either for the system of administration or for the holders of public office: 'The misfortune of this republic', he wrote, 'is that corruption is so entrenched that the magistrates take bribes from anyone who receives a contract from the state, with the result that a man who becomes a *député* or mayor already has his fortune made.'[35]

Montesquieu suggested that one reason for the avarice of the Dutch was that they were so weighed down with taxes that they had to grasp money by whatever means they could, chiefly by rapacity or theft. 'A Dutchman', he wrote, 'could die at the age of 80 without having done a single good deed.'[36] The only man Montesquieu found really estimable in Holland was the Earl of Chesterfield, the British Ambassador, and it was at the suggestion of Lord Chesterfield that he arranged in 1729 to visit England. After he had studied several republics, he felt it was time to study a kingdom. He went with an open mind: 'When I visit a country, I do not enquire whether it has good laws, but whether it executes the laws it has, because there are good laws everywhere.'[37]

In England Montesquieu found all the things he had looked for in vain in the republics of the Continent: civil liberties and religious toleration, an established Church proclaiming a minimal creed, a flourishing commerce, a monarchy which shared its sovereignty with Parliament, and a Parliament where the Upper House was composed of noblemen like himself. In short, Montesquieu discovered that the English system of constitutional monarchy succeeded better than any republic he had seen in achieving the objective of a republic, which was to combine liberty with law and enable a civil society to rule itself. The ideal which Montesquieu had derived from books did not stand up to the test of experience; he left France at the age of 39 a republican; he returned three years later a champion of constitutional monarchy *à l'anglaise*.[38]

He was by no means uncritical in his judgement of the English. He felt that the aristocracy had undermined the standing of its class by engaging in trade, and that there was far too much corruption in Parliament. 'Money is highly esteemed here; honour and virtue little.'[39] Sometimes he would lose his patience with the English: 'they don't deserve their freedom—they would sell it to the King; and if he gave it back, they would sell it again'.[40] He found it impossible to make a friend in London, he said.[41] But compared to the Dutch, the English seemed to Montesquieu to be an exemplary race: 'In London there is liberty and equality. The liberty of London is the liberty of gentlemen . . . as the equality of London is the equality of gentlemen. In this it differs from the liberty of Holland, which is the liberty of the rabble.'[42]

For the most part, Montesquieu chose to compare the English with the French, rather than the wretched Dutch. He noted that while the English paid very few compliments, they were never rude;[43] and that while the French did extraordinary things to spend money, the English did them to gain it;[44] that the English had more pride than vanity, while the French had more vanity than pride;[45] unlike the French, the English were insolent as a nation, but modest as individuals;[46] genuine, open, even indiscreet, but hating to be deceived; a people who liked simplicity and decency, respecting talent and free from jealousy.[47] His judgement is summed up in this paragraph from his *Voyages in Europe*:

England is at present the most free country in the world, not excepting any republic. I call it free because the king has not the power to do any imaginable harm, since his power is controlled and limited by statute. If the Lower House became master, its power would be limitless and dangerous, because it would then have executive power as well; instead of which at present full sovereignty is vested in Parliament and the king and executive power in the king, whose power is limited.[48]

Montesquieu believed he had discovered in England the secret of maintaining liberty:[49] and that secret was to have a divided sovereignty with countervailing forces operating between the different centres of power. He expressed the principle in these words: 'Political liberty is found only in those states where power is not abused; for it is the universal experience that every man who has power tends to abuse it. In order that no man shall abuse his power, it is necessary for things to be so arranged that power checks power.'[50]

Montesquieu developed this principle into a doctrine which has had a great influence in the world, and with which his name is always associated: the doctrine of the separation of the powers, that is, the separation of the institutions of government into the legislative, the executive, and the judiciary. It is a common criticism of Montesquieu that he misunderstood the constitution of England in thinking such separation of powers existed in that kingdom, where, in fact, the legislative and the executive and judiciary were *not* separate, since the king drew his ministers from Parliament and appointed his judges on the recommendation of his ministers. But Montesquieu's concern was less the absolute independence of the three institutions in their forms than their ability to check and balance one another in their actions; it was less the separation than the division of the powers that mattered, since it provided a permanent impediment to monopoly.

At the age of 42, Montesquieu left England to go home to his château at La Brède, where he promptly remodelled his French garden in the style of a *jardin anglais*, plunged into the study of English authors, and set to work on the preparation of his untidy masterpiece, *L'Esprit des lois*, beginning with what finally appeared as chapter 6 of Book XI on the constitution of England 'plus anglophile que jamais'.[51]

His years of wandering were now over. At La Brède he settled down to a life of thinking and writing in what Professor Starobinski calls 'la grande paix des bibliothèques.'[52] He had now a large enough income from his estates to live at leisure and buy all the books he wanted. The wife who had brought him such a handsome dowry had a fortunate Calvinist taste for frugality, and spent nothing on herself. Montesquieu passed on as little as he could to his daughter. And although he wrote disapprovingly of noblemen engaging in commerce, he took an active part in the management of his vineyards and wineries. He was noted for being rigorous in the collection of even the smallest debts and being slow to pay money he owed to others. In Paris he had had a reputation for parsimony; it was remarked that 'he never ate at his own table'. In the country he became no more generous. His guests at La Brède were struck by what they politely called the 'plainness' of the fare. Montesquieu once said to his grandson 'la fortune est un état et non pas un bien'. He made sure his daughter married her cousin so that the estate at La Brède should remain in the family.[53] His descendants still own it.

Since Montesquieu has so often been called the ideologue of the aristocracy, it is only fair to point out that he did not magnify, in his analysis of the English Parliament, the powers of the House of Lords. On the contrary, he supposed that the Upper House had no right to introduce legislation, but only that of correcting legislative measures emanating from the Commons. Parliament, as he imagined it, was divided into a Lower Chamber with the *faculté de statuer* and an Upper Chamber with the *faculté d'empêcher*, and he praised this arrangement as an example of one power countervailing another, and thus maintaining freedom.

*L'Esprit des lois* took Montesquieu twenty years to write,[54] and he had it published in Geneva in 1748 against the advice of all the friends to whom he had shown the manuscript.[55] It was placed on the Index, but it sold twenty-two impressions in two years,[56] in spite of its cost and its length: there were no less than 1,100 pages in the first edition. Its success is not altogether surprising, for the author of *Les Lettres persanes* had lost none of his cunning as a literary stylist, and *L'Esprit des lois* is perhaps the most readable work of political theory ever written.

If the construction of the book falls short of French, or Cartesian, ideals of systematic form, it has perhaps, like the *jardin anglais* Montesquieu so much admired, a hidden design and devious naturalness, which enables the author to insinuate thoughts into the mind of the reader without appearing too obviously the advocate. An example of this is Montesquieu's revision of the Classical taxonomy of constitutions. Instead of the familiar categories of monarchy, aristocracy, and democracy, corresponding to rule by the one, the few, and the many, Montesquieu divides constitutions into republics, monarchies, and despotisms, explaining that a republic, which may be either democratic or aristocratic, is a state where the people, or a section of them, retain sovereignty, that a monarchy is a state where a single person governs according to fixed and known laws, and that a despotism is a state where a single person governs arbitrarily.

This classification of constitutions is not often considered an improvement on Aristotle in terms of clarity; for the difference between a monarch and a despot is usually seen as a matter of degree rather than of kind; and if democracies and aristocracies, which can be distinguished by objective criteria, are put in the same category, it seems peculiar to separate despots from monarchs, since one is only a corrupt version of the other, and even such a fervent royalist as Voltaire said that monarchs and despots are two brothers between whom it is hard to distinguish.

But for Montesquieu this distinction between the monarch and the despot was the most important distinction political science had to make. Once he had lost his republican illusions, the difference between a democratic and an aristocratic republic seemed to him of small importance compared to the difference between despotic and constitutional monarchy—which was, as he saw it, increasingly coming to be the difference between France and England. The criterion he invoked was freedom: freedom, by definition, was negated by despotism, whereas Montesquieu's message was that a monarchy made constitutional could assure freedom, and reconcile it with law.

In Montesquieu's taxonomy of governments, each system has what he calls its 'principle': the principle of a republic is virtue; that of a monarchy is honour; that of a despotism is fear. Montesquieu does not glamorize honour; he depicts it as springing from ambition, and so he can say that 'Ambition is pernicious in a republic, but it has good effects in a monarchy, where it animates the government.'[57] Honour, in other words, springs from a desire for public glory and achievement, and where honour is the dominant value, men seek no further reward for their services to the state beyond recognition of their actions.[58] Montesquieu adds: 'Honour can inspire the finest deeds; and joined to the force of the laws, it can serve the ends of government no less than does virtue itself.'[59]

It is interesting to compare Montesquieu's remarks on the subject of self-love with those of Mandeville[60] and Adam Smith; for the economists of the British Enlightenment, the self-regarding desire of the individual to increase his private wealth leads, through the felicitous workings of an invisible hand, to the enlargement of the public good. In Montesquieu's account of royal government, the individual's desire to earn the admiration of others serves in a similar way the interest of the kingdom as a whole.

Honour, then, is something less pure and demanding than virtue, and a monarchy is correspondingly more accessible to human frailty than is a republic. In a way, the argument of *L'Esprit des lois* picks up that of *Les Lettres persanes* about virtue being the essential characteristic of the republican citizen;

but no tears are now shed over the passage from the republic to the kingdom: on the contrary, the republic is now seen as something Utopian, too ideal to be practicable. The republic is an extreme conception. Monarchy is a moderate conception, the golden mean between the impossible purity of a republic and the intolerable tyranny of a despot. The adjective 'moderate' has become one of Montesquieu's favourite words of praise.[61]

His classification of the three regimes is designed to make monarchy stand out as the most desirable system of government from the point of view of a political science which looks more to facts than to forms. And when he turns from theory to survey the world around him, much as Aristotle did in his time, to classify the constitution of existing states, Montesquieu is able to point to very few republics, in his sense of 'republic', and to monarchies vastly outnumbered by despotisms.

The main reason why despotisms are so numerous, he suggests, is that despotism is the easiest form of government to institute and maintain; 'passions', he says, 'are all that is needed to set up a despotism and keep it going; whereas in the case of a moderate government it is necessary to combine powers, to regulate and temper them, to activate them'. A moderate regime, he adds, 'is a masterpiece of legislation which chance seldom brings about and which prudence is seldom allowed to bring about'.[62]

A 'moderate constitution' is, in effect, Montesquieu's alternative name for a constitutional monarchy,[63] since, as a result of the way in which he has designed his classification of governments, it emerges as the *only* moderate system, both republics and despotisms being defined as extreme forms. The republic is extreme not only because it is Utopian; it is equally extreme (and this is something not suggested in the Myth of the Troglodytes) in being a regime without freedom. There is no freedom in the republic according to the analysis provided in *L'Esprit des lois* because sovereignty in a republic is undivided, either held entirely by the aristocratic body or held entirely by the democratic body. For Montesquieu there can be freedom only where sovereignty is not monopolized by one power, but is divided between several which can each check the others. With arguments thus formulated, Montesquieu depicts the republic not only as something unattainable by men of inadequate virtue, but as a system of government which is not the most desirable in any case.

He also deploys his theory of constitutions very skilfully so as to attack the existing regime in a devious way. His method is to specify as wholly suitable to despotism, and wholly unsuitable to monarchy, all sorts of practices that were standard at the time in France. An example of this is the use of torture, which had not only been employed for many years in France, but had been formally authorized by a criminal ordinance of Louis XIV in 1670. Montesquieu does not condemn torture with the bitter angry eloquence of Voltaire. His touch is lighter. The law, he points out, has from necessity to do many absurd things. Since men are so often liars, the law does not condemn a prisoner on the testimony of one witness; instead it does so on the testimony of two, as if two lies could yield a truth. Since women are apt to be seduced by gallantry, all children born in wedlock are counted as legitimate by the law, as if all wives were necessarily faithful. Such illogical procedures in the administration of the law are born of necessity. But what is the necessity that justifies torture? England enforces her laws successfully without torture, and so do other civilized monarchies. And if a cruel technique is proved by experience to be unnecessary, what reason can there be for employing it?

Montesquieu has one answer to this question. Torture can be useful to a despot; because the ruling principle of despotism is fear. But even here, he stops himself finding any justification whatever for torture: 'I hear the voice of nature cry out against me.'[64] He contents himself with saying that moderate penalties are suited to a monarchy and severe penalties to a despotism. Just because the principle of a monarchy is honour, disgrace in such a community is more effective than physical punishment as a penalty; and any state where punishment is not felt to be a disgrace is bound to be a tyranny. As a general rule, Montesquieu points to moderation in criminal penalties as a sure sign of a free government and the measure of its moderation in all things. And although he does not condemn capital punishment altogether, he argues for its use to be restricted to the most serious crimes—and not applied, as it was under the *ancien régime*, indiscriminately to two hundred different crimes. Applied equally to robbery and to robbery with murder, for example, hanging failed to deter a criminal from adding murder to robbery. Capital punishment was justified only when necessary as 'social surgery'.

Yet Montesquieu did not propose to eliminate punishment entirely in favour of remedial techniques. He pleaded rather for minimal penalties, and for punishment 'to fit the crime'. He also suggested that clemency was especially appropriate to a monarchy. Since a king, by definition, was a ruler who needed to be loved, clemency would be useful to him as a means of winning love. A despot, by contrast, being by definition a ruler who needed to be feared, would have no use for clemency.

Montesquieu in his role as a political sociologist seems some of the time in *L'Esprit des lois* to want to replace the Christian view of history as the unfolding of God's design with a theory of history as a succession of effects produced by antecedent causes. But he resisted the notion that a scientific approach to history entails determinism. He believed that God existed, and that God had given men free will. 'Could anything be more absurd', he demands, 'than to believe that a blind fatality produced intelligent beings?'[65] Assuredly God has laid down laws which govern the physical universe, and 'man, as a physical being, is governed by innumerable laws'. On the other hand, precisely because man is a rational, intelligent being, he is capable of transgressing the laws to which he is subject. Some of these laws are of men's own making, positive laws; but there are also laws which are antecedent to positive laws, and these are what Montesquieu calls 'relations of justice'; in more conventional terminology they are natural laws.

Montesquieu's attitude to religion was not unlike that of Montaigne or Locke. He believed in no more than a few simple propositions about the existence of God and God's benevolence; but to that minimal creed he clung with increasing confidence. In *Les Lettres persanes* he made fun of Christianity in general and the Catholic Church in particular, but in later writings he took care to avoid provocative utterances on the subject. In his biography of Montesquieu, Professor Robert Shackleton gives an example of the author's increasing wariness as revealed in successive drafts of *L'Esprit des lois*. In the first version of the chapter on religion, Montesquieu wrote: 'Under moderate governments, men are more attached to morals and less to religion; in despotic countries, they are more attached to religion and less to morals.' In the second draft of the text he introduced the qualifying words 'One might perhaps say that . . .'. In the published version, he cut out the remark altogether.[66]

Much was once made of the claim that Montesquieu was reconciled to the Church of Rome on his death-bed. An Irish Jesuit
named Bernard Routh got into the château of La Brède during
Montesquieu's last illness, and despite the efforts of the Duchesse
d'Aiguillon to prevent him from 'tormenting a dying man',
he succeeded—or, at any rate, claimed to have succeeded—in
bringing the philosopher back to the path of devotion and
repentence.

This dramatic episode is perhaps of less importance to an
understanding of Montesquieu's religious sentiments than is his
behaviour in more tranquil times.[67] He never asked his wife to
give up her Protestantism, and he was always a fervent champion
of religious toleration. At the same time, he remained on the best
of terms with his several relations who were in holy orders in the
Catholic Church. Besides, according to his sociological theory
that every country had the religion which its geographical and
climatic conditions demanded, Montesquieu held that Catholicism was the 'right' religion for France just as Anglicanism was
the 'right' religion for England. After a visit to Rome as a young
man, he said he felt glad to be a Catholic if only because that
Church had inspired such magnificent works of art. This is not to
say that he subscribed to more than a fraction of the teachings of
the Catholic Church. On the other hand, he always detested
atheism. To him the idea of a universe without God was
'effroyable' and he believed that every state must have its church.
In *L'Esprit des lois* he goes so far as to suggest that Christian
principles well engraved in the minds of the people would be more
conducive to a good political order than either the republican
principle of virtue or the monarchist principle of honour.

Montesquieu is commonly remembered in the textbooks as the
exponent of the theory of climates, and yet this was not a particularly original element in his teaching. It had already been
expounded in the sixteenth-century by Bodin, and revived by
several later writers. This theory asserted, among other things,
that climate determined people's political organization, so that
cold climate, for example, generated liberty and hot climates,
despotism. What is novel about Montesquieu's version of the
theory is that he attempts to support it with scientific evidence:
'Cold air', he writes,

constricts the extremities of the body's external fibres. This increases elasticity and favours the return of the blood from the extremities to the heart. Cold air contracts these fibres, and thus adds to their strength. Hot air, by contrast, relaxes and lengthens the extremities of the fibres, and so diminishes their strength and elasticity. People in cold climates therefore have more vigour.[68]

Montesquieu argues on the strength of these 'empirical' findings that people living in hot climates are timid, cowardly, and thus easily enslaved, while the inhabitants of cold countries are courageous and stand up for their freedom. 'Political servitude', he says, 'depends on the nature of the climate.'[69] Or again: 'Climate is the first of the causes.'

Elsewhere he seems to contradict this assertion. In keeping with his belief in free will, he argues that moral causes are more decisive than physical causes in the shaping of history. He had drawn the distinction between the two sorts of cause in *Les Lettres persanes*, and the idea of historical causality played a central role in the most important book Montesquieu published between *Les Lettres persanes* and *L'Esprit des lois*, namely his *Considérations sur les causes de la grandeur des Romains et de leur décadence* of 1734.

This is not a professional historian's book.[70] Compared, for example, to *The Decline and Fall of the Roman Empire* by Edward Gibbon, which came out half a century later, it is both less instructive and less provocative;[71] indeed Montesquieu actually took the precaution of showing the text to a Jesuit friend, Père Castel, and removing, on his advice, passages which might offend the Church. The importance of the *Considérations sur les causes de la grandeur des Romains et de leur décadence*, however, resides in its being a philosopher's book,[72] an attempt to show in the example of a certain episode in history how free will and causality are both operative in the shared experience of the human race. Drawing his inspiration largely from Malebranche, Montesquieu suggests that it is possible to be scientific without being deterministic.

Montesquieu makes much of the distinction between what he calls 'moral causes' and 'physical causes'. He introduced the distinction in *Les Lettres persanes*,[73] and in an unfinished *Essai sur les causes* he explains how the moral causes, which presuppose free will, can affect the external world, just as events in the external world can affect the mind:[74]

> The soul in our body is like a spider in its web; the spider cannot move without affecting the threads which spread out from it and you cannot touch one of the threads without moving the spider.[75]

Physical causes tend to shape history, but moral causes can prevail over physical causes. Their efficacy depends on the exercise of will. Thus, although climate shapes a people's political character, Montesquieu argues in *L'Esprit des lois* that a good legislator can overcome 'the vices of climate'.[76] Moral causes operate together with physical causes in producing what Montesquieu calls the 'national spirit' or 'general spirit'. This has been defined by a modern sociologist as 'the way of living, behaving, thinking and feeling of a particular collectivity';[77] and Montesquieu suggests that such a 'national spirit' or 'general spirit' can in turn become itself a cause of the moral sort. He argues that while a legislator will have to work against physical causes, such as climate, to promote political liberty, he will only succeed if he works with, and not against, the 'spirit'.

The notion of a 'national spirit', afterwards developed by Rousseau and given ideological force by the nationalist movements of the nineteenth-century, was not without its ideological significance for Montesquieu himself. He had suggested in the Myth of the Troglodytes that an ideal republic was a sort of family, but he wanted to give no support to the royalist idea that the nation was a family writ large, held together by the patriarchal figure of the king. For Montesquieu the nation was what would nowadays be called a sociological group, held together by the shared volition and experience of its members, their customs, language, and tradition, their common *esprit*[78] (a word for which 'spirit' is an awkward English rendering, although it is the nearest synonym we have).

Montesquieu thought it important to distinguish between the social and the political. His argument was that societies were natural, political institutions conventional. His belief in man as a naturally social animal kept him close to Aristotle and set him apart from Hobbes and Locke and the other individualist philosophers of the seventeenth century, the 'social contract' theorists who dominated liberal thought.

In *Les Lettres persanes* Montesquieu describes as absurd the enquiry of philosophers into the origins of society. If men had fled from one another, he suggests, that phenomenon would have required explanation, but no explanation is needed as to why men live together: every human being is born of another and depends on another, and all live in communities, which shows that their society is natural.[79]

And yet, denying that societies were contractual in origin, Montesquieu subscribed to the contract theory of the origin of governments; and to that extent he was a follower of Locke. That is to say, he agreed with Locke's conception of civil institutions coming into existence as the result of an agreement between the members of a given society and its sovereign.[80] And when Montesquieu abandoned his early preference for republican government in favour of constitutional monarchy, he still kept his conception of the state as something instituted by the people.

Montesquieu did not set out to define the word 'law', but he offers what looks like a definition when he writes at the very beginning of *L'Esprit des lois*: 'Laws are the necessary relationships which derive from the nature of things.'[81] David Hume expressed dissatisfaction with this formulation, as well he might, if only because Montesquieu confuses two senses of law which Hume thought it important to keep distinct: on the one hand, law as a statement of the regularities to be seen in nature—the laws of the scientists; and on the other hand, law as a set of imperative rules, law of the kind to be found in legal codes, moral interdictions, the commandments of God, and so forth.

One reason perhaps why Montesquieu did not draw out this distinction is that he remained enough of a Christian—or a deist—to cling to the traditional view that the laws of nature—the law of gravity and other scientific laws—were in a sense commands of the Creator. A stone so to speak 'obeyed' God's command in falling towards the earth's centre. But if Montesquieu never entirely lost this way of thinking, he was troubled by the difference between statements of what did happen and statements of what ought to happen.[82] Moreover a large part of his enterprise was to enquire into the relation between laws in one sense of the word 'law'—scientific laws—and laws in another sense—the positive laws of civil codes. This activity was different from that of traditional political theory, which was concerned with the relationship between the law embodied in the positive laws of civil codes and law in the sense of natural law, the ideal principles of justice to be found in God, reason or nature. Part of the originality of Montesquieu was this attempt to add the perspective of sociology to that of jurisprudence.[83]

Even so, writing both as a philosopher of law and as a sociologist sometimes led him into what look like contradictions, as, for example, in what he has to say on the subject of slavery. In Book XV of *L'Esprit des lois*, he writes: 'Since all men are born equal, it must be said that slavery is contrary to nature.'

He displays mingled indignation and trenchant sarcasm when he considers the flimsy reasons that have been advanced to justify slavery—and it should be remembered that before Montesquieu, even the most liberal political theorists, including Grotius and Locke, had tried to defend slavery, Locke indeed being a shareholder in the slave trade. It is the distinctive voice of the Enlightenment that we hear in Montesquieu when he castigates slavery with the same muted anger with which he castigates torture, as something bad in itself and evil in its consequences. Slavery, says Montesquieu, is unnecessary;[84] it corrupts the masters;[85] it prevents the slave from acquiring virtue;[86] what is more, it violates sexual morality since female slaves become the prey of their masters.

In other parts of the same book, Montesquieu seems to concede that slavery is compatible with natural law, and admits the institution of slavery in both republics and monarchies as well as in despotisms, where everybody is a slave.[87] He does not go beyond saying of natural law that it requires the humane treatment of slaves, and suggesting that slaves well treated will not revolt.[88] He notes that under a 'moderate' government the magistrate will ensure that slaves are properly fed and clothed,[89] while slaves will have a right of appeal against ill treatment by their masters,[90] and be allowed to buy their freedom.[91] He also says that there will not be 'too many slaves in a moderate state',[92] while warning, on the other hand, against a wholesale sudden emancipation. 'If too many slaves are freed at once . . . they will become a charge on the commonwealth.'[93]

One might well think that if slavery is wholly contrary to natural law, natural law cannot yield principles of regulating slavery. Yet it could perhaps be said on behalf of Montesquieu that his principles for regulating slavery have to be seen in their proper historical context, and that he sets them out only when he is considering a world—the ancient world—where slavery was taken for granted by everybody, including the most stringent moralists. Besides, there was a difference between slavery and torture; slavery had once proved itself useful, indeed necessary to progress, whereas torture had no practical utility.

Montesquieu the sociologist was much concerned to ascertain the practicalities of politics, to find out what constraints and limitations there were on men's choices, what was the *Speilraum* within which they could move. Men were free in the sense that they had free will, but the options open to them were limited by circumstances which hemmed them in; possibilities were shaped by the consequences of past decisions and choices. Men's actions did not always have the intended effect. Montesquieu cites the example of the French Protestants struggling to put Henri IV on the throne, only to be persecuted and driven out of France by Henri's successors in the Bourbon dynasty.

Reflections such as these led Montesquieu to conclude that there was little room for manœuvre in politics, and in particular little room for improvement. His historical and sociological investigations led him to adopt a decidedly pessimistic outlook. Republican states had vanished for lack of republican virtue; and even though an admirable form of moderate monarchy existed in England, Montesquieu did not think it could be readily reproduced elsewhere, since there would be different geographical and historical factors to contend with, and a different *esprit général* in the people.

In *L'Esprit des lois* Montesquieu depicted England as a 'mirror of liberty', but he did not expect France to reshape its constitution on the model of England. The character and conditions of the French people were too much at variance with those of the English people. What Montesquieu wanted was for France to recover from its own traditions and its own experience the institution and methods which would reverse the decline of the French kingdom towards despotism. In England, the balance of power was achieved by the sharing of sovereignty between the Crown, Parliament and the courts. In France equilibrium would have to be achieved by other means.

In France, Montesquieu argued, the right distribution of power should be between the Crown, the Church, and the nobility. Because he thought this, Montesquieu gave careful attention to what he considered peculiarly French in French history. Inadequate as he may have been as a historian of ancient Rome, he was as sound as any of his contemporaries on the history of the Franco-Germanic Middle Ages. There was clearly a political reason for the thoroughness of his researches: he wanted to validate the title of the French nobility to a share in the sovereignty of the kingdom and bring to light the historical basis of the fundamental or constitutional law of France.

He took care to avoid a polemical presentation of the argument. Professor Shackleton gives another example in his biography of Montesquieu's discretion.[94] In the original manuscript Montesquieu wrote 'Intermediary powers constitute the nature of monarchical government.' In the corrected version he wrote 'Subordinate intermediary powers constitute the nature of monarchical government.' In the final published version he wrote 'Subordinate and dependent powers constitute the nature of monarchical government.'[95]

The four most important of these 'intermediary' powers which he tactfully calls 'dependent' while privately eager to assert their independence are (1) the landed nobility (*les seigneurs*); (2) the clergy (*le clergé*); (3) the cities (*les villes*); and (4) the legal nobility (*la noblesse de robe*). Montesquieu never suggests that the role of the landed aristocracy is legislative; indeed he is surprisingly silent on the functions of any of these houses of the Estates-General in the French constitution. The role he assigns to the landed nobility is that of sustaining the integrity of the monarchy.

The estate of landed nobility has a moral dimension; as the votaries of honour in a system animated by honour, its members must be dedicated to the profession of arms and the administration of seigneurial justice. They must be barred from commerce, where men are governed by another ethos and represent another interest in society. Montesquieu even envisages the *seigneurs* having to give lessons in honour to the king. He recalls the story of the Viscomte d'Orte being commanded by Charles IX to massacre the Protestants in his province and replying: 'Sire, I have soldiers in my army, but no executioners. I can only employ them for things that can be done [*choses faisables*].'

Next Montesquieu looks to the clergy. He was never on easy terms with the Church, but he considered that the clergy had an important part to play in the French constitution as a weight to balance the other ruling elements. Voltaire and many other sceptical philosophers said that religion was needed to keep the common people in order, but Montesquieu said it was needed to keep princes in order: 'A prince who loves religion, and fears it, is a lion which yields to the hand which strokes it, and the voice which soothes it . . . the prince who has no religion is a terrible beast who feels his freedom only when he tears his prey to pieces and devours it.'[96]

Montesquieu did not share the view of those philosophers of the Enlightenment who held that pagan religion was somehow superior to Christianity. 'For a religion to be compelling,' he wrote, 'it must have a pure morality.'[97] The pagan religions in general did not set such an ethical goal. Christianity did. So Montesquieu preferred it. He added that it was 'less the truth or falsehood of a dogma which rendered it useful or harmful to men in civil society than the use—or abuse—that they make of it'.[98]

The third intermediary power which Montesquieu names is *les villes*, meaning those chartered cities whose rights and privileges of local government served to modify and balance the power of the central government. Here, again, is an instance of what his critics regarded as a feudal element in his thinking; for the privileges of local authorities had been one of the main targets of the modernizing policy of the Bourbon monarchs in the seventeenth-century; such local rights were still seen by most progressive theorists as residues of medievalism and obstacles to national development.

The fourth element which Montesquieu envisaged as serving to balance the power of the Crown was undoubtedly in his eyes the most important—the legal nobility as an estate and the *parlements* as an institution. The claims he makes on behalf of the *parlements* echo the claims they made for themselves at different times, especially after the Regent had restored their right to speak. According to Montesquieu, the legal nobility, unlike the landed nobility, does have a role—a central role—in legislation. As he puts the case, 'it is not enough in a monarchy for there to be intermediary orders, there must also be a repository of laws. This repository can only be the political corps itself, declaring the laws when they are made and reviving them when they are forgotten.'[99]

If Montesquieu is to be seen as an ideologue of the French *noblesse de robe*—and in a certain sense he undoubtedly was, since he argued, as he sincerely believed, that the national interest and the interest of the *parlements* were one—he offers something very different from the old *thèse nobiliare* according to which the king was simply the first nobleman of France owing his sovereignty to the authorization and consent of the other noblemen. Montesquieu advances the far more radical thesis that the king derives his sovereignty from the people—or the nation.

Far from being any kind of neo-medieval or feudal notion, this is a mark of Montesquieu's modernity. He is very modern, again, in the priority he assigns to freedom.[100] Plato and Aristotle, and most political philosophers of the ancient world, were mainly concerned with justice. The theorists of the sixteenth- and seventeenth-centuries, such as Bodin and Hobbes, were mainly concerned with peace, and one can understand why. Bodin wrote at a time when France was tearing itself to pieces in civil wars, and his political theory was a response to that situation; Hobbes, foreseeing the outbreak of civil war in England, had a similar motivation. But Montesquieu wrote at a time when civil wars in France had been almost forgotten, when more than a century of internal peace had been imposed by the mortal solicitude of absolutist patriarchal monarchs. What was absent in France (and all the more conspicuously absent by comparison with the situation in England after 1689) was the freedom that the monarchs had destroyed. And that freedom, for all his reflections on virtue and honour, was what Montesquieu put at the centre of his system. Here he goes in tandem with Locke, and however ironically, the so-called ideologue of the *noblesse de robe* proves to have much in common with the so-called ideologue of the bourgeoisie. Their conception of freedom was virtually the same. 'Political liberty', Montesquieu writes, 'does not consist in doing what you want to do . . . it is the right to do anything that the laws permit.'[101]

Montesquieu rejects Hobbes's notion that freedom is the 'silence of the laws' and rallies to Locke's thesis that political liberty depends on the existence of laws.[102] The adjective 'political' is significant; for political liberty is implicitly distinguished from anarchic liberty, where freedom does mean doing whatever you please. Political liberty can only exist in a civil society and within a framework of laws which give it meaning.

The problem for Montesquieu is to formulate the kind of laws which will protect freedom, and to identify the kind of civil institutions and processes which will ensure the rule of law. And this problem which exercised Montesquieu's mind for so many years was a problem for all his successors as political theorists of the Enlightenment. They all spoke of 'liberty', but they did not all mean the same thing by that word. Moreover, many of them wanted much else besides liberty—happiness, abundance, harmony, and the sovereignty of reason.

Montesquieu expected less. His sense of the limits of the possible, his appeal to the ancient constitution, his respect for the Gothic past, and his patrician aloofness all set him apart from the younger, more progressive and rationalistic *philosophes*. If he was the Whig of the French Enlightenment, he subscribed to little of what might be called the metaphysics of Whiggery.[103] For Montesquieu there were no natural rights to life, liberty, and property; no social contract; no radical individualism, and certainly no hints of revolution.

Instead he tried to make political science scientific. D'Alembert, one of the few professional scientists among the *philosophes* of the French Enlightenment, said of Montesquieu that he had taken his subject out of the hands of theorists who wrote about Man and Law and Society and made it the study of men and laws and societies; he had written 'less about Duty than about the means by which duties could be fulfilled'; less about 'the perfection of ideal law than about the improvement of real laws'.[104]

During his stay in England, Montesquieu had the satisfaction of being elected a Fellow of the Royal Society. English readers devoured his books with all the more pleasure because they were so unfailingly flattering to English institutions. When Montesquieu died at the age of 65 in February, 1755, the *Evening Post* in London reported:

On the tenth of this month died at Paris, universally and sincerely regretted, Charles Secondat, baron of Montesquieu, and Président à mortier of the parliament of Bordeaux. His virtues did honour human nature, his writings justice. A friend to mankind, he asserted their undoubted and inalienable rights with freedom, even in his own country, whose prejudices in matters of religion and government, he had long lamented and endeavoured (not without some success) to remove. He well knew, and justly admired the happy constitution of this country, where fixed and known laws equally restrain monarchy from tyranny and liberty from licentiousness. His works will illustrate his name, and survive him, as long as right reason . . . shall be understood, respected and maintained.[105]

It is said that a prophet is not honoured in his own land. When Montesquieu was buried in France, only one of the leading *philosophes* of the Enlightenment attended the funeral: Denis Diderot, who was not at that time greatly in sympathy with Montesquieu's kind of liberalism, but who came in the end to agree with it and develop it in a more radical direction.

# 2
# Voltaire

Voltaire was more or less a contemporary of Montesquieu; he was five years younger, but he made his name at an earlier age. If Montesquieu was the first philosopher of the Enlightenment, Voltaire was its first *moraliste*. His dramatic works are nowadays seldom read, and some of his poetry is almost unreadable. But almost everyone still enjoys his satirical novel *Candide* and his essays in favour of liberty and toleration—writings which in their time pricked the bubble of so many religious, political, and social opinions. He was not a systematic thinker like Descartes or Locke any more than he was a great dramatist like Racine or Corneille, but he had ideas and he knew how to communicate them; he was an unmatched *vulgarisateur* who captured the attention of people all over the Western world, and did much to alter their attitudes to life. He organized campaigns on behalf of the victims of persecution, got people out of prison, and filled his own house with refugees. He established his name in people's minds as a supremely amusing champion of light against the forces of darkness; and long before the age of photography, Voltaire's image was familiar to everyone through drawings and cartoons— a sprightly little skinny fellow with a wicked mocking grin. Mr Gladstone called John Stuart Mill the 'saint of rationalism'; Voltaire was its infinitely more attractive devil.

Thomas Carlyle deplored 'his entire want of Earnestness',[1] but Hippolyte Taine said it was impossible to resist Voltaire's intelligence. 'The contagion is too overpowering. A creature of air and flame; the most excitable that ever lived.'[2] And Byron, who admired him as much as anyone, described Voltaire in *Childe Harold*:

> Of fire and fickleness a child
> Most mutable in wishes, but in mind,
> A wit as various—gay, grave, sage, wild,
> Historian, bard, philosopher combined,
> He multiplied himself among mankind.[3]

Voltaire lived a very long life. He died on the eve of the French Revolution, but he had been born in the reign of the Sun King, Louis XIV, for whom he preserved an almost sentimental adulation. He was educated at a Jesuit school, and he also had a Jesuit private tutor; and when he turned against Christianity, he kept a certain sympathy for the Society of Jesus, if only because of their worldliness and superior culture, which he much preferred to the dour puritanism of the rival Catholic party of Jansenists. He was born into a middle-class family by the name of Arouet, and although he distanced himself from his family by changing his name, he was proud to proclaim himself a 'bourgeois'. He had no ambition to rise to the ranks of the nobility, a class he despised; and unlike most intellectuals, he was not ashamed to make money in business, devoting a part of every day to commercial activity.

He ended up with a château of his own, almost as splendid as that of Montesquieu. But Voltaire's was a fortune acquired by his own efforts while Montesquieu's wealth was inherited. In many respects their ideas were close enough for us to consider them as equally representative of the Enlightenment. They shared a passion for liberty and an impatience for reform. They were both hostile to the Catholic Church, and generally sceptical in matters of religion. They both wrote in favour of toleration. They both regarded English government and English philosophy as exemplary. They both cultivated a polished, urbane, and epigrammatic style, sharing the belief that works of scholarship had to be made enjoyable if they were to reach the public that mattered. And such is the ambiguity of the word 'liberal' that Voltaire and Montesquieu can with equal confidence be classed as liberals.

They were not friends. They both moved in the raffish milieu of Madame de Prie when they were each pursuing a life of pleasure as young men in Paris in the 1720s, but there is no evidence of their meeting at that time,[4] and there is a marked coolness in remarks each made about the other in later years. This does not seem to be due to any sort of professional rivalry. There was a political basis for their mutual suspicion. Each saw the other as expounding in a modern guise a familiar seventeenth-century doctrine of which he profoundly disapproved. Montesquieu, the *président* of a provincial *parlement*, the *châtelain* of a battlemented, moated castle, was seen by Voltaire as an exponent of the old *thèse nobiliare*—the thesis of Fénelon and Saint-Simon and Boulainvilliers that good government and the principles of the ancient constitution in France alike required the division of sovereignty between the Crown and the nobility, in other words, the political system of feudalism disinterred and dressed up as a formula for freedom. Voltaire, on his side, appeared to Montesquieu as a smart new champion of nothing other than the old *thèse royale*—the thesis of Bodin and Bossuet and the Bourbon kings, that good government must be centralized and absolute and, of course, wise, in order to ensure peace and prosperity for the kingdom—Voltaire only adding to these purposes the pursuit of happiness and the promotion of the rights to life, liberty, and property.

In short, Voltaire saw Montesquieu as the ideologue of the aristocracy and Montesquieu saw Voltaire as the ideologue of the royalist *bourgeoisie* which had been elevated by Louis XIV as part of his policy of subduing the nobility. There is a measure of truth in both these appraisals. Voltaire and Montesquieu wrote against a background of a struggle for more and more power by the French *noblesse de robe*, whose authority had been restored after the death of Louis XIV, and a corresponding struggle by the French *bourgeoisie* to preserve and extend the advantages they had gained during the long reign of that monarch. In these aspirations, Montesquieu was undoubtedly on the side of the nobility; Voltaire no less squarely on the side of the bourgeoisie and the Crown.

Since the word 'bourgeois' has now become almost universally pejorative, it may seem odd that Voltaire should have been so attached to his status as a bourgeois. His father, a solidly middle-class man who had married somewhat above his social rank, sent Voltaire to a fashionable college in the hope that he might become a successful lawyer and eventually raise his family to the *noblesse de robe*. The aristocracy of France was both a more accessible and a very much more numerous estate than the aristocracy of England, limited as that was to a few hundred peers. In France there were thousands and thousands of aristocratic families, very few of them able, like Montesquieu, to trace their ancestry back to Saint Louis, but all very proud of a title of nobility which might have been acquired only yesterday, bought with a piece of land or a seat on the bench of a *parlement*.

Voltaire had no ambition to rise to the *noblesse de robe*, or to follow the career of lawyer which might lead to such elevation. He wanted to be a poet and his only desire for social advancement was to lift the status of the man of letters to the highest rank of society. In this—as in most things he made up his mind to do—Voltaire could fairly claim success. Many years later, in an article entitled 'The Men of Letters' which he wrote for Diderot's *Encyclopédie*, Voltaire recalled that in his youth polite society had been composed entirely of the well-born; by the middle of the eighteenth-century, men of letters had come to dominate the social scene.[5]

This is one measure of the strength of the French Enlightenment: philosophy—or rather the particular sort of philosophy introduced by Montesquieu and Voltaire—became fashionable. Conversation in the *salons* turned aside from gossip to consider questions of beauty, truth, goodness, happiness, freedom, and Providence. Montesquieu—Monsieur le Président, Monsieur le Baron—would have been socially acceptable even if he had not become a successful author; it was Voltaire who insisted that the credentials of an author were all that was needed to put a man on a level with a prince. He, personally, always treated any nobleman he met as his equal. Some did not mind. After Voltaire became a celebrity at the age of 24 in 1718 with the immense success of his play *Oedipe* he was taken up by several grandees who prided themselves on their love of literature. But there was one nobleman named Rohan-Chabot who detested Voltaire, and, having experienced what he considered Voltaire's insolence, had him beaten up by his servants, because Voltaire was too low in station for him to fight in person. For Voltaire the worst part of the experience was discovering that none of his grand friends would take his side against Rohan-Chabot. The French aristocracy closed ranks against the bourgeois, and Voltaire found himself in the Bastille—a place in which he had already been imprisoned for nearly a year as a punishment for a joke at the expense of the dissolute Regent, the Duc d'Orléans. Fortunately Voltaire had some friends in the English aristocracy who did not desert him, and with the help of Lord Bolingbroke and Lord Stair he secured his release from the Bastille on giving an undertaking to leave France for England.[6]

He was 31 years old when he reached London for the first time and he was delighted with everything he found: in a letter written in English to a French friend, he described England as a land of liberty; and urged his friend to join him in London: 'You will see a nation fond of their liberty, learned, witty, despising life and death, a nation of philosophers.'[7]

Lord Morley said of Voltaire that he arrived in England a poet and left a sage; and undoubtedly those two years in London inspired Voltaire to take a new kind of interest in history, ethics, and politics. Like Montesquieu, who reached England in 1729 some months after his own departure, Voltaire saw in the English system of government a mirror of liberty, and he spoke of the English constitution with equal enthusiasm. But Voltaire did not admire the same features of the English government that Montesquieu admired, and some of the things which Montesquieu saw as merits, Voltaire considered to be defects.

In the first place he had a different conception of liberty. Whereas Montesquieu agreed with Locke that liberty was the right to do what one ought to do in accordance with the laws, Voltaire was content to say with Hobbes that liberty was the absence of constraint.[8] And again like Hobbes, Voltaire believed in undivided sovereignty, the great difference being that Voltaire had a passion for freedom which Hobbes did not have, and he believed, as Hobbes did not believe, that men kept in civil society their natural right to liberty and property as well as a natural right to life. To this extent Voltaire's political objectives were Lockian, and perhaps more Lockian than were Montesquieu's, for while Montesquieu subscribed to Locke's theory of divided sovereignty and Locke's conception of freedom, which Voltaire did not accept, Voltaire subscribed to Locke's individualism and Locke's theory of natural rights, which Montesquieu rejected.

Again Voltaire differed from Montesquieu in his view of Parliament; he did not discern the secret of English freedom, as did Montesquieu, in the balance of power between the legislative, the executive, and the judiciary, and he was not especially impressed by the bicameral structure of Parliament as House of Lords and House of Commons. The House of Lords had no merit in Voltaire's eyes as an instrument of representative government. Indeed he suggested that the Upper Chamber represented nothing other than the several private interests of the noblemen who sat in it. On the other hand, he was filled with respect for the House of Commons. He visualized it as a solidly bourgeois institution, not realizing, perhaps, how strong a hold the political peers had at that time over its composition.

'The House of Commons', he wrote in his *Dictionnaire philosophique*, 'is truly the nation. If the peers are in Parliament on behalf of the peerage, the House of Commons is there on behalf of the nation, since every Member is a deputy of the people.'[9]

But while Voltaire was lavish in his praise of the House of Commons, he was quick to stamp on the proposal of Montesquieu and others that the experience of the Parliament in Westminster provided a precedent for the *parlements* in France to be elevated and strengthened as legislative bodies in the interests of freedom. Voltaire argued that this was to be deceived by the ambiguity of a word: the French word *parlement* stood for a court of law, or rather the several so-called sovereign courts of law in Paris and the provinces, which were composed of noble magistrates, the *noblesse de robe*—with the duty of registering legislation prepared by the government at Versailles. Although the English word 'parliament' was rendered as *parlement* in French, the French *parlements* had nothing in common with the English Parliament, which was a national assembly of politicans (elected deputies in the Lower House) freely debating, voting on, and initiating legislation. The nearest French equivalent to the Parliament at Westminster, he pointed out, was the Estates-General, which had not been allowed to meet since 1614—not that Voltaire thought it ought to meet, since it was composed of two houses he heartily detested, the clergy and the nobility, and only one, the Third Estate, which might claim to represent the people.

Once again in opposition to the views of Montesquieu, Voltaire denied that the French *parlements* could serve to hinder the King of France from becoming a despot in the way that the Parliament at Westminster hindered the King of England from becoming a despot. 'Nowhere else in the whole globe', he protested, 'has a court of law ever attempted to share the sovereign power.'[10]

The French *parlements*, according to Voltaire, served only their own interests as a corps and a caste. Far from being potential instruments of liberty, they were the agents of oppression, packed with fanatical Jansenists, and imposing constraints far worse than those of the King's government at Versailles.

Acquaintance with England did nothing to diminish Voltaire's royalism. Indeed as he studied English history, he came to the conclusion that the English owed their freedom primarily to their kings:

Very little liberty was known in England when the nobility was strong, for the people then were victims of ecclesiastical tyrants and plunderers called barons. It was under King John that the people came to have a voice in their government . . . English liberty developed with the legislative authority of the House of Commons and the gradual emergence of a monarch who is powerful to do good, but has his hands tied to prevent him from doing harm.[11]

Like other philosophers of the French Enlightenment, Voltaire is commonly said to have favoured 'enlightened despotism', but this is not true; what he favoured was enlightened royalism, and he separated the idea of absolute from despotic sovereignty as sharply as Montesquieu himself distinguished monarchy from despotism. Although Voltaire wrote—late in life—a work entitled *Idées républicaines*, he was never enthusiastic about the republican ideal. He rejected Montesquieu's idea that the central principle of a republic was virtue. 'A republic', he wrote in his *Pensées sur le gouvernement*,

is not founded on virtue; it is founded on the ambition of every citizen, the pride which subdues pride, the desire to dominate which will not put up with another's domination. Out of this come laws which preserve equality as much as possible. A republic is a society where the diners, with equal appetite, eat at the same table until there appears a vigorous and voracious man who takes the lot for himself and leaves the crumbs to the others.[12]

Voltaire was ready to admit that a republican system might work well in small states, and he disagreed with Bayle's assertion that Macedonian monarchy was preferable to Athenian democracy: 'le gouvernement populaire est donc par lui-même moins inique, moins abominable que le gouvernement tyrannique'.[13]

For Voltaire, all government entailed limitations on freedom, and since he wanted as much freedom as possible, he argued that government should be limited to the necessary and the useful.

This was another reason why he admired England so much; there was religious toleration.

'In England, everyone is allowed to go to heaven in his own way . . . If there were one religion in England, they would have to fear its despotism; if there were two, men would be at each other's throats; but there are thirty, so they live happily and peaceably together.'[14]

The religious toleration which prevailed in England never ceased to command Voltaire's admiring attention, if only because it was such a marked contrast to the situation in France. Here he was entirely in agreement with Montesquieu, holding that religious toleration was not only good in itself but beneficial, useful to the economic life of the nation. 'If you enter the London Stock Exchange', he wrote, '. . . you will see the representatives of different nations gathered there for the service of mankind. There the Jew, the Muhammadan and the Christian do business together as if they were of the same religion, and they give the name of "infidel" only to those who go bankrupt.'[15]

Voltaire also remarked on the extent to which England had gained economically as a result of offering refuge to the Huguenot industrialists banished from France by Louis XIV. He argued that toleration was the fruit of liberty, the origin of happiness and of abundance; where there was no freedom of thought there was no freedom of trade, because the same tyranny encroached on commerce and religion alike. 'In England, commerce, by enriching the people, has extended their freedom, and this freedom has in turn extended their commerce and furthered the greatness of the state.'[16]

Voltaire was no less impressed by the English fiscal system, which seemed to him to impose its burdens fairly,[17] and not to grant privileges, like the French, to the clergy and nobility at the expense of everyone else. In England justice and prosperity went hand in hand; taxation was not a restraint on enterprise as it was in France.

Writing in English to a French friend from London, he declared: 'I think, I write like a free Englishman.'[18] He had reached England at an opportune moment. Philosophers and men of letters were held in high esteem in the reigns of Queen Anne or George I. Voltaire had some inkling of this before he crossed the Channel, for in 1718 at the age of 25 he had sent from

Paris a copy of his *Oedipe* to George I with a fulsome dedicatory epistle, and received in return a medallion and a gold watch[19]—a marked contrast to his experience at Versailles, where he 'had to hang ignobly about in the crowd at the marriage of Louis XV to gain a paltry pittance from the Queen's privy purse'.[20] In England men of letters were being liberally patronized, Prior and Gay having embassies, Addison holding the office of secretary of state, and Rowe, Philips, and Congreve all enjoying well-paid sinecures. With the accession to power of Walpole, this golden age for authors came to an abrupt—and permanent—end in England; and by 1776, when David Hume arrived in Paris, the situation had been reversed, for it was in France, Hume noted, that literary men were honoured and fêted, while in England they were held in contempt.

During his stay in England, Voltaire developed a fervent admiration for English literature which matched his enthusiasm for English government.[21] Afterwards he would boast that he alone had introduced Milton, Pope, Swift, and Dryden to France and that he was the first to explain Shakespeare to French readers. What is more he saw himself as a champion of the empiricist philosophy of Newton and Locke and Bacon against the rationalist metaphysics of Descartes and Malebranche, and thus the champion, in a sense, of science against religion. On the other hand, it must be remembered that there was a fair amount of both rationalism and religion in Locke and Newton, and this Voltaire very willingly assimilated. He was never a materialist or an atheist, as were many of the younger philosophers of the Enlightenment. Like Newton, Voltaire invoked the 'argument from design' for God's existence—the wonderfully engineered 'watch' of the universe proclaimed the existence of a watchmaker. Besides these rational grounds for his own genuine belief in God, Voltaire also thought there were practical grounds for wishing that belief to be generally held:

I want my lawyer, my tailor, my servants, even my wife to believe in God, because it means that I shall be cheated and robbed and cuckolded less often . . . God is needed to provide a divine sanction for morality. It is absolutely necessary not only for ordinary people, but also for princes and rulers to have an idea of the Supreme Being, Creator, governor, rewarder and avenger profoundly engraven on their minds . . . if God did not exist, it would be necessary to invent him.[22]

Privately Voltaire did not believe that God really intervened in the workings of the universe to secure the enforcement of morality, but he thought it important for ordinary people to imagine that he did. For himself, his faith was limited to belief in the existence of a single Creator or Supreme Being; in a word, Voltaire was a deist.[23]

There is only one God . . . Lift your eyes to the celestial globes, turn them to the earth and the seas, everything corresponds, each is made for the other; each being is intimately related to other beings; everything forms part of the same design: therefore there is only one architect, one sole master, one sole preserver.[24]

Voltaire could not go beyond his deism to accept the latitudinarian Christianity of Newton and Locke, undemanding as that version of Christianity might be considered; all the Christian Churches, with the exception of the Quakers, had too black a record of persecution in Voltaire's eyes. Indeed his own deism became attenuated with the passage of time; his Deity was originally conceived as being benevolent as well as omnipotent; but the longer Voltaire lived, the less reason could he find for ascribing goodness to the Creator. The earthquake of 1755 in Lisbon, where thousands of innocent lives were lost, convinced him that his God must have gone to sleep and allowed some fallen angel to take over the direction of the universe. The Lisbon disaster prompted what is perhaps Voltaire's best book, and certainly the one which is still most widely read, *Candide ou l'optimisme*, which makes such brilliant mockery of the idea that ours is 'the best of all possible worlds' and all 'partial evil, good misunderstood'.

And yet Voltaire was an optimist himself—more of an optimist in a sense than the optimists he attacked, Leibniz and Alexander Pope, for they at least subscribed to the Christian doctrine of the Fall of Man, whereas Voltaire believed in progress.[25] In his *Essai sur les mœurs* he argued that human history was a continuous movement of human betterment through the progressive enlargement of useful knowledge. This was the optimism which characterized most men of the Enlightenment; an optimism which went together with a curious sort of cosmic pessimism.

The English philosopher whom Voltaire praised most frequently was Locke. Late in life, he declared how he always returned to the philosophy of Locke: 'like a prodigal son returning to his father, I threw myself into the arms of that modest man, who never pretends to know what he does not know'.[26] Voltaire considered himself an adherent both of Locke's epistemological and of his political teaching. Of his debt to Locke's writings there can be no question; Voltaire's own *Traité sur la tolérance* adds little to the arguments of Locke's *Letter for Toleration*. But it is by no means evident that Voltaire subscribed to the political theory expounded in Locke's *Two Treatises of Government*. For example, Voltaire did not accept the theory of the contractual origins of society, any more than Montesquieu accepted it. Voltaire suggests that men are naturally social and that governments come into existence through conquest, not contract. His argument is that with the passage of time, the force which had originally established the dominion of one man over another came to be transformed by custom and habit and the development of civilization into a regulated government. The modern kingdom is a product of progress for which men have every reason to be grateful.

Voltaire admired the attack on metaphysics which Locke had undertaken in his *Essay Concerning Human Understanding*, and he carried that attack into the areas where Locke had stopped short—the areas of politics and law. Voltaire chose to assert the natural rights of man without invoking either the concept of a state of nature or the doctrine of natural law which had traditionally been assumed to provide the logical foundation for any theory of natural right. What Voltaire saw, and admired, in Locke was a practical philosopher. Locke had produced a doctrine of natural rights which stood up to the test of experience; in other words, what had happened in England since 1689 had shown that the 'natural rights to life, liberty and property' as Locke had defined them could be translated into positive rights which the English people were able to enjoy. In his *Dictionnaire philosophique* Voltaire restated those rights for the benefit of his French readers. They were: 'the right to liberty for a person and his property; the right to speak to the nation with voice or pen; the right to be tried in any criminal cause by a jury of independent persons; the right to be judged only according to precise and known terms of law; and to profess any religion a man pleases'.[27]

Voltaire separated the Lockian theory of natural rights both from traditional natural law and from Locke's Whiggish doctrine of parliamentary sovereignty. The Whiggish doctrine was good for England, he thought, but it was not necessarily suitable for export to other countries, and certainly not to France. The theory of the natural rights of man, however, was of universal application; natural rights were, by definition, the rights of all men everywhere; they were the rights of man as man, and the French authorities had the same duty to respect them as had the English.

It was Voltaire's sense of history which prompted him to think that the English system of government could not be copied by the French. Whereas Montesquieu, the political sociologist, said that the social circumstances and climate of France precluded any full-scale reproduction of the English model, Voltaire said it was the history of the two kingdoms which made that impossible. As Voltaire understood it, the history of England had for several centuries moved in a different direction from that of France. In medieval times, both countries had lived under much the same kind of feudal regime, with power divided between Crown, Church, and nobility; but by the sixteenth-century the Tudor monarchs had succeeded in making themselves masters in England; having nationalized the Church and used the Church's wealth to buy up the nobility, they were able to use their monopoly of power to give their kingdom the blessings of peace at a time when France was tearing itself apart in atrocious civil wars—civil wars provoked in part by religious fanaticism and in part by the belligerence of noblemen. In the seventeenth century, the situation, as Voltaire perceived it, had been reversed; the Bourbon kings, by subduing the nobility and conspiring with cardinals, had given France a century of internal peace while the English, tormented by parliamentary factions and religious sects, had relapsed into civil war. By the end of the seventeenth century, the two kingdoms had been shaped by different histories, inherited different problems and acquired a different set of institutions; so that the same remedies could not be expected to be effective in both kingdoms. In so far as Locke's political theory was appropriate in every detail for the English, it was unlikely to be suited in every detail to the French.

There was, however, another English philosopher whose

message seemed to speak precisely to the condition of France, and that was Francis Bacon. Bacon had died in 1626, but that did not mean that his message was out of date. On the contrary, it had a kind of actuality for eighteenth-century France which made him, to a greater extent even than Locke or Newton, a prophetic figure for Voltaire and indeed for the whole French Enlightenment. For Bacon was the first philosopher of science. It was not that Bacon had made any scientific discoveries of his own; he simply proclaimed the doctrine that science could save us. In a way, he was typically English in his stress on utility. Science, he suggested, was not just an intellectual exercise to give us knowledge, but a practical enterprise to give us mastery over our world. Once men knew how nature worked, they could exploit nature to their advantage, overcome scarcity by scientific innovations in agriculture, overcome disease by scientific research in medicine, and generally improve the life of man by all sorts of developments in technology and industry.

Voltaire thrilled to this vision of progress, and he was no less excited by the programme Bacon sketched out as a means of achieving it: first, the abolition of traditional metaphysics and of idle theological disputes on which scholarship was wasted; and second, the repudiation of old-fashioned legal and political impediments to the efficient organization of a progressive state. Bacon was frankly in favour of an enlarged royal prerogative at the expense of the rights of Parliament and the courts. Voltaire approved. Bacon had, in his time, the scheme of fostering the desire of James I to become an absolute monarch so that he himself might enact the role of philosopher at the elbow of a mighty king; if Bacon failed, that did not mean his method could not be tried elsewhere.

Besides, the Baconian plan had a better chance of success in France, because France had had, in Voltaire's opinion, an altogether happy experience of absolute monarchy under the Bourbon kings of the seventeenth century. One can readily understand Voltaire's admiration for Henri IV; it is less easy to understand his veneration for Louis XIV, the persecutor of Protestants, the oppressor of dissent, and the protector of the pious. It has been suggested that Louis XIV appealed to the aesthetic side of Voltaire's imagination, which saw the King as an artist imposing unity on the chaos of society. In any case, Voltaire saw no necessary threat to freedom in the centralization of royal government. On the contrary, he considered that in French experience the great enemies of liberty were the Church and the institutions controlled by the nobility, including the *parlements*. By suppressing or emasculating such institutions, a strong central government could enlarge the citizen's liberty; it had done so in the past in France and could do so in the future. It is interesting to compare this argument with Montesquieu's doctrine of power checking power to produce freedom through equilibrium. For Voltaire, one single power that can be trusted is needed not to counterbalance, but rather to subdue those other powers which menace freedom.

When Voltaire's *Lettres philosophiques* was published in Paris in 1734 it was burned by the public executioner, a sign from the Paris *parlement* of what he might expect from them in reply to his criticisms.[28] It would not be beyond their powers, after all, to burn the author with the book. On the other side, the King's government at Versailles did very little to reward his royalism; he was simply warned by Comte d'Argenson to go to ground to avoid arrest. Even though he was appointed Royal Historian in 1745, and gentleman of the King's Chamber in 1746, Voltaire alienated other courtiers with his indiscretions, and had to leave Versailles.

In the dispute between the government and the Church which followed the edict of 1749 imposing income tax on the clergy as well as other people, Voltaire produced a brilliant pamphlet entitled *La Voix du sage et du peuple* supporting the royal government and refuting the claims of the clergy to fiscal privileges. Priests, he argued, were teachers, and like all teachers they should be told by the state what to teach; not only should they be taxed like every other subject of the king, they should be disciplined like every other civil servant. Such arguments proved all too radical for a pusillanimous king, and Voltaire received no thanks from Versailles. And then in 1771, when the royal government summarily dismissed the *parlements* and replaced them with appointed magistrates, Voltaire, almost alone among the *philosophes*, gave public support to the King's action; again there were no signs of gratitude in Versailles. It is hardly surprising that Voltaire chose to live so much of his life beyond the French King's jurisdiction.

And yet he was never willing to support the French *parlements* in any of their conflicts with the King. Diderot, Holbach, and other *philosophes* came in time to see the *parlements* as some sort of guarantee of legality, a brake on the despotic tendencies of the royal government. Voltaire never changed his mind. To him the *parlements* were bigoted—often Jansenist—agents of oppression, burning books, torturing prisoners, arresting the innocent, and generally impeding any progressive legislation that the King might devise.

It is not difficult to understand Voltaire's implacable hostility to the *parlements* if we look at the famous cases he emerged from his study to publicize. The victims of persecution he defended were always victims of judicial, not royal, persecution. The *parlementaires* were the enemies of freedom, together with their allies in the Church. These were the people Voltaire had in mind when he uttered repeatedly his battle-cry '*Écrasez l'infâme!*'

The Calas case will always be remembered for Voltaire's triumphant intervention in the shameful actions of the French judiciary.[29] On this occasion it was a court at Toulouse[30] which accepted a far-fetched allegation that Calas, a Protestant, had murdered his son because that son was on the point of converting to Catholicism. Calas was duly tried, tortured, and condemned to be strangled by the executioner and burned on the scaffold.

The case attracted very little attention at the time, but one interested individual, a tradesman from Marseilles named Audibert, made the journey to Geneva where Voltaire was then living, and brought the fate of Calas to his notice. Audibert realized that while Voltaire might proclaim that everyone should be content to cultivate his own garden, Voltaire himself was the last person to obey that injunction.

'Was Calas innocent or guilty?', Voltaire asked. 'In either case his story is evidence of the most horrible fanaticism in this supposedly enlightened century . . . One must do what one can to render execrable the fanaticism which has either led a father to hang his son or led eight magistrates to break an innocent man on the wheel.'[31]

Voltaire decided to intervene. He paid lawyers and investigators to collect the facts, and once he was convinced that Calas was innocent, he started to publicize the case, writing innumerable letters to individuals and articles for publication.

His purpose was not only to clear the name of the unfortunate Calas, but to turn public opinion against the kind of religious intolerance which had prompted the injustice and against the use of torture as a method of enforcing the law. In one of his pamphlets he noted that it was not only the English—'those hard-headed people who have robbed us of Canada'—who had renounced the use of torture; even the Russians—'who not so long ago were considered barbarians'—had abolished it; and only the French 'cling to their ancient atrocious practices'.[32]

In his campaign against torture Voltaire had the support of Versailles. The government was ready to revoke the edict of 1670 which authorized torture, but the *parlements* insisted on retaining it. Malesherbes, the minister responsible for the censorship, encouraged Voltaire's friend the Abbé Morellet to publish in 1762 *A Manual for Inquisitors*, drawn from the most sadistic parts of the *Directorium* of the Holy Office of the fourteenth century. This brought the cruellest practices of the Inquisition into the light of the eighteenth century, and startled readers by the resuscitation of horrors supposed to be dead. Malesherbes told Morellet that he might imagine he was publishing a collection of unheard-of facts and forgotten practices of the Church, but the truth was that the procedures described were 'as nearly as possible identical with the criminal jurisprudence of France at that very moment'.[33]

Voltaire devoted much of his time for three years to clearing Calas's name. Finally, on the third anniversary of his death, Calas was exonerated of all guilt by the *maîtres des requêtes*, a royal court sitting at Versailles. In the words of his most recent biographer, 'It was to prove the greatest of all Voltaire's individual triumphs.'[34]

But if the Calas case was the most famous in Voltaire's career as a champion of *les droits de l'homme*, it was certainly not the only one. There was the case of a Protestant couple named Sirven, a father and mother accused of murdering their daughter because she wanted to become a nun, and sentenced to death *in absentia* by the *parlement* of Toulouse. Then there was the case of the Comte de Lally, a general beheaded in the Place de Grève on the orders of the Paris *parlement* as a scapegoat for a military defeat in India. There was also the case of a girl of eighteen being hanged for stealing eighteen napkins from a mistress who had failed to pay her wages. The case which caused Voltaire the most distress and provoked his undying hostility to the *parlements* of France was that of the Chevalier de la Barre, another eighteen-year-old, who had sung songs thought blasphemous near a crucifix at Abbeville, and was thereupon arrested, tried, tortured, and condemned by the local magistrates to have his hand cut off and his body burned by a slow fire. When the appeal came before the *parlement* of Paris, fifteen of the twenty-five noble judges confirmed the verdict and only reduced the sentence to decapitation: the Chevalier de la Barre, like the Comte de Lally, was allowed an upper-class death by the axe, but that was the extent of the *parlement*'s humanity. A copy of Voltaire's *Lettres philosophiques* was thrown on the scaffold where the victim died.

La Barre's companion in the escapade of singing the blasphemous songs, a youth named Etallonde, escaped from France to be promptly, and pointedly, invited by Frederick II to Potsdam and offered a commission in the Prussian army. Frederick had played a key role in the drama of Voltaire's life, and at one time raised hopes that he might become the kind of 'philosopher-king' who would realize Voltaire's dream of enlightened absolute monarchy. Louis XV, unenlightened in his philosophy and unappreciative of Voltaire's genius, was a disappointment. King Stanislas of Poland, while both an intellectual and an admirer of Voltaire, had the marked disadvantage of being no longer on his throne; but Frederick of Prussia was every inch a monarch. He invited Voltaire in the most flattering terms to join his court in Germany, and Voltaire went, full of the highest expectations. It was a doomed enterprise. Like Plato in Syracuse, or Francis Bacon at the court of James I, and Denis Diderot, some years later, at the court of the Empress Catherine, Voltaire was destined to find himself unable to control the mind of a monarch who considered himself a philosopher already. Voltaire soon learned that Frederick had no desire to receive advice on how to rule, but only to receive the critical guidance—or rather the praise—of a literary man on his literary endeavours.

Voltaire did not like living in Prussia in a cold climate, surrounded by handsome soldiers but denied the company of beautiful women,[35] and expected to flatter a vain, despotic king. Frederick's hostility to religion was hardly an adequate basis for enduring friendship with Voltaire. Besides, Voltaire could not dissimulate his disapproval of Frederick's policy of building up a powerful army and then going to war. Voltaire was by way of being a pacifist, and war was an evil which he felt had to be ascribed, for the most part, to kings. 'War', he wrote,

'is something invented by men, by those three or four hundred persons scattered over the globe who are known as kings or princes and who are said—perhaps because of the harm they do—to be the image of divinity on earth . . . War is undoubtedly a fine art, which destroys the country-side, and which kills forty thousand or a hundred thousand men a year . . . And what is most marvellous about the infernal enterprise is that every Chief of murderers has his colours blessed and invokes God's name solemnly before he sets forth to kill his fellow men.[36]

Disappointment at the court of Frederick of Prussia made a dent in Voltaire's royalism. Some commentators claim that he became a democrat in his later years, and even publicly proclaimed himself to be one. The evidence for this is the dialogue written in 1768 entitled *L'A.B.C.*, where Voltaire has one of the speakers say:

I'll admit to you that I could easily put up with a democratic government . . . I enjoy seeing free men making the *laws* under which they live, as they have made their *houses*. It pleases me that my mason, my carpenter, my blacksmith who helped me build my dwelling, my neighbour the farmer, and my friend the manufacturer, all rise above their craft and know the public interest better than the most insolent Turkish governor. In a democracy, no day labourer, no artisan, need fear anyone or contempt . . . To be free, to have none but equals, that's the true life, the natural life of man.[37]

Leaving aside the patronizing tone of Voltaire's reference to the democratic classes,[38] we must remember that this dialogue dates from the period of his connection with Geneva.[39] There is nothing inconsistent in Voltaire's favouring democracy in Geneva or the cantons of Switzerland and royal absolutism in France, since he had always said that a political system must suit the character of the country concerned. Geneva was small enough, and had experience enough of republican government, for democracy to be a sensible system for its people.

Voltaire's *Idées républicaines*, often cited as evidence of his having been converted in old age from royalism to republicanism, dates from this same period. In fact *Idées républicaines* is a tract for the Genevans, as the journalist Friedrich Melchior Grimm explained in his *Correspondence littéraire* in January 1766, when the work first appeared:

The genius who lives at Ferney finds this a good moment to say his word about the quarrels that are dividing the republic of Geneva. He has published, continuing to hide himself from us, a little work of forty-five pages large octavo *Idées républicaines*, '*par un membre d'un corps*' [*sic*]. This is not a humorous work. It contains very sensible ideas, and without entering into the Genevan bickering, it proposes very wise solutions.[40]

Voltaire's attitude to the politics of Geneva changed as he came to know that city better.[41] On the surface Geneva was an almost ideal republic. Underneath it was a city of intolerance and strife. The people were divided into three classes; a patriciate of rich families, a hundred or two; a middle class of citizens, 1,500 adult males; and a lower class of *natifs* and *habitants* composing the majority of the population of 25,000 souls.

Originally Voltaire's friends in Geneva were members of the patriciate. When he first settled in the city in 1755 it was the patrician Tronchin who acquired his house, Les Délices, in his name, since Catholics were not allowed to own property in Geneva. Voltaire could then see nothing wrong with an arrangement whereby the richest and most cultured inhabitants directed the republic; the government seemed thoroughly enlightened, and even the Calvinism of the established Church appeared to have mellowed with time into a harmless unitarianism.

Gradually certain aspects of the regime began to trouble Voltaire. There was the incident of one Robert Covelle, condemned to genuflect before the consistory of Geneva as a sign of repentance for fathering an illegitimate child. Covelle refused to kneel, and Voltaire, who greeted him with mock ceremoniousness as '*Monsieur le Fornicateur*', proclaimed the right of a free man to stand upright before his accusers.[42] When Rousseau's *Émile* and *Social Contract* were burned in Geneva in 1762, and an order issued for the author's arrest, Voltaire was horrified. He detested Rousseau and Rousseau's opinions, but he believed in every author's right to freedom of expression, and he sprang to Rousseau's defence.[43]

By this time Voltaire had given up the house in Geneva, and

installed himself in the Château of Ferney just beyond the frontier. But he continued to intervene in the affairs of the republic. When Rousseau in his *Lettres écrites de la montagne* described the patrician council of Geneva as 'twenty-five despots' Voltaire was forced to agree. So Voltaire deserted his patrician friends to support the middle-class citizens in their endeavour to restore the authentic republican constitution of their state. Voltaire's *Idées républicaines* puts the case of republicans in a republic—and in so far as it is anti-aristocratic, it is in no way at odds with the anti-aristocratic elements in those writings where Voltaire advocates royalism for a kingdom. Both are pleas for undivided sovereignty; where the *nation* is sovereign *its* sovereignty should be absolute: where the *king* is sovereign *his* sovereignty should be absolute.

Voltaire's basic political philosophy had not changed. He did not advocate the introduction of republican ideas into kingdoms: he only proposed that a republic should be governed according to republican principles. Besides, he drew from history the lesson that republican constitutions were only suited to small states, and frankly he did not think much of tiny states; apart from Geneva, he sometimes spoke, with ill-concealed contempt, of 'the republic of San Marino and the canton of Zug'.

Even the republicans of Geneva disappointed Voltaire in the end. He found that the middle-class citizens were no better democrats than the patricians. For once these citizens had achieved satisfaction, the lower classes of the city—the *natifs* and *habitants*—asked in turn for rights and liberties to be extended to them, as they had been promised when the citizens needed their help against the patricians; to this plea the citizens replied with the same violence with which the patricians had formerly reacted to their claims. Fearing lower-class rebellion in 1770, the middle classes took up arms, killed three *natifs*, wounded more, and put a hundred or so in prison.

Voltaire, disgusted by the hypocrisy of the Genevan citizens, became the champion of the plebeian cause, and tried to persuade the French government to establish at Versoix, near the frontier, a place where persecuted workers from Geneva could find refuge on French soil. It was an ironical situation, since Geneva had itself grown up as a city of refuge from French persecution. In the event the Versoix project came to nothing, but Voltaire, all on his own as chatelain of Ferney, found homes and jobs for dozens of exiled *natifs*. It was a characteristic act of Voltaire as practical reformer and benevolent *seigneur*.

Read in the light of these circumstances, Voltaire's *Idées républicaines* cannot be taken as evidence of any sort of conversion of the author to a republican ideology; on the other hand, it does indicate a diminution of his earlier contempt for the popular classes, and a greater belief in the capacity of the ordinary man, if only he were decently educated, to enact the role of citizen.

Voltaire once described himself as an 'Epicurean'. 'Stoicism', he wrote,

is undoubtedly better than Christian moral teaching. It breeds a better character. A Stoic must earn salvation by living well, whereas a Christian needs only a last-minute repentance after thirty years of crime to be assured of eternal bliss. But I am not a Stoic. I am rather an Epicurean. I do not think life is to be endured: I think it is to be enjoyed.[44]

In his later years Voltaire moved closer to Stoicism, but it would perhaps be better to describe him with a modern word as a utilitarian. He did not seek happiness for himself alone; he wanted it for everyone. The famous formula of Cesare Beccaria, 'la massima felicità del massimo numero', was one which well expressed Voltaire's own measure of the good, and Jeremy Bentham, who corresponded with Voltaire, acknowledged him as his 'master'. Even so, Voltaire did not carry his utilitarianism to the lengths of those theorists who believed that the elimination of poverty should be a matter of public policy and that the state should tax the rich in order to redistribute wealth among the poor. Voltaire retained a more typically bourgeois outlook. One of the reasons why he admired Locke so much was that Locke took such care to justify a natural right to property, and put that right together with the rights to life and liberty. When Voltaire read Rousseau's *Discourse on the Origin of Inequality* one of the things which enraged him most was Rousseau's suggestion that the right to property was somehow fraudulent: 'What!' Voltaire wrote in the margin of his text, 'has a man no right to the fruit of his labour?'[45]

Voltaire was very much a man of property. In the course of a long life he made a great deal of money—some of it by shrewd organization of the publication of his books, some by inheritance from his father, much more by shrewd investment, and some by luck in a lottery—if 'luck' is the word for finding a loophole in the rules which enabled him to sweep in the prize.

Towards the end of his life he said that he had once thought nothing of money, but had then seen so many men of letters poor and despised that he resolved not to augment their number: 'I turned myself into a hammer to avoid being used as an anvil. The first efforts to make money are painful, but it soon becomes very satisfying to watch one's wealth accumulate; and in old age, when money is most necessary, it is almost a duty to be rich'.[46]

The wealth he acquired enabled Voltaire to live in luxury—especially at his château at Ferney, where he had his private theatre and his private chapel (the only one dedicated, he explained, to God alone). He was delighted to find in the writings of the economists of his time reasons to believe that luxury was socially advantageous. Among his favourite economists was J. F. Melon, author of *Essai politique sur le commerce*, published in 1734. Melon argues in these pages that commerce consists in the exchange of what is superfluous for what is necessary. The more prosperous a country, the more advantage it will gain from trading with other nations. Commerce elevates a country from savage customs to the benefits of civilization. The wealth acquired by one section of a society will have useful effects for all the other sections; the high consumption of some will provide a profitable market for the production of others. The desire of each to increase his well-being will lead to the enjoyment of luxury, which Melon defines as 'extraordinary sumptuosity produced by wealth and secure government'.[47] With the passage of time, yesterday's luxuries become today's necessities; and thus the innocent pursuit and enjoyment of luxury become motives of general progress.

Voltaire not only read Melon; he also read Bernard Mandeville, and was at the same time attracted and repelled. If Voltaire's poem in defence of luxury, *Le Mondain*, reproduces the arguments of Melon, its sequel, *La Defense du mondain*, is closer to Mandeville, but Mandeville without his naked cynicism.[48]

Mandeville, as Voltaire understood him, maintained that it was vice that kept the economic system moving. The vanity of women made them demand more and more clothing, indeed more elaborate and original styles of clothing every season; and this is what kept the textile industry active together with the wholesalers and retailers of clothes. The greed of men made them demand ever greater refinement in their food and drink, and this generated business for farmers and vintners and purveyors of every sort. The avarice of merchants prompted them to risk their capital in the hope of gain, and this made industry and commerce possible. Even the dishonesty of thieves made work for locksmiths and policemen.

Voltaire, with his special reverence for property, was particularly scandalized by this last of Mandeville's suggestions. After all, he protested, there was poison in many medicines, but that did not mean that poison could be praised as what cured patients. However, under the influence of Madam du Châtelet, his bluestocking mistress, who admired Mandeville to the point of translating his work into French, Voltaire came to see more merit in *The Fable of the Bees*.

Mandeville's argument was that men could not have both the comforts of life and virtue and innocence. The comforts of life—luxury, wealth, power—were the products of vice. A virtuous people according to Mandeville would not do much or change much (and here one is reminded of Montesquieu's Troglodytes); a virtuous people would be frugal, public-spirited, and weak; they would have no dynamic, and nothing would motivate their economy. On the other hand, a vicious people, greedy for more and more private satisfaction, would be active, industrious, and adventurous, and their economy would therefore become prosperous and powerful.

It pleased Voltaire that Mandeville should cut short the cackle and the cant about virtue; but Voltaire, for all his scepticism, was not a cynic. He took an altogether more kindly view of man's sociability than did Mandeville. He believed that men acquired altruistic habits as a result of living in families, and that nature had instilled in everyone both compassion for others and a *bienveillance générale*. He could not accept Mandeville's suggestion that morality was bred entirely from the so-called vice of pride, society exacting good behaviour from its members only by making them ashamed of being ill regarded by their neighours. Indeed, Voltaire refused to treat as vices what Mandeville considered vices, or as virtues what Mandeville called virtues, nor could he accept the suggestion that Sparta was morally better than

Athens. He agreed with Mandeville that Sparta was the city of austerity but he could see no evidence of greater virtue among the Spartans; on the contrary, he regarded Sparta, with its militarism and regimentation and its massacres, as morally repugnant. In the end he came to see Mandeville—a Dutchman who wrote in English—as an inverted Calvinist, taking Calvin's conception of what virtue was and then mocking virtue. Voltaire had an altogether different conception of virtue: right or good actions were those which either diminished the amount of suffering in the world or which increased the amount of happiness.

In other words, Voltaire's moral philosophy was that of Beccaria. When Beccaria's famous book *Dei delitti e delle pene* (*On Crimes and Punishments*) came out in 1765 Voltaire read it in Italian, pronounced it 'philosophical'—his highest word of praise, and added: 'The author is a brother.' He then produced a short commentary[49] on the book which shows us Voltaire drawing out the policy implications for France of Beccaria's penal theories. Voltaire insists on the importance of keeping the province of law separate from that of morality. Prisons and penalties should not be used as forms of retribution, but as a means of deterrence and reform. Society must protect itself, but no man should assume the office of God and inflict punishment on sinners. Penalties could be justified only in terms of utility. The death penalty was rarely, if ever justified: and torture was as useless as it was odious. 'True jurisprudence is to prevent crime, not to put to death the unfortunate.'[50]

Just procedures were needed in the administration of laws—fair and open trials, strict rules of evidence, and so forth—and in the making and codification of laws. It was very necessary for laws to be both uniform and intelligible; the only test should be that of social advantage and the public interest.

It was in his thoughts about law that Voltaire came closest to Montesquieu, which is not altogether surprising in view of the fact that Beccaria, who inspired him, had been inspired in his turn by Montesquieu. But Voltaire was close to Montesquieu in many other ways as well. Despite the differences between them, they shared an intense belief in freedom. For both Voltaire and Montesquieu the central problem of politics is how to contrive government so that men may be at the same time free and ruled. Montesquieu proposes a solution on Aristotelian lines: men can be both free and ruled if they are ruled by law rather than by men, and he argues that this can be accomplished if sovereignty is so divided that one power can balance and correct the others. Voltaire's solution is to entrust the protection of freedom to an enlightened sovereign whose power is undivided and entirely committed to the promotion of his people's rights and happiness.

The weakness of Voltaire's formula is that it allows for no institutional corps to ensure that the sovereign adheres to such policies. There is no appeal to the law, since Voltaire's sovereign would be the ultimate arbiter of the law. There is no appeal to God, since Voltaire's God had been shown by the Lisbon earthquake to be asleep. There is just one way by which Voltaire might be thought to be able to solve his problem: by proposing that the sovereign should be answerable to and, if need be, controlled by the people.

Indeed as he grew older and became less confident of finding an enlightened monarch among the actual princes of the world, it seems that Voltaire moved towards adopting this solution, advocating not democracy (except perhaps for the Swiss), but something which resembles democracy—that is, a populistic absolutism—a conception of the undivided sovereignty of a monarch being derived from the authorization of the people constantly renewed—'le plébiscite de tous les jours', in the phrase of Ernest Renan. It is not as appealing to the Anglo-Saxon mind as is Montesquieu's solution, but it gives an intimation of, and suggests an intellectual justification of, something which actually emerged in French political experience after Voltaire's time—the centralized rule of a Napoleon I, a Napoleon III or a Charles de Gaulle, drawing its authority not from intermediate institutions in the state but from a direct appeal to the electorate.

Voltaire never faced squarely, with Locke, the question of the people's right to decide whether their sovereign had abused his office, and their corresponding right to dismiss him. Voltaire, who had no wish to be an apologist of revolution, shrank from pressing his argument to such disturbing conclusions. But those revolutionary implications were there, and one can well understand why, apart from such extraordinary rulers as Frederick and Catherine, the monarchs of Europe regarded Voltaire with a certain dread. He was their friend, their champion and advocate. The trouble was that he swept away, one by one, all the things that made a king feel safe on his throne: religion, tradition, habit, customs, and the established order of society. He gave people new reasons for obedience, but he took away their old motives for obedience. And thus, paradoxically, Voltaire proved to be even more subversive of absolute government in defending it than Montesquieu in attacking it.[51]

# 3

# Rousseau

As everyone knows, Rousseau had an odd sort of upbringing. In many ways it was an unfortunate one, but its peculiarity must have contributed to the originality of his work. Like Kierkegaard and John Stuart Mill and Bertrand Russell, he was not allowed to go to school, so that he was both deprived of the benefits and spared the disadvantages of a conventional education. When he started to read the philosophers of the past, his mind was untouched by the opinions of ushers and dons. He read Machiavelli and Hobbes without being fully forewarned of the wickedness of their doctrines. His uninstructed mind responded to their arguments, and when the time came, he carried political philosophy forward in those channels into which Machiavelli and Hobbes had propelled it. Inevitably he acquired something of the same bad name.

Rousseau took from Hobbes the idea that man was originally solitary and that all human society was contractual, not natural.[1] The development of this idea is to be found in the *Discourse on the Origin of Inequality*[2] and the *Essay on the Origin of Languages*.[3] Rousseau adopted Hobbes's idea that men had lost their original freedom when they entered civil society, but he took from Machiavelli a further idea: that men could recover freedom—or find a new kind of freedom—in a well-ordered republic. The development of this second idea is to be found in Rousseau's most celebrated work of political philosophy, *The Social Contract*.[4]

Where Montesquieu is a theorist of parliamentary monarchy, and Voltaire a champion of enlightened royalism, Rousseau expounds a third political ideology—republicanism. But it is a special sort of republicanism, not based, like Montesquieu's early idealization of republican government, entirely on images of Classical Antiquity, for Rousseau had had actual experience of living in a republic—one of the very few in the modern world—Geneva, and Geneva was as important in the formation of

Rousseau's political thought as Florence was in that of Machiavelli.

Only one of Rousseau's books is called *The Social Contract*, but in fact two quite distinct types of contract are depicted in his writings: the first the social contract which 'must have happened' generally at an early stage of human evolution; the second the one which would need to take place if men are to live together in freedom. The idea of human societies being contractual in origin springs from a recognition that human beings are not social beings in the ways that ants and bees, for example, are social; nature does not impel each of us to do always what is advantageous for the group or tribe. We may have, some of us more than others, altruistic feelings which drive us to do for the community as much as, or more than, we do for ourselves; but even that entails a process of reasoning, thinking out what course of action would be best for society. There is no instinct driving each individual to perform an allotted social role as there is in the social insects. Each human being has to decide what actions he is to undertake, and where there is this freedom there is controversy. People do not all agree as to what is to be done for the good of all, even if all agree that the good of all should be promoted. Every human being has a mind of his own; and every human being's instincts are self-protective. Men are a race of autonomous individuals.

Rousseau believed more than most philosophers in the radical individualism of natural man; yet he also believed that man was, as Aristotle said, a political animal, a *zoon politikon*. How can we reconcile these beliefs? The answer lies perhaps in the ambiguity of a word which figures prominently in all eighteenth-century thought: 'nature'. Nature, for Rousseau, stood opposed to culture; natural man was original man as he lived in the savage state under the rule of nature alone. But nature was also a force that demanded the attention of man in the civilized state. There its commands were of a different order, and were often unheeded; unheeded to such an extent that Rousseau could even claim that modern man was alienated from nature and, as a result of this, that man had lost both his happiness and his freedom.

It was in the autumn of 1753 that the Academy of Dijon announced an essay competition on the question 'What is the origin of inequality among men, and is it authorized by natural law?' Rousseau responded promptly. 'If the Academy has the courage to raise such a question', he said to himself, 'I will have the courage to respond.'[5] Rousseau did not in his final treatment of the subject have much to say about the second part of the question—as to whether inequality was authorized by natural law: what interested him was the problem of origins. He tells us that he went for long walks in the forest of Saint-Germain to reflect on the life of man as it must have been before civilizations began: 'I dared to strip man's nature naked, to follow the evolution of those times and things which have disfigured him; I compared man as he made himself with man as nature made him, and I discovered that his supposed improvement had generated all his miseries.'[6]

The theme of apparent progress concealing actual regression was not a new one for Rousseau. He had expounded it in an earlier, prize-winning essay he had written for the Academy of Dijon, his *Discourse on the Sciences and the Arts* of 1749. There Rousseau had argued that the more science, industry, technology, and culture became developed and sophisticated the more they carried human societies from decent simplicity towards moral corruption. Paradoxically, this discourse was a great success among the very people Rousseau attacked: the fashionable *salons* and scientific circles of Paris, in which he himself moved at that time. What Rousseau said in his first discourse was not particularly original, for similar attacks on modern culture had been made by reactionary writers, both Catholic and Puritan. Rousseau's argument amazed the public because it came from a supposedly progressive author, one of the leading collaborators of Diderot's great *Encyclopédie*, an enterprise dedicated to the ideals of scientific progress and the improvement of knowledge. Some readers were left in doubt about the author's sincerity, but time was to prove that he really meant what he said. Progress, Rousseau insisted, was an illusion. The human race had taken a wrong turning, or more than one wrong turning. In the second discourse Rousseau wrote for the Academy of Dijon, the *Discourse on Inequality*, he carried his analysis much further back in time.

On this occasion, Rousseau did not succeed at Dijon, but the work was altogether more original and remarkable than the earlier discourse which won the prize. In less than a hundred pages Rousseau outlined a theory of human evolution which prefigured the discoveries of Darwin;[7] he revolutionized the study of anthropology and linguistics,[8] and he made a seminal contribution to political philosophy.[9] Even if his argument was distorted by his critics, and perhaps not always well understood by his readers, it altered people's ways of thinking about themselves and their world, and even changed their ways of feeling.

Rousseau begins his enquiry by noting that there are two kinds of inequality among men. The first consists in natural inequalities, arising from differences in strength and intelligence, agility, and so forth; the second consists in artificial inequalities, which derive from conventions which men themselves have introduced into society. Rousseau claims that it is because of these artificial inequalities that some men are richer than others, some more honoured than others, and some obeyed by others. He takes the object of his enquiry to be to discover the origins of such artificial inequalities, since there would be no point in asking why nature had come to bestow its gifts unequally. He therefore sees his first task as that of distinguishing what is properly and originally natural to man from what man has made for himself. This he thinks can only be done by going back in time to ascertain what man was like before he had formed societies or groups. The way to learn about natural man was to rediscover original man. Although Rousseau did not advance the view later put forward by Darwin that man evolved from a cousin of the apes, he did suggest that man developed from a primitive biped, related to the orang-utan, into the sophisticated creature of modern times, and that this evolution could be understood largely as a process of adaptation and struggle.[10]

Rousseau does not claim to be the first to try to explain human society by contrasting it with a pre-social state of nature; he simply argues that earlier writers, such as Hobbes and Locke (whose works, with which he was at any rate partially familiar in French translation, had greatly impressed him), had failed in the attempt.

They have all felt it necessary to go back to the state of nature, but none of them has succeeded in getting there . . . all these philosophers, talking ceaselessly of need, greed, oppression, desire, and pride, have transported into the state of nature concepts formed in society. They speak of savage man and they depict civilized man.[11]

The philosopher Rousseau has most in mind here is Hobbes. In Hobbes the state of nature is represented as one of war of each man against all men; human beings are seen as aggressive, avaricious, proud, selfish, and afraid; and on the basis of this analysis of natural man, Hobbes asserts that without the mortal solicitude of an absolute sovereign to bind them together in the civil state, men's lives must be 'solitary, poor, nasty, brutish and short'.[12] Rousseau argues, against Hobbes, that all the unpleasant characteristics of the human condition derive not from nature but from society; and that if we look far enough back in our search for the origins of man and reach the true state of nature, we shall find a being who is admittedly (as Hobbes says) solitary, but is otherwise healthy, happy, free, and good.

Rousseau envisages original man as being removed only to a small extent from the beast, 'an animal less strong than some, less agile than others, but, taken as a whole, the most advantageously organized of all'.[13] Natural man has an easy life. 'I see him satisfying his hunger under an oak, quenching his thirst at the first stream, finding his bed under the same tree which provided his meal, and, behold, his needs are furnished.'[14]

In Rousseau's state of nature there is no scarcity and no ill health. He notes that the savages who still exist in the modern world are reported by explorers[15] to have robust constitutions, free from the diseases which afflict men in Europe, where the rich are overfed and the poor underfed, and everyone is harassed by the desires, anxieties, fatigues, excesses, passions, and sorrows which civilization generates. Domesticated men, like domesticated animals, says Rousseau, grow soft, whereas in the state of nature they are fit because they have to be fit in order to survive.

Accustomed from infancy to the inclemencies of the weather, and the rigours of the seasons, used to fatigue, and forced to defend themselves and their prey naked and unarmed against other wild beasts or to escape from them by running faster than they, men develop a robust and almost immutable constitution. Children coming into the world with the excellent physique of their fathers, and strengthening it by the same exercise which produced it, thus acquire all the vigour of which the human race is capable. Nature treats them exactly as the law of Sparta treated the children of its citizens: it makes those who are well-constituted strong and robust, and makes the others die.[16]

The reference to Sparta is significant here: for Sparta, as he understood it, was for Rousseau an ideal republic;[17] and one of the reasons why it was ideal is that it enabled men to recover something of what they lost when they left the state of nature.

Even though Rousseau emphasizes the similarities between the life of original man and the life of a beast, he nevertheless depicts man as being, from the beginning, radically different from other animals in possessing two characteristics. These two characteristics do *not* include the one traditionally held to distinguish man from beast, that of reason. For Rousseau what makes man unique among living creatures is first, his freedom, and secondly, his capacity for self-improvement. Here, whether Rousseau is right or wrong, he is arrestingly original.

Natural man is free for Rousseau in three senses of the word 'freedom'. First, he has free will. This is a crucial form of freedom for Rousseau. Hobbes and most of Rousseau's friends in the circle of the *Encyclopédie* were determinists,[18] believing that man was a 'machine', albeit more complex than any other machine in nature, but subject to the same laws of cause and effect. Rousseau was willing enough to use the metaphor of a machine, but he claimed that whereas among the beasts nature alone 'operated the machine', in the case of human beings the individual contributed to his own operations, in his capacity as an autonomous agent. 'The beast chooses or rejects by instinct; man by an act of free will.'[19]

This metaphysical freedom, or freedom of the will, is for Rousseau a defining characteristic of man, and as such is possessed by all men in all conditions, whether of nature or society. But there are two other forms of freedom which he sees men as enjoying in the state of nature, but not necessarily having in society. One of these freedoms man could not possibly possess in civil society, and that is anarchic freedom—freedom from any kind of political rule. This would, of course, be absolute in the state of nature since the state of nature is by definition a condition in which there is no government and no positive law. The third freedom enjoyed by man in Rousseau's state of nature is personal freedom, the independence of a man who has no master, no employer, no superior, no one on whom he is in any way dependent. While Rousseau's remarks on anarchic freedom are ambiguous, there is no uncertainty about the value and importance he attaches to personal freedom. This is the great advantage the savage has over the civilized man. In the civilized world, most men are enslaved; in the state of nature no one can enslave anyone else:

Is there a man who is so much stronger than me, and who is, moreover, lazy enough and fierce enough to compel me to provide for his sustenance while he remains idle? He must resolve not to lose sight of me for a single moment . . . for fear I should escape or kill him.[20]

Besides enjoying *liberté* in these three senses, Rousseau's natural man differs from the beasts in possessing *perfectibilité*. This word must not be translated, as it often is, as 'perfectibility', because Rousseau did not assert in his *Discourse on Inequality*, or anywhere else, that man was perfectible; all he claimed was that man had the capacity to better himself by his own efforts. He never suggested that man would ever be perfect, or even that man was on the road towards perfection.[21] The French verb *perfecter*, as he used it, means simply 'to improve'; and the capacity for *perfectibilité* which Rousseau attributed to human beings was nothing more than a *capacity for self-improvement*.

The story of human evolution as Rousseau unfolds it is in many ways a melancholy one, marked, in the first place, by man's loss of two of the three sorts of freedom he enjoyed in the state of nature, and then by his misuse of his capacity for self-improvement to do things which have made him worse instead of better.

Original men, or 'savages' as Rousseau sometimes chooses to call our forebears as they lived in the first state of nature, were simple beings, with no language, very little capacity for thought, few needs, and, in consequence, few passions. 'Since savage man desires only the things which he knows and knows only those things of which possession is within his power or easily obtained, then nothing ought to be so tranquil as his soul or so limited as his mind.'[22] For such a being, the exercise of will, desire, and fear will be the whole of his inner experience: even the fears of a savage are limited to apprehension of present danger. He can fear pain, but not death, because he has no concept of death; anxiety, that disease of the imagination, is unknown to him.

Conceptual thinking, Rousseau suggests, developed only with speech; and in the early stages of life on earth, men needed no language:

Having neither houses nor huts, nor any kind of property, everyone slept where he chanced to find himself, and often for one night only; as males and females united fortuitously, according to encounters, opportunities, and desires, they required no speech to express what they had to say to one another, and they separated with the same ease.[23]

Here we have a denial of the view that the family is a natural society, and in a long footnote to the *Discourse on Inequality* Rousseau offers a detailed criticism of Locke's argument that nature itself impels human males and females to unite on a settled basis to feed and shelter their young.[24] Rousseau agrees with Locke that a man may have a motive for remaining with a particular woman when she has a child, but he protests that Locke fails to prove that a man would have any motive for staying with a particular woman during the nine months of her pregnancy:

For it is not a matter of knowing why the man should remain attached to the woman after the birth, but why he should become attached to her after the conception. His appetite satisfied, the man has no longer any need for a particular woman, nor the woman for a particular man. The man has not the least care about, nor perhaps the least idea of the consequences of his action. One goes off in one direction, the other in another, and there is no likelihood that at the end of nine months either will remember having known the other.[25]

The point Rousseau is making here is that while it is undoubtedly advantageous to the human race that there should be permanent unions between males and females, it does not follow that such unions are 'established by nature'.[26] However, it will be observed that in *The Social Contract*[27] and other later writings, Rousseau himself speaks of the family as a 'natural society'; and in later pages of the *Discourse on Inequality* itself he speaks of a father being master of his child 'by a law of nature'. Is this a case of Rousseau contradicting himself? Perhaps not. For Rousseau, as we have noticed, uses the word 'natural' in more than one sense: first for everything that belongs to the state of nature, and then for what nature does to human beings once they have left the state of nature and started to live in society. Behaviour which is not natural in the savage *becomes* natural in the civilized condition. Rousseau has a great deal to say about the transformation which man undergoes as he moves from the one state to the other. His reasoning looks less paradoxical if one follows his argument in detail.

A question he refuses to answer is: 'Which was more necessary, previously formed society for the institution of languages, or previously invented languages for the establishment of society?'[28] He limits himself in the *Discourse on Inequality* to saying that men's first words were natural cries. General ideas came into men's minds with the aid of abstract words, so that the development of language itself helped to create the difficulties with which civilized man torments himself. The savage, living by instinct, has no moral experience; he has no notions of right and wrong. In the state of nature man is good, but there is no question of his being virtuous or vicious. He is happy, free, innocent—and that is all: 'One could say that savages are not wicked precisely because they do not know what it is to be good; for it is neither the development of intelligence nor the restraints of laws, but the calm of the passions and men's ignorance of vice which prevent them from doing evil'.[29]

There is here in Rousseau the germ of an idea developed more fully by his contemporary and friend David Hume, namely the idea that all men's actions are prompted by passions and that while calm passions generate harmless behaviour, violent passions drive men to do evil to themselves and others. Rousseau maintains that men's passions in the state of nature are both calm and few in number, and therefore innocuous, whereas in society their passions become so multiplied and intensified that the consequences are ruinous.

Man in the savage state has one sentiment or disposition which Rousseau speaks of as a 'natural virtue', and that is compassion or pity. He suggests that this virtue can be witnessed even in animals, not only in the tenderness of mothers for their young, but in 'the aversion of horses against trampling on any living body'.[30] He goes on to argue that this natural feeling of pity is the source of all the most important social virtues, such as kindness, generosity, mercy, and humanity. He adds a characteristic reflection on the corruption of this excellent sentiment among the men and women of modernity; because they are so removed from nature, they no longer feel pity. In 'the state of reason', as Rousseau calls it, people cease to identify themselves with the suffering being, as they do in the state of nature; this is because reason 'breeds pride . . . and turns man inward into himself'.[31]

In the modern world, it is the least educated people, the ones in whom the power of reasoning is least developed, who exhibit towards their suffering fellow men the most lively and sincere commiseration. Rousseau does not miss the opportunity here of pointing an accusing finger at his fellow philosophers:

It is philosophy which isolates a man, and prompts him to say in secret at the sight of another suffering: 'Perish if you will; I am safe.' No longer can anything but dangers to society in general disturb the tranquil sleep of the philosopher or drag him from his bed. A fellow man may with impunity be murdered under his window, for the philosopher has only to put his hands over his ears and argue a little with himself to prevent nature, which rebels inside him, from making him identify himself with the victim of the murder. The savage man entirely lacks this admirable talent.[32]

If Rousseau's state of nature has so few disadvantages, the reader is bound to ask, how did men ever come to leave it? Rousseau depicts this departure taking place by a series of stages. The first really important transformation of the human condition was the creation of what Rousseau calls 'nascent society', a process he envisages as having evolved over a long stretch of time. He locates as the central feature of this development the institution of settled domiciles or 'huts'. Once men made homes for themselves, the prolonged cohabitation of males and females led to the introduction of the family; and it is this which marked— according to Rousseau's theory—man's departure from the true state of nature, where the individual was solitary and sexually promiscuous, into a condition where men formed the habit of living under the same roof with a mate and were therefore no longer alone.

Rousseau speaks of this passage of man from the state of nature to 'nascent society' as the 'epoch of a first revolution which established and differentiated families' and which introduced 'property of a sort'.[33] This 'property of a sort' must, however, be distinguished from the full concept of property—that of lawful ownership—which emerges only after a further revolution. All that man has in 'nascent society' is a feeling of possession of the hut he occupies. This feeling may have produced many quarrels, but, Rousseau adds, 'since the strongest men were probably the first to build themselves huts which they felt themselves able to defend, it is reasonable to believe that the weak found it quicker and safer to imitate them rather than try to dislodge them,[34] and to have refrained from attempting to dispossess them from fear of blows rather than from any respect for ownership.

'Nascent society' is the period of human evolution which Rousseau regards as almost ideal: it is the Garden of Eden in his vision of the past.[35] Human beings had become gentler and more loving than they were in the savage state. No longer were individuals solitary and indifferent to the fate of others. Settled homes produced finer feelings. 'The first movements of the heart were the effect of this new situation, which united in a common dwelling husbands and wives, fathers and children. The habit of living together gave birth to the noblest sentiments known to man, namely conjugal love and paternal love. Each family became a little society, all the better united because mutual affection and liberty were its only bonds.'[36]

While man in 'nascent society' was no longer solitary, he was not yet the enemy of his fellow creatures. Midway between 'the stupidity of brutes' and 'the disastrous enlightenment of civilized men' he was 'restrained by natural pity from harming anyone'.[37] It was the golden mean between the 'indolence' of the primitive state of nature and the 'petulant activity' of modern pride; it was the best time the human race had ever known, 'the true youth of the world.'[38]

The reader is bound to ask why, if the simple condition of 'nascent society' was so delightful, did men ever quit it? In the *Essay on the Origin of Languages*, Rousseau suggests that primitive men were driven to organize more developed societies as a result of 'natural disasters, such as floods, eruptions of volcanoes, earthquakes, or great fires;'[39] as if only a miracle could explain their catastrophic passage to a condition of unhappiness. In the *Discourse on Inequality* he provides an alternative explanation for the development of organized society: economic shortage. As the number of persons on earth increased, the natural abundance of provisions diminished; no longer able to feed himself and his family on the herbs he could find, the individual had to start eating meat and to unite with his neighbours in order to hunt game in groups.

Thus associations larger than the family were formed, and 'nascent society' became 'society'—although as yet still an anarchic or pre-political society. This development produced important moral and psychological changes in men and women.

Ceasing in the context of the family to be a solitary person, each became in the context of society an egoistic person.

Even within the family, important changes took place. Individuals lost their independence. Women began to bear more children, and so became less capable of providing for their nourishment and protecting them. They had to rely on their mates. Women became weaker in the context of the family home. Males and females were no longer equal as they had been in the state of nature. Differences between the sexes increased as women became sedentary in the house, and men became ever more active as they roamed around, with male companions, looking for food and clothing and furnishings for their dwellings.

As men accumulated these more refined commodities, they began to develop 'needs'—that is, an attachment to things of which 'the loss became more cruel than the possession was sweet'.[40]

Language, too, developed with the demand for communication, first within the family and then between neighbours, and association between neighbours led to the formation of communities. It was at this point that inequality between one man and another originated: 'people became accustomed to judging different objects and making comparisons; they gradually acquired ideas of merit and of beauty, which in turn produced feelings of preference'.[41]

As ideas and sentiments were cultivated, the human race became sociable. People met in front of their huts or under a tree; singing and dancing became their amusements; and each looked at others, knowing that others looked at him. Each wanted to excel in his neighbours' eyes: 'He who sang or danced the best, he who was the most handsome, the strongest, the most adroit or the most eloquent became the most highly regarded; and this was the first step towards inequality, and at the same time towards vice.'[42]

Men began to base their conception of themselves on what other people thought of them. The idea of 'consideration' entered their minds; each wanted respect, and soon demanded respect as a right. The duties of civility emerged even among savages; a man who was wounded in his pride was even more offended than a man who was wounded in his body, and each 'punished the contempt another showed him in proportion to the esteem he accorded himself'.[43]

In society, says Rousseau, man becomes 'denatured'. His *amour de soi-même*, or self-love, an instinctive, self-protective, self-regarding disposition derived from nature, is transformed in society into *amour-propre*, or pride, the desire to be superior to others and to be esteemed by them.

One must not confuse self-love and pride: two passions very different in their nature and in their effects. Self-love is a natural sentiment which prompts every animal to watch over its own conservation and which, directed in man by reason and modified by pity, produces humanity and virtue. Pride is only a relative, artificial sentiment born in society, prompting each individual to attach more importance to himself than to anyone else and inspiring all the injuries men do to themselves and to others.[44]

Another important development took place in human experience at the stage of pre-political association. Sex became a destructive factor.[45] Rousseau claims that sexual desires are weak in the state of nature because they are like those of animals, directed to any available partner. In the social state sexual desires become strong as they come to be concentrated on a chosen person. In other words, there emerges not only conjugal love, but romantic love:

As a result of seeing each other, people cannot do without seeing more of each other. A tender and sweet sentiment insinuates itself into the soul, and at the least obstacle becomes an inflamed fury; jealousy awakens with love; discord triumphs and the gentlest of passions receives the sacrifice of human blood.[46]

Sex, a trivial thing in the state of nature, serves from the earliest stages of civilization both to bring human beings together as lovers and to divide them as rivals. Romantic love has an evolutionary purpose, for while conjugal love keeps people within their own little family, romantic love carries them into a wider society.[47] It is a motor of community; but at the same time it undermines sociability by the bitter conflicts it provokes as a consequence of competition between suitors for a particular person's favours.

Love is seen by Rousseau as being even more important for women than it is for men. It is an instrument of their purposes. He asserts: 'Love is cultivated by women with much skill and care in order to establish their empire over men, and so make dominant the sex that ought to obey.'[48] How does this come about?

Rousseau's argument is that women, weakened as they are domesticated, and grown to be dependent on men to an extent that men are not dependent on women, have to use cunning to make men stay attached to them. Each woman must make some man love her enough to shelter, feed, and protect her, and keep her as his cherished mate. In order for women to make men as dependent on them as they are dependent on men, they must dominate men, and dominate them by devious manœuvres and manipulations, since they cannot dominate them by force. Rousseau maintains that in order to understand sexual relationships in society it is necessary to stress the differences between male and female, and not to imagine, as feminists imagine, that the sexual equality which prevailed in the state of nature can continue among the civilized.

There are, however, some inequalities which Rousseau does deplore. The inequalities which he sees as most inimical to freedom and to nature are those which arise from the division of labour:

So long as they applied themselves only to work that one person could accomplish alone and to arts that did not require the collaboration of several hands, men were as free, healthy, good and happy as their nature allowed, and they continued to enjoy among themselves the sweetness of independent intercourse; but from the instant that one man needed the help of another, and it was found to be useful for one man to have provisions enough for two, equality disappeared, property was introduced, work became necessary, and vast forests were transformed into cultivated fields which had to be watered with the sweat of men, and where slavery and misery were soon seen to germinate and flourish with the crops.[49]

Agriculture, then, together with metallurgy, led to those inequalities which Rousseau laments. 'It is iron and wheat which first civilized men and ruined the human race.'[50] As Rousseau reconstructs the past, the division of labour first took place between smiths, forging tools, and farmers, exploiting the land so as to produce food for both farmers and smiths. The cultivation of the soil led to claims being made for rightful ownership of the piece of land which a particular farmer had worked; in other words, it introduced what Rousseau calls the 'fatal' concept of property: 'Things in this state might have remained equal if talents had been equal, and if, for example, the use of iron and the consumption of foodstuffs had always exactly balanced each other; but this equilibrium, which nothing maintained, was soon broken.'[51] The difference between men's capacities and their circumstances produced even greater inequalities in men's possessions, which in turn led to a war between each and all.

At this point Rousseau's argument recalls that of Thomas Hobbes. And indeed while Rousseau rejects Hobbes's claim that the state of nature is a state of war between all men, he gives a Hobbesian picture of the state of society as it was before the introduction, by a 'social contract', of the institutions of government and law. The great difference between Rousseau and Hobbes is that Rousseau argues in the *Discourse on Inequality* that a social condition, and not a state of nature, immediately preceded the introduction of civil society. Rousseau, as we have seen, claims that the state of nature was peaceful and innocent, and that it was only after the experience of living in society that men were led to institute government—led to do so because conflicts over possessions arose with the division of labour. Nascent society 'gave place to the most horrible state of war'.[52]

This state of war in pre-political society is seen by Rousseau as having different causes from the state of war depicted by Hobbes. Hobbes speaks of a war between equals; Rousseau sees a war provoked by inequality, by what he calls 'the usurpations of the rich and the brigandage of the poor'.[53] War begins when the idea of property is born and one man claims as his own what another man's hunger prompts him to seize, when one man has to fight to get what he needs while another man must fight to keep what he has. For Hobbes war sprang from natural aggressiveness; for Rousseau war first began with the unequal division of possessions in the context of scarcity, coupled with the corruption of human passions which was the work of culture rather than of nature.

Both Hobbes and Rousseau envisage men finding the same remedy for the state of war between each and all: namely the institution, through common agreement, of a system of positive law which all must obey. But whereas Hobbes's social contract is a rational and just solution equally advantageous to all, Rousseau's social contract, as it is described in the *Discourse on*

*Inequality*, is a fraudulent contract imposed on the poor by the rich. In *The Social Contract*, Rousseau describes an altogether different sort of social contract—a just covenant which would ensure liberty under the law for everyone. But that is something into which men must enter in full knowledge of what they are doing. In the *Discourse on Inequality*, Rousseau is describing a contract taking place in the remote past,[54] when men first passed, most of them without much intelligence, from anarchic communities into civil society. In that situation Rousseau imagines the first founder of civil government as a wily rich man saying to the poor: 'let us unite . . . let us institute rules of justice and peace . . . instead of directing our forces against each other, let us unite them together in one supreme power which shall govern us all according to wise laws'.[55] The poor, who can see that peace is better than war for everybody, agree; they do not see that in setting up a system of positive law they are transforming existing possessions into permanent legal property, and so perpetuating their own poverty as well as the wealth of the rich. And so, as Rousseau puts it, 'all ran towards their chains, believing that they were securing their liberty'.[56]

It should be noticed that in his account of the fraudulent social contract, Rousseau speaks of the rich dominating and deceiving the poor, not of the strong dominating and intimidating the weak:

The first man who, having enclosed a piece of land, thought of saying 'This is mine' and found people simple enough to believe him was the true founder of civil society. How many crimes, wars, murders; how much misery and horror the human race would have been spared if someone had pulled up the stakes and filled in the ditch and cried out to his fellow men: 'Beware of this imposter: you are lost if you forget that the fruits of the earth belong to everyone and that the earth itself belongs to no one!'[57]

Of course Rousseau knew that the past could not be undone. He was not recommending that people should return to 'nascent society' or primitive anarchism; if he deplored the choices that men once made, he nowhere suggested, as did some later socialist theorists,[58] that communal ownership of the fruits of the earth could be re-introduced in modern times. On the contrary, Rousseau insisted that he was writing of a past which was exceedingly remote and could never be recovered. He went on to argue that since the original foundation of governments, societies had gone through further radical transformations.

Once civil societies had been instituted, the power conferred on rulers led to the division of men into the strong and the weak. In the next stage, legitimate power was converted into arbitrary power, and this divided men into masters and slaves. Although Rousseau does not go into detail, he obviously sees the degeneration of political systems from primitive law into absolute despotism as the reflection of the further degeneration of the human animal. Living under government did nothing, in Rousseau's view, to arrest the moral corruption of the individual. It ended the war of each against all to the advantage of the rich, but in the end it did little good to anyone, rich or poor. This was because civilized man cannot be happy. The savage, says Rousseau, has only to eat and he is at peace with nature 'and the friend of all his fellow men'.[59] But social man is never satisfied: 'first of all it is a matter of providing necessities, then providing the extras; afterwards come the luxuries, then riches, then subjects, then slaves—he does not have a moment's respite'.[60] As men's needs become less natural, the desire to satisfy them becomes more impassioned, so that civilized man wants in the end to 'cut every throat until he is master of the whole universe'.[61]

But although Rousseau paints this charmless portrait of modern man, he denies that nature is responsible for man's defects: 'Men are wicked; melancholy and constant experience removes any need for proof; yet man is naturally good; I believe I have demonstrated it. What then can have depraved him?'[62]

Rousseau ascribes responsibility to the changes that have come about in men's constitution as a result of the cultural factors they themselves have introduced into the world. Besides this, he names acquired defects of character in the individual.

Once again, Rousseau stresses the fatal role of *amour propre* in the life of civil man; the role is not unlike the part played by pride and vainglory in Hobbes's account of natural man. For both philosophers, the psychological or moral causes of human conflict are much the same, the main difference being that Hobbes regards the egoism of man as a product of nature whereas Rousseau insists that it is a product of society. It is at once an outcome of men's progress and the cause of their discontent. 'If this were the place to go into details', he writes,

. . . I would observe to what extent this universal desire for reputation, honours, and promotion, which devours us all, exercises and compares talents and strengths, and I would show how it excites and multiplies passions; and how, in turning all men into competitors, rivals, or rather enemies, it causes constant failures and successes and catastrophes of every sort by making so many contenders run the same course; I would show that this burning desire to be talked about, this yearning for distinction . . . is responsible for what is best and what is worst among men, for our virtues and our vices, for our sciences and our mistakes; for our conquerors and our philosophers—that is to say for a multitude of bad things and very few good things.[63]

The tragedy of modern man, as Rousseau sees it, is that he can no longer find happiness in the only way it can be found, which is living according to his nature. Natural man enjoys repose and freedom; social man, on the contrary, is always active, always busy, always playing a part, sometimes bowing to greater men whom he hates, or to richer men, whom he scorns; always ready to do anything for honours, power, and reputation, and yet never having enough: 'The savage lives within himself; social man lives always outside himself; he knows how to live only in the opinion of others and it is, so to speak, from their judgements alone that he derives the sense of his own existence.'[64]

As an indictment of civilization, Rousseau's *Discourse on Inequality* would seem to offer no possibility of redemption, no prospect for social man to recover freedom, happiness, or authenticity. But Rousseau's other writings are less discouraging; there we find indications of a way to salvation. The basis of hope is his belief that man is naturally good. If culture is responsible for all that has gone wrong, is not culture something that can be modified?

Rousseau's earlier *Discourse on the Sciences and the Arts*[65] had argued only that certain forms of culture were corrupting, not all forms of culture. And in the preface to his *Discourse on Inequality* there is a clear promise that a certain type of civil society can restore to men, even in the modern world, the freedom, happiness, and authenticity which the human race in general has lost in the course of its evolution.

The preface to the *Discourse on Inequality* takes the form of a

dedication to the republic of Geneva, and in those pages
Rousseau holds up that little state as a model to the world: a civil
society which has escaped the corruption of the rest. It is
undoubtedly an idealized portrait of Geneva that he gives us. But
the important thing is that it is there: it enables us to put down
Rousseau's *Discourse on Inequality* without a feeling of total
despair.

Voltaire, who detested Rousseau, could find no redeeming
feature in the *Discourse on Inequality*: 'I have received, Monsieur, your new book against the human race, and I thank you',
he wrote to Rousseau after he had sent him a copy. 'No one has
employed so much intelligence to turn men into beasts. One starts
wanting to walk on all fours after reading your book. However,
in more than sixty years I have lost the habit.'[66]

Voltaire had not the patience to try to understand what
Rousseau had been attempting to do—to provide a genuinely
scientific account of the facts of the human condition before
developing a speculative theory which might point the way to
improvement. Rousseau's image of Geneva was a central feature
of that further theory.

In dedicating his *Discourse on Inequality* to the citizens of
Geneva he congratulates them on being 'that people which,
among all others, seems to me to possess the greatest advantages
of society and to have guarded most successfully against the
abuses of society'.[67] Rousseau is proud to number himself among
those citizens:

Having had the good fortune to be born among you, how could I reflect
on the equality which nature established among men and the inequality
which they have instituted among themselves, without thinking of the
profound wisdom with which the one and the other, happily combined in
this republic, contribute in the manner closest to natural law and most
favourable to society, to the maintenance of public order and the well-
being of individuals?[68]

The republic of Geneva was a country unlike others, and
Rousseau, who was born there in 1712, had been brought up to be
an eager and uncritical patriot. It had been an independent city-
state since the middle years of the sixteenth century, when its
constitution was formulated—or reformulated—by a law-giver
of genius, Calvin.[69] But the circumstances of its institution were

not simple. Before it acquired independence, sovereignty of the city was effectively divided between the bishops of Geneva and the dukes of Savoy, and the burghers had, by playing one ruler against the other, acquired for themselves an extensive range of civil rights. The bishops gave the burghers powers to use against the dukes, but the ungrateful burghers used those powers in turn against the bishops, and rid themselves in time of both their sovereigns. They had not intended, however, to proclaim themselves a republic; they aspired only to seek incorporation as a canton in the Swiss confederation. This purpose was thwarted as a result of the Reformation, which divided the Swiss among themselves: the Genevans had counted on joining the confederation on the basis of existing alliances with Fribourg and Berne, but as Fribourg remained Catholic and Berne turned Protestant, Geneva could not please one canton without antagonizing the other. In the event Berne proved more useful to the Genevans in turning out the duke and the bishop, so the Genevans chose to become Protestant. By this step they alienated Fribourg and the other Catholic Swiss cantons with the result that Geneva's entry into the Swiss confederation was vetoed until the nineteenth century.

Calvin enabled the Genevans to make a virtue of necessity: denied membership of a larger nation, they learned from him how to construct a peaceful little nation of their own. They instituted an autonomous, independent city, where the people themselves were sovereign. Administration was placed in the hands of elected elders; and the guidance of the people entrusted to the clergy of the national Calvinist Church. The republican constitution was a skilful mixture of the democratic, the aristocratic, and the theocratic elements. Almost by a miracle, it survived as an independent city-state in an age of expanding kingdoms and empires. But not entirely by a miracle. In Calvin's lifetime Swiss troops from the friendly Protestant canton of Berne surrounded Geneva's frontiers, and after Calvin's death, when Geneva became a centre of international banking, the rulers of Europe's larger powers preserved Geneva's neutrality in order to protect their own financial interests. And so despite having no natural defences whatever, the city-state of Geneva kept its autonomy and republican constitution at a time when the other small republics of Europe fell into the hands of monarchs.

Rousseau had been brought up by his ardently patriotic father to think of Geneva as the one state in the modern world which had recovered the glory of the ancient republics.[70] He read as a child the works of Plutarch, and could boast 'I was a Roman at the age of twelve.'[71] In his *Confessions*, Rousseau says that admiration for ancient Rome 'helped to create in me that free and republican spirit, that proud and strong character, impatient of any yoke or servitude, which has tormented me all my life in situations where it has been least appropriate'.[72]

In the dedication to his *Discourse on Inequality*, Rousseau explains why he considers Geneva the nearest to an ideal state to be found on this earth. It is small; with a population of only several thousand, every citizen can be acquainted with all his fellow citizens and everyone's life is open to the gaze of others; it is a state where everyone's private interest coincides with the public interest; where no one is subject to any law except the law he has made and imposed on himself; where the constitution has stood the test of time; where military virtues are cultivated but wars are not engaged in; where the magistrates are chosen by all but are vested with undisputed authority; and where democracy is 'wisely tempered'.

This is not at all an accurate description of Geneva as it had become in the middle of the eighteenth-century, but it is what Calvin had designed Geneva to be, what Geneva should have been, and what the rulers of Geneva in all their public pronouncements claimed that Geneva was. To the author of the *Discourse on Inequality* the myth of Geneva was more important than the reality of Geneva. For it is that myth which holds out the possibility of what might be called the renegotiation of the social contract. The old fraudulent social contract which had marked the introduction of government into human experience could be re-enacted as a genuine social contract, not a device by which the rich would cheat the poor, but a means of combining liberty and law.

Geneva, which Rousseau visited for several months after he had written the *Discourse on Inequality*, proved to be a disappointment to him. He came in time to realize that it was far from being the 'wisely tempered democracy' he had described in his dedication. But he did not forsake the idea of an authentic social contract as a means of reconciling liberty and law. He did not falter in his republicanism. This is what inspired his next most important essay in political theory—the book he called *The Social Contract*, which was published in 1762, some seven years after the *Discourse on Inequality*.

The *Discourse on Inequality* was coldly received by the authorities of Geneva; *The Social Contract* was actually banned. It was burned on the orders of the censors, and a warrant was issued for the author's arrest. And yet Rousseau could say, with complete sincerity, that in *The Social Contract* he had presented Geneva as an example to all governments: 'People were pleased to relegate *The Social Contract* with the *Republic* of Plato to the realm of illusions: but I depicted an existing object . . . My book proposed one state as a model, and in just that one state it has been burned!'[73]

Thomas Hobbes was in Rousseau's mind when he wrote *The Social Contract* just as he had been when he wrote the *Discourse on Inequality*. Even if his knowledge of Hobbes was imperfect, he had read enough of Hobbes either in French translation or Hobbes's own Latin to be excited by him; and to regard his theory as a challenge that must be answered.

Hobbes, as Rousseau understood him, argued that men had to choose between law and liberty, between being governed and being free. For Hobbes freedom meant the absence of opposition:[74] 'the liberties of subjects depend on the silence of the law'.[75] Freedom went with anarchy: law to be effective, meant the rule of an absolute and undivided sovereign. Men loved freedom, but the consequences of anarchy were so appalling that any sort of government was better than no government at all. Hobbes's social contract was a covenant made between men to surrender collectively their natural rights to a sovereign in return for the peace and security of a civil order which that sovereign could secure by holding all men in awe.

Rousseau did not agree that freedom was antithetical to the constraints of government. Freedom was not the absence of opposition, but the exercise of ruling oneself. He believed it was possible to combine liberty and law, by instituting a regime which would enable men to rule themselves. Such an arrangement would entail, as Hobbes's system did, a covenant being made between individuals to surrender their natural rights to a sovereign: but that sovereign should be none other than the people themselves, united in one legislative corps.

Rousseau not only rejects Hobbes's idea that men must choose between being free and being ruled, but asserts that it is only through ruling themselves that men can recover their freedom. In the *Discourse on Inequality* Rousseau speaks of the three kinds of freedom men enjoy in the state of nature, one, and perhaps two of which they lose on entering society. In *The Social Contract* he speaks of another kind of freedom which they can experience only in society: political freedom. And this is something altogether superior to mere independence.

In *The Social Contract* Rousseau speaks less of the innocence of savage man, and more of his brutishness. Man in the state of nature is described as a 'stupid and unimaginative animal' who becomes 'an intelligent being and a man' only as a result of entering civil society. Assuredly, as a result of the development of passions and sophistry which society breeds, men have generally grown worse with the passage of time; but that is because culture, instead of improving men, has corrupted them—the theme of Rousseau's early *Discourse on the Sciences and the Arts*, to which he returned again and again. Culture is bound to change men, and if it does not make them better, it will make them worse.

In the state of nature a man cannot, by definition, be a citizen. But once he has quit the state of nature and entered society, a man's nature can only be realized if he becomes a citizen. In this sense Rousseau accepts Aristotle's definition of man as a *zoon politikon*. Here again we meet the two senses of 'nature' in Rousseau's argument. Just as the family, unnatural in the state of nature, becomes natural in society, so does political freedom, totally alien to the savage, become natural for the civilized man.

In a way, Rousseau's response to the challenge of Hobbes is wonderfully simple. Clearly men can be at the same time ruled and free if they rule themselves. For then the obligation to obey will be combined with the desire to obey; everyone in obeying the law will be acting only in obedience to his own will. In saying this, Rousseau was going a good deal further than liberal theorists such as Locke, who associated freedom with the people's consent to obey a constitutional monarch to whom they entrusted sovereignty. For Rousseau there is no investment or transfer of sovereignty: sovereignty not only originates in the people, it stays there.

Rousseau's solution to the problem of being at the same time ruled and free might plausibly be expressed as 'democracy'. But this is a word he seldom uses, and even then his use of it looks paradoxical. We have noted that in the dedication to the *Discourse on Inequality* he praises the republic of Geneva as a 'democracy wisely tempered', but in *The Social Contract* he writes: If there were a nation of gods, it would govern itself democratically. A government so perfect is not suited to men.'[76] There is in fact no contradiction here, in view of the particular use Rousseau makes of the word 'government'. He carefully separates government, as administration, from sovereignty, as legislation. He maintains that legislation must be democratic, in the sense that every citizen should participate in it, and participate in person. This is the democratic element in the constitution of Geneva which Rousseau has in mind when he speaks of that state as a 'democracy wisely tempered'. At the same time, he rejects— as unsuited to men—democratic administration. The participation by all the citizens in the administrative or executive government of the state he considers altogether too impractical and Utopian an arrangement to be desirable in practice. Executive government, he argues, must be entrusted to duly elected magistrates or ministers.

In the dedication to his *Discourse on Inequality* Rousseau declares: 'I would have fled from a republic, as necessarily ill governed, where the people . . . foolishly kept in their own hands the administration of civil affairs and the execution of their laws.'[77] He stresses the need for a state to have 'chiefs' (*chefs*):

I would have chosen a republic where the individuals, content with sanctioning the laws and making decisions in assemblies on proposals from the chiefs on the most important public business . . . elected year by year the most capable and upright of their fellow citizens to administer justice and govern the state.[78]

The point Rousseau dwells on is that superiority in public office shall correspond to superiority of capability and rectitude. Such a system he can call 'aristocratic' in the true Classical sense of that word: government by the best. This is clearly the sense he has in mind when he speaks in *The Social Contract* of an elective aristocracy as 'the best form of government';[79] and in doing so he does not contradict the preference expressed in the *Discourse on Inequality* for a wisely tempered democracy—for what he means there is democratic legislation, wisely tempered by an aristocratic administration, democratically elected. He contrasts this sort of aristocracy with an aristocracy based on heredity, characteristic of feudal regimes: 'the worst form of government'.[80]

In *The Social Contract* Rousseau draws attention to the dangers inherent in a system which separates the executive, the aristocratic body, from the legislative, the democratic body. He points out that while it is desirable for the business of administration to be entrusted to magistrates or chiefs, those magistrates will naturally tend with the passage of time to encroach on the sacred territory of legislation, and thus to invade the sovereignty of the people, and finally to destroy the republican nature of the state. 'This is the inherent and inescapable vice which, from the birth of the body politic, tends relentlessly to destroy it, just as old age and death destroy the body of a man.'[81]

Rousseau says nothing about this 'vice' in his dedication to Geneva of his *Discourse on Inequality*. One can suggest a reason for this. He did not realize, when he wrote that dedication, the extent to which the magistrates of Geneva had invaded the sphere of democratic sovereignty; but by the time he wrote *The Social Contract* he had woken up to the reality of the political situation of his supposedly ideal city-state.

The republican constitution of Geneva had not changed since Calvin established—or re-established—it in the 1530s, but much had altered behind the façade. The main institutions of the republic were the General Council, the Council of Two Hundred, and the Council of Twenty-Five. The General Council was the democratic body, to which every male citizen over the age of twenty-five belonged, and which had the power to enact laws, to elect the principal magistrates, and to approve or reject proposals concerning defence, alliances, taxation, and so forth. Its members had the vote, but no right to speak or initiate legislation. The Council of Two Hundred was in effect the debating forum, and the Council of Twenty-Five, the instrument of executive government.

What had happened in the two centuries since Calvin's time was that the Council of Twenty-Five had progressively taken over control of the state, dominating the Council of Two Hundred, summoning the General Council as seldom as possible and then only to give mute assent to the magistrates' proposals for legislation and their list of candidates for executive office. What is more, the members of the Council of Twenty-Five had come to be drawn from an ever narrower circle of Genevan society, a group of patrician families which contrived to keep all the offices of state for themselves and their nominees. In effect, a hereditary nobility had grown up in Geneva—not an open avowed patriciate like that of Berne, but one which clothed itself in all the forms and rhetoric of Classical republican ideology.

At the same time the citizen class shrunk progressively. In the sixteenth century, the majority of adult males in Geneva were enrolled as burgesses and citizens. By the end of the seventeenth century those citizens constituted a minority, a middle class of about 1,500 adult males in population of 25,000. Below there was a disfranchised lower class, not only excluded from the voting register, but denied access to the more lucrative trades of the city.[82]

Rousseau was born into a family of equivocal social standing. His paternal grandfather was a superior artisan and burgess who had been engaged in political activity on behalf of citizens' rights against the patrician magistrates: a 'liberal' we might call him, anachronistically. Rousseau's father seems to have been more of a 'conservative'. He had married a woman of superior social status, not quite in the patrician class, but in the upper academic class, and living among the élites at the fashionable centre of town. Rousseau was born in one of the smartest houses; and although his mother died soon after his birth, and Rousseau had to move down the hill to live in humble quarters, he was brought up by his father to think of himself as a superior person, and to take an uncritical view of the political arrangements of his native city-state. Writing about Geneva many years later, Rousseau recalled a military festivity he had witnessed as a child with his father:

My father, embracing me, was thrilled in a way that I can still feel and share. 'Jean-Jacques', he said to me, 'love your country. Look at these good Genevans: they are all friends; they are all brothers. Joy and harmony reign among them. You are a Genevan. One day you will see other nations . . . but you will never find any people to match your own'.[82]

Rousseau ran away from Geneva when he was 16 because he was wretchedly unhappy in his work as an engraver's apprentice, and he did not return to the city for any length of time until the age of 42—just after he had written the *Discourse on Inequality*. When he wrote *The Social Contract* several years later he had learned rather more about the way things were in Geneva, and one cannot doubt that his warnings about the tendency of the executive government to invade the rights of the legislative were based on this newly acquired awareness of what had happened over several generations of Genevan history.

Perhaps we should not be surprised that *The Social Contract* was banned and burned in Geneva. Rousseau could well protest that he had provided in his pages an advertisement for Geneva: 'I took your constitution as my model for political institutions.'[84] But at the same time he showed how such a constitution came to be undermined; in fact, there was no hiding the implication that the constitution of Geneva had been undermined in just that way. There were other features of Rousseau's argument that were bound to be offensive to people who proclaimed themselves not only good republicans but good Christians.

For although Rousseau distances himself from that universally detested atheist and materialist Hobbes, he does so only to align himself with a political philosopher of equally ill repute, Machiavelli. For Rousseau saw in Machiavelli, not the supposed champion of monarchy who wrote *Il Principe*, but the ideologue of republicanism who wrote the *Discorsi*. Like Machiavelli, Rousseau was in love with the political systems of Antiquity: that is what he meant when he said 'I was a Roman at the age of twelve.'[85] In time he came to prefer Sparta to Rome, but only because it remained more perfectly republican.

Rousseau does not tell the whole truth when he says that in writing *The Social Contract* 'I took your constitution [of Geneva] as my model'; for he also took another constitution as his model. At the end of his exploration of the idea of what a civil society must look like if it is successfully to combine liberty and law, we find Calvin's Geneva fortified with further institutions and practices derived from Sparta.

Rousseau insists that citizens can only be free—can only be citizens in the true sense of the word—if they in person make the rules under which they live. The idea of representative or delegation is wholly unacceptable to him. He writes very critically of the parliamentary system of legislation by elected deputies. 'The

English people believes itself to be free; it is gravely mistaken; it is free only during the election of Members of Parliament; as soon as the Members are elected, the people is enslaved, it is nothing.'[86]

Here again we must note the special meaning Rousseau attaches to freedom. Political freedom entails participation in legislation—as distinct from the unimpeded enjoyment of rights. It is freedom as it was understood in Sparta: freedom expressed in active citizenship. And like the Spartans, Rousseau limits citizenship to adult males. There is only one kind of representation in his system: the head of the family represents the women and children. Genevan women had always been excluded from the citizens' roll, and in his dedication to the *Discourse on Inequality*, Rousseau proposes that the women of Geneva should 'command' only in the context of the family: 'The destiny of your sex will always be to govern ours', he tells the women of Geneva. 'Happy are we so long as your chaste power, exerted solely within the marraige bond, makes itself felt only for the glory of the state and the well-being of the public! It was thus that the women commanded at Sparta and thus that you deserve to command in Geneva.'[87]

The difference between male and female is an important feature of Rousseau's political theory.[88] He had once worked as a research assistant to an early pioneer of feminism, Mme Dupin,[89] and he had no patience with her kind of argument for equal rights. Instead of equality between the sexes, Rousseau proclaims a sort of equilibrium between them: men should rule the world, and women should rule men. One of Rousseau's criticisms of the modern world—of which France is his prime example (and from which Geneva is held to be an exception)—is that women have acquired an undue predominance. How has this come about? Rousseau has already explained in tracing the history of 'nascent society' how women, becoming dependent on man in the context of domestic life, have to strive to make men correspondingly dependent on them. Since sexual desire is (according to Rousseau) less intense in the male than in the female, females have to stimulate it, and they do this by hiding their sexual charms, making themselves mysterious and playing hard to get. In a word, they acquire modesty.

This strategy is advantageous to everyone. When women are elusive, men are not only spared the ordeal of being devoured by women's voracious sexual appetites, but are also 'civilized', that is, trained in the art of pleasing women. Once the male's sexual desire has been elevated to a ruling passion, and once the female refuses to satisfy that desire unless the male does a great many tricks to earn his reward, then it becomes as important for men to study how to please women as it is for women to study how to please men.

One of the reasons why male sexual desire is weak in the state of nature is that there are plenty of females in the forest and no limits to the mating season. The situation is reversed in society by the introduction of female modesty, a somewhat bogus virtue as Rousseau describes it, but one very necessary to the female if she is to transform the male's weak lust into a strong passionate love.

Modesty is not natural (in a way it goes against nature), but it is suggested to women by nature, together with shame, 'to arm the weak in order that they shall enslave the strong'.[90] Here again we meet the two senses of 'nature' in Rousseau's writings. By original nature, women are immodest and shameless; in the social context, nature propels them, for their own protection, towards shame and modesty. The ambiguity of the situation is reflected in women's actual behaviour. It is pride which enables women to triumph over themselves, and become chaste; but the same pride makes them want to have the whole world at their feet.

Rousseau deplores the fact that in modern times women have been able to satisfy this extravagant desire. He believes it is right that women should rule men privately, but that it is men's task to rule the world publicly. This again is part of his republican ideology; it is as a republican that he attacks the sexual arrangements which prevail in the decadent kingdom of France. There he discerns a deplorable form of sexual uniformity in which men have come to resemble women by becoming equally effeminate; they have been reduced to being the foppish slaves of women in society and of a despot in the state.

In Sparta things were different; there austerity, manliness, and military virtues prevailed, and Rousseau is eager for Geneva to keep Sparta in mind as a model. The women of Sparta knew that their duty was to rear citizens, not to aspire to be citizens themselves. Rousseau sees no place for women in legislative activity because his conception of the citizen is that of a citizen-soldier, and women cannot be asked to bear arms (they are too frail and too precious as mothers of future soldiers), nor can a good wife and mother be relied upon always to put the interests of the state before the interests of her own family, as a good citizen must. Women's skill lies in the use of hidden, personal, devious power; whereas public politics requires impersonal, rational legislation and open forthright utterance, for which men are suited by nature. The abilities of each sex, as Rousseau sees them, are distinct; man is the 'arm' and woman the 'eye' of the partnership. If everything is in its place, there will be no confusion of roles; privately women will rule men, and publicly men will rule the state.

*The Social Contract* begins with a sensational opening sentence: 'Man was born free, but he is everywhere in chains.'[91] But the argument of the book is that men need not be in chains. When a state is based on a genuine social contract (as opposed to the fraudulent social contract depicted in the *Discourse on Inequality*) men receive in exchange for their independence a better kind of freedom, true political freedom or republican freedom. In entering a civil society based on the right kind of social contract, man loses his 'natural liberty and his absolute right to anything that tempts him', but he gains 'civil liberty and the legal right of property in what he possesses';[92] to this is added the moral liberty which makes a man master of himself, 'for to be governed by appetite alone is slavery, while obedience to a law one prescribes to oneself is liberty'.[93]

In this formulation of Rousseau's argument we confront a serious problem. It is easy to understand that an individual can be said to be free if he prescribes to himself the rules he obeys in his life; but how can a group of people be said to be free in prescribing for themselves the rules they obey? An individual is a person with a single will; but a group of people is a number of persons each with his own will. How can a group of persons have *a* will, in obedience to which all its members will be free? For it clearly must have such a single will, if any sense is to be made of Rousseau's proposition.

Rousseau's response to the problem is to define his civil society as an 'artificial person' so that people become *a* people, a people with a single will, which he calls 'la volonté générale', or general will. The social contract which brings the civil society into being is itself a pledge, and that civil society remains in being as a pledged group. When Ernest Renan in the nineteenth century defined the nation as a 'plebiscite renewed every day' he expressed exactly Rousseau's conception: the republic is the creation of will, of a will that never falters, in each and every member, to further the public, the common, the national interest—even though it might sometimes compete with personal interest. Of course, no one can be expected to cease to desire his own good; but as each individual is transformed into a citizen, he acquires besides his private will a public or general will, and identifies his own good with the public good.

Rousseau sounds very much like Hobbes when he says that under the pact by which men enter civil society everyone makes a 'total alienation of himself and all his rights to the whole community'.[94] However, it must be understood that Rousseau represents this alienation as a form of exchange—men give up natural rights in return for civil rights; the total alienation is followed by a total restitution, and the bargain is a good one because what men surrender are rights of dubious value, unsupported by anything but an individual's own powers, rights which are precarious and without a moral basis, while what men receive in return are rights that are legitimate and enforced. The rights they alienate are rights based on might; the rights they acquire are rights based on law.

There is no more haunting passage in the whole of *The Social Contract* than that in which Rousseau speaks of forcing a man to be free.[95] But it would be wrong to put too much weight on these words, in the manner of those who consider Rousseau a forerunner of modern totalitarianism. He is 'authoritarian' in the sense that he favours authority, but his authority is carefully distinguished from mere power, and is offered as something wholly consistent with liberty—being based on the expressed assent and credence of those who follow it. Rousseau does not say that *men* may be forced to be free, in the sense of a whole community being forced to be free; he says that *a* man may be forced to be free, Rousseau is thinking here of the occasional individual who, as a result of being enslaved by his passions, disobeys the voice of law, or of the general will, within him. The general will is something inside each man as well as in society generally, so that the man who is coerced by the community for a breach of that law is, in Rousseau's view of things, being brought back to an awareness of his own true will. Thus in penalizing a law-breaker, society is literally correcting him, restoring him to his own authentic purposes. Legal penalties are a device for helping the individual in his struggle against his own passions, as well as a device for protecting society against the antisocial depredations of law-breakers. This explains the curious footnote where Rousseau writes: 'In Genoa the word *Libertas* may be seen on the doors of all the prisons and on the fetters of the galleys. This use of the motto is excellent and just.'[96]

For Rousseau there is a radical dichotomy between true law and actual law. Actual law is what he describes in the *Discourse on Inequality* and again in *Émile*, where he writes: 'The universal spirit of laws in all countries is to favour the stronger against the weaker, and those who have against those who have nothing.'[97] True law, which is what he describes in *The Social Contract*, is different. It is just law, and what assures its being just is that its rules are made by a people in its capacity as sovereign and obeyed by the same people in its capacity as subject. Rousseau is confident that such laws cannot be oppressive on the grounds that no people would forge fetters for itself.

The distinction between true law and actual law corresponds to the distinction Rousseau draws between the general will and the will of all. The general will is a normative concept, and its rightness is part of its definition. The will of all is an empirical will: the only test of the will of all is to ascertain what all actually do will. Rousseau takes care to note the logical distinction between 'right' and 'fact'.

Why should I abide by the decision of the majority? Because by the deed of the social contract itself, to which everyone must subscribe and pledge (there is no question of a majority decision here: you either pledge or you are out of civil society altogether) each contractant agrees to accept the decision of the majority in the formulation of the laws. It is also understood that the members of the majority, whose decision is accepted as binding, do not will as a majority, but simply as interpreters of the general will—so that it is a majority interpretation of the general will which is binding, not a majority will. This is how it becomes morally obligatory for the minority to accept those decisions.

However, Rousseau is troubled by the fact that the majority of citizens are not necessarily the most intelligent. Indeed, he agrees with Plato that most people are rather stupid. 'The general will is always rightful', but it is sometimes mistaken.[98] Hence the need for a lawgiver, to draw up for the people and on behalf of the people the constitution or system of laws under which the people is to live.

One of the most striking chapters in *The Social Contract* is that in which Rousseau writes 'to discover the rules of society that are best suited to nations there would need to exist a superior intelligence',[99] and he then goes on to invoke the names of such supermen as Lycurgus, Calvin,[100] and Moses.[101] He does not only praise these great founders; he notes their technique—which is that of claiming that they have received their constitution from a supernatural source. He quotes Machiavelli on this point, quoting—admittedly in Italian—the following paragraph from Machiavelli's *Discorsi*:

The truth is that there has never been any lawgiver who in introducing extraordinary laws to a people did not have recourse to God, for otherwise his laws would not have been accepted.[102]

Rousseau does not suggest here that the lawgiver should really have God's authority, only that he should *pretend* to: the lawgiver 'puts his own laws into the mouth of the immortals, thus compelling by divine authority persons who cannot be moved by human prudence'.[103]

This passage is all the more remarkable in view of Rousseau's insistence in so many of his writings on the importance of sincerity. In this *Letter to Monsieur d'Alembert*, for example, he attacks the profession of the stage at great length, arguing that the art of acting is one of 'counterfeit . . . the art of assuming a personality which is not one's own, of simulating passions one does not feel, saying things one does not believe'.[104] He contrasts the actor's role with that of the political orator, who 'speaks only in his own name' and says nothing other than what he thinks, so that the man and the persona are identical'.[105] It is strange, therefore, that Rousseau should advise the most important orator of all, the lawgiver, to have recourse to dissimulation, and to suggest to the crowd that the proposals he has thought out himself have been given to him by the deity.

The Machiavellian element in Rousseau's thinking comes out even more conspicuously in the chapter in *The Social Contract* which he calls 'The Civil Religion'. This is a chapter which caused particular shock and indignation in Geneva, and it is only surprising that Rousseau did not expect it to do so. Its argument is asserted aggressively: Christianity is the true religion, but it is worse than useless as a civil religion.

Christianity is a wholly spiritual religion, concerned solely with the things of heaven; the Christian's homeland is not of this world. The Christian does his duty, it is true, but he does it with profound indifference towards the good or ill success of his deeds . . . The essential thing for Christians is to go to paradise, and resignation is but one more means to that end . . . [In war] all will do their duty, but they will do it without passion for victory; they know better how to die than to conquer.[106]

In this chapter Rousseau does not quote Machiavelli by name, but he repeats Machiavelli's arguments against Christianity, that it teaches monkish virtues of humility and submission instead of the manly virtues a republic needs—courage, virility, patriotism, love of glory and of the service of the state. Rousseau agrees with Machiavelli: there can be no such thing as a Christian republic, 'for each of these terms contradicts the other'.[107] He does not go so far as Machiavelli in proposing a revival of bloodthirsty pagan rituals, but he does propose a civil religion with minimal theological content which will fortify and not impede (as Christianity impedes) the cultivation of republican virtue.

It is understandable that the authorities of Geneva, profoundly convinced that the national church of their republic was at the same time a truly Christian church and a nursery of patriotism, should consider Rousseau's arguments both subversive and heretical. Rousseau's insistence on the need for a non-Christian civil religion is the measure of the extent to which his own ideal of a republic went beyond the model of Calvin's Geneva.

Sparta is Rousseau's model in the later chapters of *The Social Contract*. This was spotted by one of his earliest and most cogent critics, Benjamin Constant.[108] A native of Lausanne, and an inhabitant of the neighbouring canton of Vaud, Constant knew Geneva well, and was familiar with the myth which Rousseau shared with so many of his compatriots that this city-state had revived in a modern state the best republican features of the ancient world. Constant saw in *The Social Contract* an attempt to treat this myth as a reality. He argued that the ancient city-state could not be revived in the modern world, first, because the large-scale nation-state had become the standard form of political organization; and secondly, because the ancient republics were not desirable anyway—Sparta in particular being no better than a 'warrior's monastery'.

Constant focused his attack on Rousseau's endeavour to revolutionize men's conception of freedom,[109] to replace the idea of 'modern liberty'—something which men could and should enjoy at the present time—with the idea of 'ancient liberty'—something which had its place only in the lost world of Antiquity. Invited to surrender 'modern liberty' for the sake of 'ancient liberty', men were being offered a meretricious illusion in place of a practicable and realistic objective.

'Ancient liberty', as Constant explained it, meant 'direct personal participation in the government of one's own state'; it was 'whatever ensured its citizens the largest share in exercising political power'.[110] By contrast, 'modern liberty' was 'whatever guarantees the independence of citizens from their government'.[111] In the ancient republics, a man believed himself to be free to the extent that he exercised his political power. In the modern world, Constant suggested, men experienced their freedom in doing what they chose to do, enjoying the right to express opinions, to come and go, to assemble and worship as they pleased, and to dispose of property. Modern liberty was largely a matter of freedom *from* interference in the pursuit of one's own lawful ends.

Constant, who lived long enough to see Rousseau's concept of 'ancient liberty' invoked by Robespierre and others to justify some of the worst excesses of the French Revolution as expressions of popular sovereignty, was sharply critical of Rousseau's argument. But he was not entirely hostile. He suggested that some element of 'ancient liberty' should be added to 'modern liberty' to give it a more active content:[112] he believed that everyone's liberty should include, besides the right to be left alone, 'the right to exert influence on the administration of government, either through the election of some or all of its public functionaries or through petitions, remonstrances, and demands'.[113]

In effect Constant was the first to draw from Rousseau what the world as a whole came in time to learn from him: namely the desire to add a democratic dimension to its understanding of freedom. In response to this demand, representative governments since the late eighteenth-century came to be progressively democratized. The United States led the way: other states followed. Universal suffrage became the norm, even under those regimes where 'parliamentary' or 'legislative' assemblies were powerless. Democratized representative government is not what Rousseau understood by 'a wisely-tempered democracy', but his plea for *his* kind of democracy, for *his* kind of 'ancient freedom', was so eloquent that it impelled men's thoughts towards the improvement of 'modern freedom'. Rousseau did not become a 'legislator for mankind'; but he stirred the imagination of men, first with his disturbing picture of what had happened to them in the course of their evolution, and secondly with his exhilarating picture of what they might become if they were to remake the institutions under which they lived. There is both an optimistic and a pessimistic side to Rousseau's political theory. It was the optimistic side which captured more attention and which has earned him the reputation of a prophet of democracy.

# 4
# Diderot

Diderot is almost always spoken of as the most attractive philosopher of the French Enlightenment. All his contemporaries—except Rousseau after he had quarrelled with him—thought well of him. He is also the most elusive of the *philosophes*. In the first half of his career, Diderot published almost everything he wrote; later, he put his manuscripts away in a drawer, and it was only after his death that his best books were published. It is hard to say what prompted him to withhold them from the Press. It was certainly not lack of courage, for Diderot was the most fearless writer of his time.

The *Encyclopédie*, which he edited, is the great monument of the Enlightenment, and it was the product of a bold and unremitting struggle, which Diderot had often to undertake alone. He was a victim of censorship, persecution, and imprisonment; he was betrayed by his publisher and deserted by his collaborators, but he battled on doggedly for what he always thought of as a *cause*. He understood philosophy not simply as the enlargement of knowledge, or even the enlargement of useful knowledge, or even the enlargement of useful knowledge plus the improvement of men's conduct; besides all this it was a fight against traditional beliefs and the institutions which upheld them.

Like Rousseau, Diderot had a hard life. They were born within a few months of each other and they arrived in Paris at about the same time, two ambitious young men from the provinces seeking fame and fortune in the republic of letters. It is often said that a generation separated Diderot and Rousseau from Montesquieu and Voltaire. But it was something more than age. Montesquieu and Voltaire were grandees; in their different ways they both became famous writers before they were 30, whereas Diderot and Rousseau had a long wait for recognition. Moreover, Diderot and Rousseau never ceased to be short of money; they contemplated life from garrets, while Montesquieu and Voltaire looked out on the world from the windows of their stately châteaux. Naturally their perspectives were different, especially in matters of economics and politics.

Diderot is every bit as paradoxical a philosopher as is Rousseau; perhaps even more so. His political writings do not add up to a system in the sense that Rousseau's do. Diderot will have to be called a 'dialectical' thinker, in that he has a way of pushing a thesis to its limits and then stepping back to argue against it. Professor Wade suggests that 'whereas Voltaire debates with the public, Diderot debates with himself'.[1] It may be denied that Voltaire even debated with the public, since he talked without listening; but Diderot did undoubtedly debate with himself, and to that extent he is a philosopher in the style of Socrates. He is also a very intense and creative thinker, pouring out ideas like flames from a volcano, in all directions at once.

One consequence of this is that commentaries on Diderot are as often as not attempts to impose on Diderot's thinking a systematic order which he failed to arrange himself, and this is particularly true of his political ideas. He has been depicted as an exponent of liberal pluralism, of constitutional monarchy, of enlightened despotism, of socialism, even of communism, and passages in his writings can be invoked to support any of these interpretations, some more plausibly than others. He is a great favourite with Marxists, and he has come to be highly honoured in the Soviet Union. There is more than one reason for this: Diderot's papers, acquired by Catherine the Great, are in Leningrad, and with the Russian flair for turning every fragment of its *patrimoine* to the service of national self-esteem, Diderot had only to be shown to be ideologically acceptable in order for him to be revered as a forerunner of Lenin.

Since Diderot attacked metaphysics and religion, wrote ungracious words about the rich, and was an early critic of colonial policies which Lenin later denounced as 'imperialism', it cannot have been difficult to make him sound like a hero of the Soviet Union. It was only necessary to ignore his doubts about materialism, his belief in economic freedom, his passion for individual liberty, and his arguments in favour of checks and balances against monolithic government.

Like many other philosophers Diderot had different views at different times of his life, and while he cannot be said to have given unreserved assent to any doctrine at any period, there are certain discernible phases in the unfolding of his political thought. The first corresponds to the period of his collaboration and friendship with Rousseau, when he tried to work out a materialist theory of politics which was an alternative both to Hobbes's materialist theory and to Rousseau's non-materialist theory. The second coincides with Diderot's activity as editor of the *Encyclopédie*, when he attempted to set forth a scientific theory of absolutism which was an improvement on Voltaire's. The third originates in his association with Catherine the Great, when personal experience of a despotic regime impelled him to work out a political theory which had much in common with that of Montesquieu. In the final phase, when he became increasingly critical of the colonial expansion of European monarchies, he returned to a position which is closer to that of Rousseau.

Although Diderot never followed the example of Montesquieu and Voltaire in visiting England, he read English, and owed much to English philosophers, especially Bacon, Shaftesbury, and Hobbes. He had learned English less from scholarly curiosity than in order to find work as a translator, for Diderot had to earn his living solely as a writer—and was one of the first men in France to do so.[2] He refused to follow his father's advice and become either a priest or a lawyer; and he had no private means. His father was a master cutler in Langres, where Diderot was born in October 1713. He had thus much the same kind of bourgeois origins as Rousseau, born in 1712 the son of a watchmaker of Geneva—the most notable difference between them being that while Rousseau was largely an autodidact, Diderot received a superior Jesuit education, which left him with a highly sophisticated mind and an unwavering hostility to Christianity in general and to priests in particular.

It is not easy to say what Diderot owed to Rousseau and Rousseau to Diderot in the course of their many conversations together. Rousseau, undoubtedly, had the genius, Diderot the culture; Rousseau the temperament of a Plato, Diderot that of an Aristotle; Rousseau the insight into unseen things; Diderot the eye for the visible, with no less imagination, and perhaps rather more admirable qualities of character. Rousseau complains in the *Confessions* that Diderot tried to dominate him, and even to insert some of his black thoughts into the *Discourse on*

*Inequality*;[3] but if Diderot did try to impose his ideas on Rousseau, Rousseau for his part succeeded in making Diderot apply his mind to certain subjects and to think about them in certain ways.

On several crucial points of social theory they seem always to have disagreed. Whereas Rousseau argued that man was solitary by nature and social only by convention, Diderot insisted that man was naturally social. Diderot may well have arrived at this belief as a result of reading (and translating) Shaftesbury; at any rate, the natural sociability of man was a key element in the theory of civil society which he attempted to construct on the basis of a naturalistic conception of the universe.[4]

Like Rousseau, Diderot was an evolutionist, but he told a different story of man's evolution. He argued that man was originally a social animal in the way that flocks or herds of beasts are social, having altruistic sentiments which united neighbours together on peaceable and friendly terms. In time, differences of natural strength led to certain members of these human societies dominating others, so that the flocks or herds came to be transformed into packs, that is, groups controlled by masterful and aggressive leaders. At a further stage of evolution, Diderot suggested, these packs based on violence were transformed into civil societies based on contract; force was thus changed into right, and the ferocious chiefs became civilized as anointed kings.[5]

From this account of the origin of political societies Diderot drew more than one set of conclusions. The first was an idealized primitivism: the argument that man was designed by nature to live in amicable communitarian association with others, without being intimidated by bullies or having to tame those bullies by introducing systems of positive law. Here we have a much more 'Utopian' image of man than that suggested by Rousseau, for whom man, if originally innocent, was also utterly solitary. Diderot's original man, social by nature, is the real 'noble savage', so often mistakenly thought to have been an invention of Rousseau.

We meet Diderot's noble savage again in a book which dates from his later years, his *Supplément au voyage de Bougainville*.[6] This is written in Diderot's favourite dialogue form, which prevents us from being sure which voice is that of Diderot himself. The participants in the conversation discuss Bougainville's reports of the societies he encountered in Tahiti and other islands of the South Seas. They understand him to have found people who live happily and wholly according to natural impulse, a people with no institutions of private property or of marriage. These people engage without inhibitions in sexual congress; the word 'incest' does not exist in their language. The very idea of crime is unknown to them. They are content to live frugal, healthy lives; or rather they were content before Bougainville arrived, and the lives of the Tahitians were ruined by the modern Christian culture that the French mariners took to their islands, a culture which introduced the concepts of sin, guilt, greed, chastity, and jealousy, together with diseases hitherto unknown.

One has the impression, reading the *Supplément au voyage de Bougainville*, that Diderot himself is using the experience of Tahiti as an argument for anarchistic communism, but in a letter to a friend we find him writing:

Shall I tell you a fine paradox? It is true that I am convinced that the only real happiness for the human race lies in a social state in which there would be no king, no magistrate, no priest, no laws, no 'mine' and 'thine', no movable property, no landed property, no vices, no virtues. And this social state is damnably *ideal*.[7]

Indeed in later sections of the *Supplément* itself, Diderot seems to dismantle the romantic image of Tahiti and to suggest that behind the façade the Tahitians are neither happy nor innocent. He points out the flaws of primitivism; he warns us not to be deceived by an all too beautiful fantasy. The *Supplément* is 'Utopian' only in the very exact sense that it belongs to the same genre as Sir Thomas More's *Utopia*, a dialogue in which the author's own attitude is veiled, and which every reader must interpret for himself.

The second set of conclusions which Diderot drew from his doctrine of the natural sociability of man was that the history of human societies was a felicitous development from the rule of force to the rule of law; so that side by side with his doctrine of original innocence, which had much in common with that of Rousseau, Diderot developed a doctrine of progress which was at odds with Rousseau's thinking, although he came in the end to question progress as he questioned most things.

It was the doctrine of progress which led Diderot to advocate for a time that policy of authoritarian government and social engineering which prompted nineteenth-century historians to speak of 'enlightened despotism' and to ascribe it to Diderot and the other philosophers of the French Enlightenment as a shared political creed. In fact, only very minor *philosophes* advocated enlightened despotism. What Diderot favoured at a certain period was a kind of absolutism, along the lines of Voltaire's 'enlightened royalism', the rule of the philosopher-king. Even Diderot's attachment to this doctrine was characterized by reservations, and in his later years he rejected it entirely. He was drawn to it in the first place by the teaching of Francis Bacon, who was also the inspiration of the *Encyclopédie*, of which Diderot was appointed editor at the age of 33.

Originally the idea had been for Diderot to translate into French *Chambers's Encyclopaedia*, a routine job of the kind to which he had reconciled himself in the course of earning his living as a free-lance writer; but he succeeded in transforming the enterprise into the fulfilment of a grand design envisaged by Francis Bacon nearly a century and a half earlier: the assembly of all available knowledge, and especially scientific and technical knowledge, in a systematic compendium. This was intended to be no mere scholarly edifice, but an instrument of progress; a guide to salvation through science. For Diderot, as for Bacon himself, science was less a theoretical activity designed to furnish knowledge of nature than a practical activity designed to give man mastery over nature, a mastery to be used, in Bacon's words, 'for the benefit and use of life'.[8]

Bacon's programme for salvation through science called for a number of innovations: no more wasting time on traditional metaphysics or Classical texts, but the institution of laboratories, colleges, research stations, and academies for scientific activity, and, what is more, a strong centralized government unhindered by medieval obstruction from parliament and law courts to ensure that the policy was put into effect. Diderot, enthralled by Bacon's vision, resolved to produce, instead of a mere translation of *Chambers*, a comprehensive survey of the kind Bacon had proposed; a record of scientific achievement which would also be a work of propaganda for the new Baconian faith. In a letter to Voltaire, Diderot wrote:

This shall be our device: no quarter for the superstitious, for the fanatical, for the ignorant, or for fools, malefactors, or tyrants. I would like to see our brethren united in zeal for truth, goodness, and beauty—a rather more valuable trinity than the other one. It is not enough for us to know more than the Christians; we must show that we are better, and that science has done more for mankind than divine or sufficient grace.[9]

The *Encyclopédie* was advertised in 1750 as a work to be in ten volumes of text, with two volumes of plates. It grew to be a work of seventeen volumes of text and eleven volumes of plates. It ran to twenty million words and absorbed twenty-five years of Diderot's life.[10] He considered the plates to be as important as the text, because they illustrated not just the forms of nature, but the instruments and techniques of work. Industry, or what he called 'manufacturing', Diderot regarded as even more important than agriculture as an instrument of progress; for 'manufacturing', as he put it, 'is the activity which sets men free'.[11] He took it upon himself as editor of the *Encyclopédie* to visit all the workshops of artisans and all the little factories he could find in Paris to make sure that the illustrators he employed made accurate drawings of the most up-to-date machines and processes.

One thing Diderot was not qualified to do was to supervise the strictly scientific articles; and here he had, at any rate for the first few years, a co-editor in d'Alembert. Jean le Rond d'Alembert, who had started life as a foundling on the steps of the Church of Saint-Jean le Rond, was four years younger than Diderot, but he had risen at an early age to fame as a scientist in the fields of geometry and physics, and was already well established in Paris at a time when Diderot was an unknown literary journalist. D'Alembert provided for the *Encyclopédie* the scientific expertise that Diderot lacked. If less hostile to religion, he shared Diderot's belief in the doctrine of salvation through science; but he did not have the same willingness to suffer for that belief.

Diderot's own courage was remarkable. When interrogated by the police, he denied having written things he had written, but he would not desist from his activities. He was put in prison at Vincennes, just as Voltaire had been put in the Bastille; but he did not think of quitting Paris when he was released, as Voltaire had done, and as Voltaire urged him to do. Diderot continued to publish the *Encyclopédie* in France, courting further persecution, when Voltaire begged him to remove it to safety in Holland or Switzerland. When further trouble threatened—in 1758—his co-editor d'Alembert resigned and several of his most eminent contributors, including Charles Duclos and Marmontel, dissociated themselves from the *Encyclopédie*. But Diderot carried on defiantly; and in the end his courage was rewarded. The *Encyclopédie* proved to be a prodigious success.

Almost all the writers connected with it became fashionable. The *parlements* and the Church remained hostile, but the government at Versailles, which was constantly at odds with the *parlements* and which had no great love of the Church, ceased to make serious efforts to suppress the *philosophes*. Diderot's friends took over all the leading cultural institutions of the kingdom, and after the death of Louis XV an *encyclopédiste*, Turgot, actually became for a time the first minister of the government. Diderot himself, however, accepted no honours. He was too jealous of his freedom, and did not feel the need that Voltaire felt to build up a fortune to protect his independence. He preserved his liberty by living frugally.

I have referred to Diderot's disagreement with Rousseau on the subject of human sociability. He disagreed with him also on the subject of determinism. On this question it was Diderot, rather than Rousseau, who took the side of Hobbes. Partly as a result of reading Hobbes, Diderot was persuaded that the whole universe was a vast machine and that human beings were simply small machines within the larger system, operating according to the same laws of cause and effect as everything else in nature. Such a system appeared to Diderot to exclude free will altogether, and he regarded philosophers who tried to be at the same time determinists and libertarians as illogical and unscientific. In a letter he wrote in 1756, Diderot declared:

The word 'freedom' has no meaning: there are and there can be no free beings; we are simply the product of the general order of things, our physical organization, our education, and the chain of events. These things exert an irresistible influence over us. One can no more conceive of a being behaving without a motive, than one can conceive of one arm of a balance moving up or down without a weight.[12]

If there was no free will, could there be any morality? Diderot was ready to admit that there could be no morality as traditionally understood, and that public policy could not be based on the assumption of free will. It would be necessary to establish the enforcement of justice and the suppression of crime on deterministic principles. Diderot suggested that actions traditionally seen as crimes could be considered as falling into two categories: those which injured society and those which contravened the rules of the Church. The latter Diderot proposed to eliminate from the class of crimes altogether. When there was no injury to persons—as in sodomy, incest, blasphemy, and so forth—he said there was no crime. Where there was an injury to persons—as in murder, theft, assault, and so on—he suggested that it was a case not so much of wrongdoing as of aberration or mental sickness. On the basis of his theory that all men were by nature social, he argued that any antisocial behaviour must be unnatural; and hence that the individual who acted in an antisocial manner—that is, the criminal—must be acting against his own nature as well as against nature in general. He needed corrective treatment, not punishment.

On these grounds Diderot put forward a radical theory of penology according to which judges and prisons would be replaced by doctors and mental hospitals (here he undoubtedly foreshadows the penology of the Soviet Union as well as the jurisprudence of Jeremy Bentham). He was not soft-hearted in all this. Indeed he accused other progressive penologists, such as Beccaria and Voltaire, of being humanitarian in a sentimental way, of seeking to soften punishments instead of eliminating punishment altogether and replacing it with scientific remedies— remedies which might well have to be unpleasant because they would have to act as deterrents as well as cures. Diderot said he hoped that all aberrant persons could be 'modified' by re-education as therapy; if not, as he expressed it bluntly, society would have to 'destroy the malefactor on the public square'.[13]

Social surgery did not stop short of the death penalty; and if Diderot in general favoured prolonged imprisonment rather than death, it was because he believed that fear of the 'torture' of a whole life behind bars would be more effective in keeping potential malefactors in order than fear of a quick death on the scaffold.

Few philosophers have explored the practical implications of determinism so boldly as Diderot, and yet, Diderot being Diderot, we soon find him expressing doubts about it all. It occurred to him that determinism might lead to fatalism, for if every single thing that happens is the result of a preceding cause, then there would seem to be no point in wishing that things were different from what they are. If, for example, all the political institutions, the laws, the morals, and manners of France were determined by sociological and other factors, it would be futile to criticize them and suggest that they might be different—unless, of course, one could see oneself as determined by the causal process itself to act an initiating role in the sequence of events.

Diderot, however, was most unwilling to see himself as determined by anything. If he denied free will, he had a passionate belief in human freedom in other senses of the word 'freedom'. One such sense was the autonomy of a man who was master of his own life. Diderot was resolved that he would never be anyone's servant or employé. Since he had no private means, it was not easy for him to stick to this design. It became even harder after he married his working-class mistress (which is something Rousseau firmly refused to do), for Madame Diderot was demanding, complaining, and always berating her husband for the hardships she had to endure in a Bohemian existence with an ill-paid *homme de lettres*. But for Diderot himself the freedom of the free lance was infinitely precious. He despised those writers and scholars who took jobs as clergymen or functionaries, or sold themselves to rich patrons or ministers or kings in order to live comfortably. He even felt guilty himself when late in life he accepted the patronage of Catherine the Great. In doing so, he compared himself to Seneca entering the service of Nero. One of the very last things Diderot wrote was a defence of Seneca which was really a defence of himself against the accusations of his own conscience.

Diderot's conception of human freedom was not simply one of the individual's autonomy; he also developed something very like John Stuart Mill's notion of freedom as 'self-realization'. In spite of the belief that men were little machines, with two 'mainsprings', the brain and the diaphragm, Diderot argued that each individual machine was unique. He asserted this theory most forcefully in his *Réfutation* of Helvétius. This celebrated *philosophe* (who was not a contributor to the *Encyclopédie*) had argued that all human beings were virtually identical in construction and further that by means of the right training and motivation anyone could be made to do anything that anyone else could do. Diderot rejected this somewhat extreme form of behaviourism. The variety of human achievements, he claimed, not only showed that men had different upbringings and lived in different environments, but that they possessed different innate aptitudes.

Diderot went beyond the mere observation of such differences. He attached great value to them. Like John Stuart Mill, he had the highest admiration for people who cultivated their own originality. He said it was from the ranks of *les originaux* that men of genius sprang. He was even attracted by wicked men, and evidently enjoyed writing about them in the occasional works of fiction he found time to write—in *La Réligieuse*, for example, and *Jacques le fataliste*—which illustrate the great variety of human characters in the world.

One of the reasons why Diderot admired 'originals' was that they achieved that freedom which is 'self-realization', the unimpeded expression of a man's own individuality. This form of human freedom seemed to him to be even less widely enjoyed than freedom as 'independence', so there was no question of Diderot ascribing it to everyone, as champions of free will ascribed that to everyone. He simply thought that people who achieved such freedom were the best people, and he had a low opinion of those who gave it up for the sake of a comfortable life:

I hate all those sordid little things that reveal only an abject soul: but I do not hate great crimes; first because beautiful paintings and great tragedies are made out of them; and secondly because noble and sublime deeds share with great crimes the same quality of *energy*. [14]

When Diderot writes like this, we seem to be far from the rationalism of the eighteenth century and closer to the spirit of romanticism or existentialism; and indeed Diderot, no less than Rousseau, presages much that was to be said by philosophers who rejected the Enlightenment. Already, in Diderot's own thinking, there is a conflict between his love of freedom and his attachment to the ideology of progress.

Diderot remained, however, a materialist in his attitude to religion, becoming if anything increasingly an atheist. His conception of the universe as a vast machine was much the same as Voltaire's, but he ceased to accept the argument that the watch-like nature of the system proved the existence of a divine watch-maker, who deserved men's adoration. One explanation of this development is that Diderot's materialism was not based, as was Voltaire's, on the seventeenth-century physical sciences as practised by Newton. Diderot was influenced rather by the biological sciences of his own time, where nature was studied in its animate forms and not in the lifeless geometrical categories of astronomy. Nature for Diderot was a living machine, an organism. And having life in it already, it did not need an external spirit to breathe life into it—it did not need, as the Newtonian universe seemed to need, God. And if God was unnecessary, why introduce him?

Voltaire had said that God must be introduced because his existence was needed to make people act morally. Voltaire had a low opinion of men's characters; but Diderot did not need to accept this argument, precisely because he thought that men were social—that is to say, good—by nature. He claimed that there existed in all men what he called the 'general will of the human race', a will which impelled every individual to act in the interest of the whole species although each had also a 'private will' directed to his own interest. Diderot's *volonté générale* is obviously not to be confused with Rousseau's concept of the same name. Rousseau's 'general will' is a political concept, based on the reflection that if a number of essentially individualistic men are to live together as a civil society, every one must will the conservation and general good of that group. However, the human race as a whole is clearly *not* a civil society, united by covenant or agreement for any common end. In the jargon of sociology, the human race is a *series*—a large number of persons existing at the same time. What is distinctive about Diderot is that he saw the human race as something more than a *series*; he saw it as a natural group, a whole held together by the *volonté générale* which nature had implanted in each member of the race. Moreover Diderot regarded the human race as something which was worthy of much the same kind of veneration which the Christians addressed to God.

'Man', he wrote in the *Encyclopédie*,

is, and must be, the centre of all things. If we banish man, the whole noble spectacle of nature becomes no more than an inert and woeful scene . . . it is the existence of man alone which makes the existence of everything else significant.[15]

In passages such as these there are echoes of the philosophers of Greek Antiquity. Indeed, although Diderot wanted to follow the advice of Bacon and forget Greek philosophy in order to concentrate on modern science for the sake of serving the interests of humanity, he found himself, in asking what were the interests of humanity, thrown back to the Greek philosophers. And there we meet him alternating between the Epicureans and the Stoics: 'You can make yourself a Stoic; you are born an Epicurean.'[16]

Diderot's sympathy for the Epicurean philosophy did not impel him to become, with Voltaire, an apologist of luxury: and his economic theory put him at odds with other *encyclopédistes* besides Voltaire. Diderot agreed with the champions of luxury that the production of high-quality artefacts was advantageous to the nation as a whole—to the rich, in providing them with ornaments of life; to the poor, in providing opportunities for skilled artisan work. But Diderot favoured the production only of useful goods—not 'luxury' goods in the sense of ostentatious and wasteful finery with which the rich could indulge themselves while the poor were starved of necessities. 'The rich', he wrote, 'eat too much and suffer from indigestion, while the poor eat too little and suffer from malnutrition. It would be good to put each on the diet of the other.'[17]

Diderot was a man with a social conscience. He was troubled by the wretched conditions which prevailed where men were forced—by hunger—to work in dangerous trades like mining, smelting, and lumbering; and he would never accept, as Voltaire did, Mandeville's suggestion that very low wages were a necessary means to keep workers from idling.[18] As for the argument of Helvétius that the poorest classes in society were the happiest, Diderot protested that Helvétius being immensely rich, had no experience whatsoever of what it meant to be poor.[19] Helvétius knew *about* reality; but he did not *know* reality.[20] Diderot's own impoverished condition was not such as to blind him to the miseries of the working classes, and when they complained, he upheld their right to do so.

Sympathy for the poor prompted Diderot to reject the arguments of Turgot and Morellet and the other physiocrats in favour of free trade, a policy based on the theory that unrestricted commerce advanced the wealth of all. The physiocrats were Diderot's friends and contributors to the *Encyclopédie*, but he opposed their economic theory when he saw that it did not stand up to the test of concrete experience. In the early 1760s, when the French government acted on the proposals of the physiocrats and abolished restrictions on the grain trade, a series of bad harvests led to shortages, excessive charges, hoarding, monopolies, and the exploitation of hunger on the part of merchants unrestrained by law. Diderot judged that an economic policy which produced so much suffering and so much profiteering was a bad policy, and he rallied to the side of the leading opponent of free trade among contemporary economists, the Abbé Fernando Galiani, author of *Dialogues sur le commerce des blés*.

Diderot entered the controversy with a pamphlet entitled *Apologie de l'Abbé Galiani*, in which he attacked the physiocrats on two grounds: first, for thinking that one could solve practical problems in the light of abstract principles, and secondly, for hardening the hearts of the comfortably off against the sufferings of the poor. 'Is the sentiment of humanity not more sacred than the right to property?'[21] he demanded. Diderot had never shared Voltaire's attachment to the doctrine of a natural right to property. He recognized a right to property, but only on grounds of utility, which would set limits to it; not on grounds of natural law.[22]

In the language of our own times, Diderot was to the left of both Rousseau and Voltaire. If, as he undoubtedly did in his years with the *Encyclopédie*, he leaned towards absolutist government, it was neither towards the republicanism of Rousseau nor the royalism of Voltaire. There was in Voltaire a nostalgia for the past, for *le grand siècle*, a hint that he would enjoy playing the part of a secular Richelieu to a monarch with total power; in Rousseau there was a nostalgia for Sparta as well as for Calvin's Geneva. Diderot's absolutism looked to the future, and it was of a kind to eliminate politics altogether. Teams of experts would plan; the monarch would authorize; and professionals would execute the plan. Diderot's rule of science would have introduced government by social scientists; in effect, the kind of people who wrote for the *Encyclopédie*, neither very grand people nor very humble ones, but men from the educated bourgeoisie with a vocation for public service. The contributors to the *Encyclopédie* were sometimes spoken of as clergy who had lost their faith; but they can also be seen as bureaucrats who had not yet found their mission.

For a time Diderot was prompted by one of his physiocratic friends, Mercier de la Rivière, to advocate an absolutism of an all-pervasive kind, the total rule of experts. One can see how he arrived at this position. Society, as Diderot saw it, was composed of individuals impelled by *la volonté générale* to maximize the happiness of all, but ignorant, for the most part, of the means of achieving that end. The great majority should therefore agree to allow the minority of experts who did know what methods and policies would maximize happiness to take the decisions. All so-called political problems were thus seen as practical problems, to be solved in the light of what Mercier de la Rivière called 'l'évidence'—a word which Diderot adopted, with enthusiasm. 'Evidence' he declared, 'is the key to reform: we do not need to listen to opinions; what we must do is collect the facts.'[23]

However, Diderot the dialectician, having thus pushed the Baconian gospel of salvation through science to these positivist extremes, proceeded to dismantle the edifice. He began by calling into question the empiricist methodology on which it all rested. He put forward objections to empiricism which have been advanced in our time by such critics as Karl Popper and Arthur Koestler. Diderot suggested that science was not primarily an exercise of observation and induction, but largely a matter of imagination and conjecture.

The element of imagination in science Diderot spoke of as 'l'esprit de divination',[24] the capacity to 'smell out' hidden connections by pursuing vague ideas, suspicions, hints, and even fantasies 'which the mind, when excited, easily takes for accurate pictures'.[25] The true scientist for Diderot was not essentially different from the artist; both required 'a delicate awareness derived from a sustained observation of nature' and both required intuition. In an eloquent passage in his *Pensées sur l'interprétation de la nature* he wrote:

Nature is like a woman, who likes to disguise herself and whose different disguises, revealing now one part of her, now another, permit those who follow her assiduously to hope that one day they will know the whole of her person.[26]

Once he had abandoned Baconian induction in science, Diderot could hardly be expected to cling to the Baconian absolution in politics which went with it; he would no longer have any good reason for sacrificing freedom for the sake of efficiency. Here we are introduced to the political theory of Diderot's later years, which mark a return, in several respects, to the liberalism of Montesquieu, for whom, all his life, Diderot had kept a deep personal esteem; he was the only *philosophe* who walked in the procession at Montesquieu's funeral.

Ironically Diderot worked out this later theory just at a time in his life when it looked as if he might be given the opportunity of realizing the Baconian dream of directing the policy of an all-powerful monarch. Catherine the Great, who held despotic sway over the vast territories of the Russian Empire, was captivated by the ideas of the French Enlightenment, and took a particular interest in the work and the person of Diderot. In 1765, she had learned, among other things, that he was more than usually worried about money because of the impending marriage of his daughter. The Empress thereupon offered to buy his library. Her terms were extremely generous; she undertook to pay at once, but would not expect delivery of the books until after Diderot's death; moreover she would appoint him for life as salaried custodian of the library while it remained under his roof.

Voltaire was excited when he heard the news: 'I embrace you', he wrote to his friend, 'and I embrace also the Empress of All the Russias. Would one have suspected fifty years ago that the Tartars would so nobly reward in Paris the virtue, the science, and the philosophy that are so ill used by our own people?'[27]

Diderot soon discovered that the Empress was as interested in the political ideas as in the philosophy of the Enlightenment, and showed every sign of willingness to learn. Already as a result of reading Montesquieu and Beccaria she had decided after four years on the throne to convene an assembly of the Russian Empire to meet in the summer of 1767 to draw up a new code of laws which would have as its purpose the promotion of the greatest happiness of the greatest number of her subjects.

Diderot, who had never been taken in by the pretensions of Frederick II of Prussia to be a philosopher-king, saw in the Empress Catherine the living embodiment of the sage he had described in his *Le Réve de d'Alembert*, a great soul who understood that in order to make her people happy she needed to consult them about their wishes. He imagined her addressing her people in these words: 'We are all made to live under laws. Laws are only laid down in order to render us happier. No one, my children, knows better than you yourselves the conditions under which you can be happy. Come therefore and teach me. Come and express your thoughts to me.'[28]

It seems that Diderot, when he wrote those words, had not yet read the *Nakaz*, or *Instructions*, which Catherine had drawn up for the imperial assembly she had convoked. It was a document which leaned heavily on the jurisprudence of Beccaria, banishing torture, restricting the use of the death penalty, and generally proposing to promote the reform of criminals rather than retribution. Nor did Diderot at first realize that the Empress intended to consult her imperial assembly only for the purpose of reforming the laws, and then to dissolve it for good. He imagined her addressing the assembly in the words of Henri IV of France: 'Je vous ai fait assembler pour recevoir vos conseils, pour les croire, pour les suivre: en un mot pour me mettre en tutelle entre vos mains.'[29]

Diderot did not immediately accept Catherine's invitation to visit her in St. Petersburg. Rather surprisingly—if anything Diderot did can be surprising—he sent instead Mercier de la Rivière, the exponent of an extreme form of absolutism which he called 'le déspotisme légal'. In the event, Mercier's sojourn in St. Petersburg was disastrous for several reasons, and in the summer of 1773 Diderot decided that there was nothing for it but to yield to the imperial will and go to St. Petersburg himself. He was now nearly sixty, and had no experience of foreign travel; but he was fortified by Catherine's confidence in him and the assurance that he would be able to expound to her in private conversation his ideas on government and politics. Those ideas had no longer much in common with the theories of Bacon or Mercier de la Rivière.

An essay entitled *Sur la Russie*, written some months before Diderot went to St. Petersburg, expresses grave doubts about the wisdom of the Empress in inviting to her capital 'men of genius from foreign countries'. Diderot suggests here that she ought really to have modernized the economic and industrial base of her country before calling in philosophers to tell her how to govern it.

He notes that Russia is not France or England; it has no educated middle class from which an enlightened bureaucracy or corps of experts could be recruited; it has no skilled mechanics or engineers; and no factories. Russia, in short, is simply not ready for the Enlightenment.

In another document, Diderot proposed that reform in Russia should start at the bottom, 'by invigorating the mechanical arts and the lower occupations'. He adds: 'Learn how to cultivate the land, to treat skins, manufacture wool, make shoes, and in time . . . people will then be painting pictures and making statues.'[30] This quotation comes from his *Mémoires pour Catherine II*, which seems to have been written after his return from Russia, and which needs to be read together with his *Observations sur le Nakaz* for an indication of Diderot's political thought at this period.

He begins the *Mémoires* with some reflections on French history: 'The first fault, the original sin of the French people', he writes, 'was to have handed over all public power to the king.'[31] He suggests that in the original pact of submission, the French people ought to have set up an institution to act as 'a barrier to defend the people against the arbitrary power of a wicked or stupid sovereign'.[32] The *parlement* of Paris had never enacted this role because its members served their own interest and not the national interest. Even so, Diderot considered the king's suppression of the *parlement* in 1771 a great misfortune, since it transformed France 'from a monarchical state to a completely despotic state'.[33]

It is clear from all this that the closer Diderot came to absolutism, the more keenly he disapproved it. In his *Observations sur le Nakaz* he wrote:

There is no true sovereign except the nation; there can be no true legislator except the people.

The first act of a well-made constitutional code should bind the monarch to obey the law. Any monarch who refused to take such an oath would declare himself in advance to be a despot and a tyrant.[34]

In another paragraph Diderot specifies the kind of institution an assembly of deputies must be if it is to represent the will of a free people, and he suggests that it would be wise 'to fix the rights of these intermediate powers and fix them in such a way that they cannot be revoked even by the legislator himself or by his successors'.[35] With the example of England in mind, he writes, 'Good government is that in which the freedom of individuals is least restricted, and the freedom of sovereigns as much restricted as it is possible to be.'[36]

Elsewhere in the same treatise, Diderot considers whether political institutions should be fortified by religious ones, only to reject the idea: 'Religion is a support which always ends by toppling the house. The distance between the altar and the throne can never be too great.'[37]

Although Diderot remained on good terms with the Empress throughout his stay in St. Petersburg, he soon realized that he was not going to persuade her of the wisdom of a parliamentary constitution. The imperial assembly she had convoked had failed to reach any conclusions after 203 sessions, and was adjourned indefinitely in December 1768. She had never any intention of setting up a permanent parliamentary body which could block or hinder her use of power in any way. She had wanted only a short-term legislative assembly to draw up a code which would make her personal rule more efficient, more enlightened, more legitimate; and once the code was approved, the assembly was to be dissolved.

Diderot used to meet Catherine almost daily to discuss matters which he was authorized to introduce as subjects for conversation, and the French Ambassador reported in December 1773: 'the conferences with Catherine continue without interruption and get longer from day to day'.[38] Her pleasure in his company did not, however, signify assent to his ideas. She is reported to have said to him once, 'You forget, Monsieur Diderot, in your plans for reform, the difference between our two positions: you work on paper, which puts up with everything. I, poor Empress, work on human skin, which is altogether more sensitive, ticklish, and resistant.'[39]

She told the Comte de Ségur some time later:

I frequently had long conversations with Monsieur Diderot, but with more curiosity than profit. Had I placed faith in him, every institution in my empire would have been overturned; legislation, administration, politics, and finances would all have been changed for the purpose of substituting some impracticable theories.[40]

Diderot left Russia in many ways a disappointed man,[41] and a few months spent in Holland on his way home reinforced his belief that free government was more valuable than good government. There is an eloquent paragraph in his so-called *Fragments échappés* which seems to date from this period:

It is sometimes said that the most felicitous government would be that of a just and enlightened despot; but this is a very bold assertion. It could easily happen that the will of this absolute master was at odds with that of his subjects. Then, in spite of his justice and his enlightenment, he would be wrong to strip them of their rights even for their own good . . . it is never permissible for a man, whoever he is, to treat his fellow men as a herd of cattle. If they say 'We like it this way and we want to stay as we are' then one should try to educate them, to undeceive them, to lead them to more sensible views by means of persuasion, but never by means of force.[42]

The theme of liberty is a dominant one in all Diderot's political writings in the last years of his life (and he was to live for ten more years after his return from Russia). Soon after the rebellion of the American colonists against the British Crown in 1775, Diderot produced the book which has contributed much to his reputation as a revolutionary: *La Révolution de l'Amérique anglaise*. This is a fairly wide-ranging defence of the American action, with summaries of the Declaration of Independence and of Thomas Paine's *Common Sense* and various other pamphlets which Diderot had read in English. It also sets forth a general doctrine of revolution which invokes at the same time a utilitarian and a natural rights argument:

If people are happy under the form of their government they will keep it. If they are unhappy, it will not be your opinions or mine, but the impossibility for them to endure that government any longer which will determine them to change it—a salutary moment which the oppressor will call 'revolt', but which is nothing other than the legitimate exercise of an inalienable and natural right of men who are oppressed, and indeed of those who are not oppressed.[43]

*La Révolution de l'Amérique anglaise* is the least original and perhaps also the least interesting of Diderot's writings on politics, and has to be seen as part of a flood of pamphleteering that came out in France in the late 1770s in support of the American rebellion.[44] The Versailles government, seeking revenge for the French defeat by the British in Canada, sponsored the American rebels not only with military and naval aid, but by the dissemination of revolutionary propaganda. It is often said that the Enlightenment provided ideological impetus for the French Revolution; it could equally be argued that Louis XVI, by encouraging the Americans to rebel against their king, put his own head on the block, since every argument set forth to justify the American action against George III could be—and was—used by discontented elements against his own regime. But since the intervention in America had cost French taxpayers a great deal of money at a time when the French treasury was low, the American cause had to be made popular in France.

Diderot's contribution to this exercise differed from others in that he, characteristically, went beyond the defence of the American rebels to call into the question the right of these rebels to be in America in the first place. Much of this later argument he did not publish under his own name, but in the form of contributions, only recently identified as his, to *L'Histoire des deux Indes*, published under the name of Diderot's friend the Abbé Guillaume Raynal.[45] Here new questions are introduced. Who are the American colonists? They are Europeans, not true Americans. Many of them are religious enthusiasts; they have sailed to the New World, elbowed out the native redskins, and developed the land with the aid of African slaves.

Diderot, like every other philosopher of the French Enlightenment, disapproved passionately of slavery; what is more, he joined Rousseau in considering the redskins to be in many ways superior to Europeans. And so we meet the dialectical Diderot once more. He can justify the American colonists' rebellion against the British Crown, but only with arguments which undermine their right to be colonists. One of the reasons given for the claim that Diderot was a forerunner of Lenin is that he was an early critic of imperialism. However, Diderot did not use the word, and he did not attack what Lenin attacked as 'imperialism' —'the last phase of capitalism'. What Diderot criticized was something with an older history, the endeavour of more advanced peoples to take over the territories of more primitive peoples. In his *Supplément au voyage de Bougainville* he had indicted the visiting Europeans for corrupting the innocent; in the *Histoire des deux Indes* he attacks the increasingly aggressive endeavours of the European rulers to build empires and colonies overseas. 'A new kind of fanaticism has developed,' he wrote, 'the search for continents to invade, islands to plunder, peoples to despoil, subjugate, and massacre.'[46]

The *deux Indes* of this book's title are the 'Indies' of the West, that is the whole of the New World, north and south, and the 'Indies' of the East—India and beyond. A few, very few such places were 'empty'; most were not. Diderot wrote: 'Reason and equity allow colonies to be established only in a country where no other people is already living. For thus one can earn the right to it by work. A country that is wholly deserted and uninhabited is the only one that can be legitimately appropriated.'[47]

Diderot's history of the Spanish conquest of South America is as hostile as are most such histories written by French, English, or Dutch authors, but unlike those historians, Diderot does not suggest that the Spanish imperial enterprise was uniquely cruel. He sees injustice in all empire-building, using arguments which would hardly be expected of an *encyclopédiste*. For empire-building was favoured by progressive opinion in the eighteenth century as it was in the nineteenth, because it was seen as a means of diffusing the advantages of modern science, technology, medicine, and so forth in undeveloped areas of the globe. If Diderot as much as Rousseau stood against the current of opinion, it was because, for all his devotion to the Baconian *ethos*, he shared many of Rousseau's doubts about the advantages of modern progress and had an even greater belief in the nobility of the savage. Precisely because he believed that man was naturally social, Diderot could count on the possibility of finding simple uncorrupted societies in the modern world.

In his *Discourse on Inequality* Rousseau describes the experience of a Hottentot in South Africa who is brought up by a Dutch benefactor, but finally refuses to be 'civilized' in the European fashion; Rousseau praises his determination to return to his origins.[48] Diderot goes further. He urges the Hottentots to get out their bows and poisoned arrows and kill the Dutch settlers before those so-called benefactors can destroy their native culture with their gifts of beads and Bibles.[49]

Such is the voice of the radical Diderot. But at the same time and in the same book another voice can be discerned—not the Abbé Raynal's, but Diderot's other voice—the conservative-liberal voice of the follower of Montesquieu warning Louis XVI against the dangers of too rapid reforms: 'All innovations should be gradual . . . To create or destroy suddenly is to corrupt the good and make the evil worse.'[50]

It is no good listening to one of Diderot's voices, and pretending that it is Diderot's definitive word. There are as many Diderots as their protagonists in his dialogues. He is the least Cartesian, the least 'French', of the *philosophes* of the Enlightenment; and at the same time the closest to the thoughts and the problems of later generations, for whom he may be supposed to have intended the writings which he concealed from his own contemporaries. He believed in a better future, and he wrote for his posterity.

# 5

# Holbach

Of all the leading philosophers of the French Enlightenment, Baron d'Holbach remains the least well known. His numerous works have seldom been reprinted and are difficult to find except in specialized libraries. Yet his name is familiar enough; in almost every history of the intellectual life of France Holbach is mentioned, either as the most systematic eighteenth-century exponent of materialism, or as the leader of intellectual society, the richest of the *encyclopédistes*, the one in whose house the others met and dined, the host to foreign philosophers on their visits to Paris, and the benefactor of any friend who found himself in need.

With the characteristic tendency of intellectuals to bite the hand that feeds them, the *philosophes* often spoke ungraciously about Holbach. Rousseau accused him of leading a hostile conspiracy; Voltaire and Buffon condemned him as a man without judgement. Even Diderot, his closest friend, said of Holbach, 'He has benevolence only in his head; his idea of doing good to others is to engage in an argument; he has no heart.'[1]

And yet Diderot perhaps more than anyone else had reason to be grateful to Holbach, for Holbach was no ordinary contributor to the *Encyclopédie*, but the author of over four hundred of the most important articles, notably those on applied science and technology; he was a loyal supporter of Diderot when the authorities threatened action against the *Encyclopédie* and other contributors withdrew from the enterprise.[2]

Holbach's *Système de la nature* is a remarkably modern book, more sophisticated than other expositions of eighteenth-century materialism, such as Helvétius on *l'Esprit* or La Mettrie on *L'Homme machine*; it adumbrates much that is nowadays known as 'logical positivism' or 'behaviourism' and foreshadows ideas developed in our time by such philosophers as Gilbert Ryle and B. F. Skinner. Holbach is a clear and robust stylist, and he does not mince his words on sensitive matters as most of his contemporaries felt it necessary to do. Considering the provocative

tive nature of his writings, it may seem surprising that he was never imprisoned, like Voltaire and Diderot, or exiled like Rousseau, or reduced, like Helvétius, to silence; but Holbach had a simple way of protecting himself: he brought out his books under the names of respectable authors recently deceased. His *Système de la nature*, for example, was published as the work of the late Monsieur de Mirabeau of the Academie Française. Since Holbach had no belief in life after death, he had no fear of meeting in another world writers whose names he had so shamelessly filched.

In his works on ethics, Holbach suggests that prosperity is the reward of virtue, but his own material advantages owed more to good luck and the French system of inheritance. He lived to the age of 66 in uninterrupted opulence, and died in the comfort of his own bed just before the outbreak of the Revolution which was inspired in part by his ideas and which destroyed the world in which he flourished.

Rousseau described Holbach as the 'son of a parvenu',[3] and others have questioned his title of nobility. But modern research has established its authenticity. Holbach inherited his barony, with his substantial fortune, from an uncle who had been a *fournisseur* to Louis XIV and been ennobled for his services. The title was French, the family, German. Holbach was born in December 1723 at Edesheim in the Palatinate, where he was baptized Paul-Heinrich Dietrich, a name he afterwards Gallicized as 'Thiry'.

Helvétius also came from Germany, but his origins were French, his forebears being Huguenots who had left France to escape religious persecution in the seventeenth century and then returned under royal patronage. Helvétius had made a fortune as a tax farmer before he turned to philosophy. He was never a contributor to the *Encyclopédie*, and was regarded by Holbach as something of an amateur. Holbach had good grounds for considering himself a professional. He had been exceptionally well educated in Germany and afterwards in Holland at what was then the best university in Europe, Leiden. He specialized in two fields: English empiricist philosophy and the several natural sciences which were more advanced in Protestant countries than they were in France—geology, mineralogy, and metallurgy. He also took an intense interest in anti-clerical and atheistical literature, and translated several polemical books of this kind from

German and English into French. At Leiden he became a close friend of the English radical John Wilkes.

When Holbach established himself in Paris at the age of 26 in 1749, he proved himself extremely useful to Diderot. For while Diderot aimed to realize in the *Encyclopédie* the Baconian dream of organizing a conspectus of all the sciences, he had no qualifications as a scientist. D'Alembert, appointed by the publishers to provide the expertise Diderot lacked, deserted him when persecution threatened; besides, d'Alembert was a specialist in the traditional abstract sciences, physics and mathematics, whereas Diderot wanted to give greater prominence to the biological sciences, applied sciences, and moral sciences, and it was in these areas that Holbach was at home.

Moreover, Holbach with his Paris *salon* and his country château at Le Grandval provided places in which Diderot as editor of the *Encyclopédie* could meet his contributors and discuss their work. Twice a week Madame d'Holbach gave a dinner party in Paris, and working weekends took place at Le Grandval where the hospitality, as Diderot reported, had all the elegance of Paris and 'was perhaps even more sumptuous'.[4] The price of all this was putting up with Holbach talking philosophy from morning to night. Diderot sometimes yearned for the more worldly and frivolous conversation to be enjoyed in the *salon* of Mme Helvétius. He once wrote from his study saying: 'The only happiness I feel a little is not being tormented by the Baron.'[5]

Holbach is sometimes spoken of as being very 'German' in his temperament, partly by reason of his industry and thoroughness —for he is known to have written at least thirty-five books besides the four hundred articles he produced for the *Encyclopédie* and partly because of his tendency to push things to extremes. He was certainly among the most radical of the philosophers, in his atheism and his materialism if less so in his politics. He detested anything that savoured of compromise. And yet in many ways Holbach, with his passion for systems, for clear and distinct ideas, and his impatience with irregularity and unbridled imagination, was the model French rationalist, just as Diderot, with his aesthetic fantasies, his dialectical thinking, and his love of the extraordinary, was close to the ideal type of a German romantic. If they were both 'Baconians', Holbach no more than Diderot can be fairly described as a champion of enlightened despotism. Holbach's political ideas may come as a surprise to the reader who knows only his writings on metaphysics and morals, for his attachment to the Baconian gospel of salvation through science might prompt one to assume, with several historians, that he also subscribed to Bacon's ideas on politics; but this was not the case.

Holbach's radicalism expressed itself in taking ideas which he shared with other *encyclopédistes* and pushing them to extremes. His atheism might seem a shade obsessive as well as excessive. More than half the books he wrote are directed against Christianity; even his masterpiece, *Le Système de la nature*, is one volume of philosophy and another, slightly larger, volume of atheist polemics. Holbach considered that his views on religion were more logical than those of his fellow philosophers. He did not seek like Voltaire to replace the God of the Christian tradition with a Supreme Being of his own invention; he felt that every argument against orthodox religion was equally an argument against so-called 'natural religion'.[6] Nor did Holbach propose like Rousseau to initiate a civil religion with a simple set of dogmas to sustain civic virtue. He had no patience with the view held by so many philosophers that it was necessary for ordinary people to believe in God as a means of upholding morality. He came closer to the opinion of Marx that religion was an influence the popular classes would be better off without, only he did not call it an 'opiate' but a stimulant, an 'eau de vie' which excited the people's lust for sensations and made them feast on the thrills of burning heretics, persecuting dissenters, and torturing prisoners.

Even so, Holbach did not advocate the actual suppression of religious institutions. Acknowledging that religious faith was more precious to some people than their physical property, he felt it would be wrong to rob them of it.[7] All religious cults, he argued, should be tolerated until such time as people could be weaned away from them, and such re-education could not be expected to take effect overnight. What Holbach found hard to stomach were arguments such as Pascal's, that there was nothing to be lost by betting on the unverifiable claims of Christianity being true.

Holbach had an equally uncompromising attitude in philosophy. It was the general view of the philosophers of the Enlightenment from Montesquieu onwards that one must look to science for knowledge; Holbach pushed this policy to extremes: all so-called knowledge which is not scientific, he suggests, is meaningless. He proclaimed himself, as did most of the *encyclopédistes*, a follower of Locke, but in his *Système de la nature* he offers a positivist's criticism of Locke: 'How has it come about', he asks,

that the profound Locke . . . and all those who, like him, have recognized the absurdity of the theory of innate ideas, have not drawn out the immediate, the necessary consequences? . . . Why have they not had the courage to apply this clear principle to all the chimeras with which the human mind has so long and so vainly occupied itself?[8]

This is a characteristic demand of Holbach's: why have they not drawn out the necessary consequences? The consequences he saw as necessary included the total banishment of metaphysics—something less harmful than religion, but just as unscientific. What had been called the queen of the sciences, Holbach condemned as a mere system of words.

In his chapter on the soul, he protests against the bifurcation of man into mind and matter, and he attributes this to the influence of Descartes. What is called the soul, he suggests, is simply a way of considering the body in relation to some of its functions. We have no experience of disembodied souls, and Holbach claims that neither the ancient philosophers nor the earliest doctors of the Church 'had any thought of the soul being immaterial'[9]

He suggests that our peculiar capacity for thinking, feeling, and behaving in certain distinctively 'human' ways prompts us to talk of mens' souls or minds; but that such words should be understood as a sort of shorthand, not implying the existence of what Holbach—anticipating Gilbert Ryle—calls an 'occult power'. Because the words 'mind' and 'soul' mislead people, Holbach proposes to dispense with them; 'they convey no sense that is accessible either to us or to those who invented them, and therefore cannot be of the slightest use for science or for ethics'.[10]

Holbach admits a distinction between what he calls 'the physical man' and 'the moral man', but maintains that the distinction is not based on any division within man himself; it simply expresses our different ways of understanding man. The physical man is the man we see jumping when he is burned; he is the man whose actions are the effects of causes we can observe. The moral man is the man whose actions are the effect of causes we cannot observe, and which we attribute in our ignorance to the occult power called the mind. For example, we see a man running away from a battlefield, and we judge him to be animated by fear—we cannot see what is motivating him so we attribute it to a 'cowardly soul' within him.

This common way of thinking, Holbach continues, breeds even more extravagant fantasies, such as the idea that the soul can survive the body, which, he protests, is just like believing that a clock could continue to chime after its works have been destroyed. The belief in the freedom of the will is in Holbach's eyes another popular illusion that needs to be demolished. How does it originate?

When we go back to the sources of our actions, he argues, we find that they are always the necessary results of our desires and wishes, over which we have no control. People have believed that we are free because we have a will, and the power to choose, but 'they have not paid attention to the fact that our wishes and desires are necessarily caused by objects or factors which are entirely independent of us'.[11]

Diderot was evidently shocked by Holbach's idea that determinism meant the total elimination of moral responsibility. In a letter he quoted with dismay Holbach's assertion that 'a human being who injures me acts no more freely than a tile which falls from the roof and hits me on the head and is therefore no more to be blamed'.[12] Diderot suggested that Holbach was in effect a fatalist, and some of Holbach's remarks seem to confirm this judgement. For example, we find him writing: 'O vain and feeble Man! You claim to be free. You do not see the chains that bind you. Do you think your weak will can force nature to stop her eternal march, or change her course?'[13]

But fatalism was a charge that Holbach would not accept. He claimed that the elimination of free will did not remove the possibility of altering the future. If all actions are caused, then the intervention of new causes can modify men's actions; if every choice is conditioned, different conditions will generate different choices. According to Holbach, it was the sceptics, such as Montaigne and David Hume, who were the true fatalists; for these were philosophers who could find no solid basis for challenging the imperfections of existing institutions, and so resigned themselves to accepting and even supporting whatever habit, custom, and tradition had established. A perpetually open mind, Holbach thought, was useless; the sceptics, resting their heads 'on the pillow of doubt', appeared to him to be the most rigid of conservatives.[14]

Holbach, for his part, was a believer: an ardent believer in nature. But nature has more than one meaning in Holbach's philosophy. First of all, nature is everything that is. All the movements we observe in the world, including those movements we speak of as human actions, are movements governed by the laws of nature; this is why there can be a science of human behaviour as well as a science of astronomy.

Secondly, nature appears in Holbach's writings as a sort of Supreme Ruler. At the end of his *Système de la nature*, he gives nature a voice and makes it—or her—speak to the human race in these words:

O Man, in following the impulse I have implanted in you to strive every instant of your life for happiness, do not resist my sovereign law. Labour to your own felicity . . . You will find the means clearly written in your own heart . . . Dare to liberate yourselves from the yoke of religion, my supreme rival . . . It is in my empire that freedom reigns . . . Come back, wandering child, come back to nature. She will console you. She will banish cares from your heart. O man, be happy![15]

There are more passages in Holbach's ethical writings of a similar kind, pleas which would seem to make sense only if man is assumed to have the freedom to obey—or disobey—the supreme ruler, nature. For there can be no doubt that Holbach is saying that it is open to man either to obey the laws of nature and flourish, or disobey the laws of nature and suffer. Nature, in other words, enacts the role in Holbach's system which God performs in religious systems. Nature is the fountain of all that is good. Truth, reason, and virtue he describes in a poetic phrase as the 'three daughters of nature'; and he goes on to suggest that nature upholds morality by punishing vice with diseases and death and rewarding virtue with happiness.

There is, however, a third sense of 'nature' as it appears in Holbach's theory. This is sometimes distinguished as 'undeveloped nature' or 'brutish nature' and sometimes as 'corrupted nature'; it is responsible for those impulses which turn men away from virtue. Moreover, Holbach was more alive to the power of such evil impulses than were most philosophers of the Enlightenment. Despite his opulent style of living, he was a puritan; and he drew between happiness and pleasure a sharp distinction which puts him at odds with the utilitarians, with Helvétius and other moralists of the Enlightenment for whom happiness was to be measured by the felicific calculus, or the predominance of pleasure over pain.

Holbach simply could not believe the stories of Bougainville and Diderot which suggested that the natives of Tahiti were both happy and sexually promiscuous.[16] Since such practices were immoral, Holbach reasoned that the Tahitians *must* be unhappy as well as ignorant. 'There are countries', he wrote, 'where public opinion attaches merit to the most abominable conduct . . . From this we conclude that human reason has not yet been sufficiently developed in many countries for the people to distinguish what is really good from what merely appears to be good.'[17]

The cult of nature for Holbach is manifestly not a policy of liberation, of freeing men from constraints which hinder natural enjoyment.[18] The enthronement of good nature requires a constant struggle against bad nature. He calls the system of government that is needed to procure this end ethocracy, or the rule of morality. This is a regime which fits into no taxonomy of constitutions familiar to political science, either that of Aristotle or that of Montesquieu; but it has striking resemblance to the theocracies of Savonarola and Calvin. It is ironical that so impassioned an atheist as Holbach should be placed in the same category as those fervent Christian reformers, but they were his direct forerunners as champions of a political order ruled by morality, albeit in their case of a morality conceived as divinely ordained.

The extremes, we are often told, meet; ethocracy is puritan politics without puritan theology. Holbach's determinism poses analogous problems to those posed by Calvin's predestination; and the places of God and the Devil in Calvin's scheme are taken by good nature and bad nature in Holbach's. For both, morality can become supreme in earthly societies only as a result of a continuous struggle against immorality; and the two theorists have curiously similar ideas about the institutional arrangements that are needed to ensure the rule of morality.

Most philosophers of the French Enlightenment admired the English political system as much as they admired English philosophy—at any rate, until the North American wars of the 1770s diminished their Anglomania, they tended to follow the lead of Montesquieu and Voltaire in considering the English constitution 'the mirror of liberty'. If they did not all have the same conception of liberty, or the same notion of how the English system worked, nearly all of them considered England the best governed country in Europe. Holbach thought differently. He received a highly critical account of English politics from his radical friend of Leiden University days, John Wilkes, and when he went to see England for himself for six months in 1756 he formed a most unfavourable opinion of both the government and the people.[19] The inequality between rich and poor appeared to him to be even more shocking and gross than it was in France; English politicians seemed to him to be wholly unprincipled and Parliament, corrupt. Reversing the judgement of Voltaire, he said that the King of England was free to do harm but had his hands tied when he wanted to do good. Holbach complained that English universities paid no attention to science and scant attention to any other branch of scholarship. The English people did not know the difference between freedom and licence, and far from being a 'mirror of liberty', the whole kingdom was a 'mirror of anarchy'. The standards by which Holbach judged England were not those of liberalism, but of ethocracy: and the criteria he invoked were probity, purity, and equity.

The one lesson that Holbach proposed to derive from English experience was the need to subordinate freedom to discipline, law, and virtue. He disagreed with Montesquieu's view that virtue was not compatible with royal government, and suggested that both in republics and in monarchies 'virtue and honour should be inseparable'.[20] Since Holbach was writing mainly for French readers, one can understand why his book concentrates on monarchies, and discusses ways in which virtue can be made to prevail under the sovereignty of a king.

The first essential, he suggests, is that the king himself should be virtuous. How is that to be assured? To begin with, the state should take the education of heirs to the throne out of the hands of the royal family, and give the princes a civil upbringing to fit them for their high office. Next, the king himself should be shielded from the corrupting influence of courtiers and flatterers.

Since all are agreed that a king must be loved, the state must ensure that he deserves to be loved. And just as princes must be educated for kingship, so must the people be educated for citizenship. Like Calvin, once again, Holbach proposed a system of free and compulsory public instruction, on the grounds that 'the happiest state is that which contains the greatest number of enlightened people'.[21] The aim of all education should be the improvement of morals at the same time as the enlargement of knowledge. The teaching of history, for example, should be designed to show pupils how *virtue* has contributed in the past to the glory and prosperity of nations, and how *vice* has brought about their decay. The teaching of sciences should be directed to awakening the pupil's awareness of the usefulness of science as distinct from the purely academic content. There should be no wasting of time, Holbach suggests, on dead languages; but there should be daily teaching of a 'moral catechism' and a 'moral code', so as to prepare children for a life of virtue. Moreover, this education should be provided for girls as well as boys, for the 'experience of Sparta', Holbach writes, 'demonstrates that women can acquire a patriotism, a greatness of soul and wisdom of which men themselves are incapable in corrupt and enslaved nations'.

Despite the stress he put on education, Holbach did not agree with Helvétius that education could do almost anything in shaping a child's character. He rejected Helvétius' claim that inherited factors were nothing and environmental factors everything, so that, given the right training, any child could be made to do whatever the teacher designed he should do. Holbach agreed that education was necessary to produce good citizens, but argued that it was not enough to prevent some from backsliding into vice. Legislation was also needed, together with the continued direction of society by the state to ensure that the people were kept in the path of virtue.[22]

Holbach was a good enough Lockian to proclaim every man's rights to life, liberty, and property, but he added a warning: 'liberty is a dangerous weapon in the hands of a corrupt people'.[23] How, then, can liberty and virtue be kept alive in tandem?

First, Holbach recommends sumptuary laws. These must begin at the top: 'it is not with ostentatious palaces that a prince should impress his subjects, but by the wisdom of his administration'.[24] The frugality of the monarch should match that of his people, and, what is even more important, his chastity should be exemplary: 'the royal palace should be a sanctuary into which nothing impure can enter'.[25]

There is a place for nobility in Holbach's model kingdom, but not for the kind of landed aristocracy that dates from medieval feudalism. 'Feudalism', he wrote, 'was nothing but a massive brigandage, and a nobility of blood based on ancient or Gothic lineage is worthless.'[26] Nobility as it is known in eighteenth-century France is a 'frivolous and empty distinction', and the ethos of the *noblesse de race* which exalts 'idleness, military prowess, luxury, gambling, and gallantry' is no good for anyone. An aristocrat is useful only in his capacity as landowner, and members of that class, Holbach suggests, should be made to apply themselves to managing and improving their estates, organizing farms, developing industries, and transforming the countryside into a source of social wealth. Their class would then become a genuine aristocracy with a wholly new set of values: work, production, service.

Holbach did not carry his enthusiasm for this idea to the point of removing himself to his own very large estates in Germany in order to manage and improve them, any more than he imposed sumptuary laws on the life-style of his château and his *hôtel particulier* in Paris; his perception of his own function was within the aristocracy of the mind, as a hard-working philosopher who was also a convenor of meetings of other philosophers, the head of an invisible college. He made no attempt, as did Voltaire, to defend the privileges of the rich. Indeed, he suggested that great fortunes were generally the fruit of injustice, and he argued that it was one of the duties of the state, in a society where there were great disparities of wealth, to subdue the rich and take care of the poor.[27] He stopped short of the proposals of such contemporaries as the Abbé de Mably that the state should actually redistribute wealth. He was strongly critical of Helvétius' doctrine of human equality.[28] His only contribution to the birth of socialism was to question the right of the rich to own the wealth they held. He considered belief in democracy to be absurdly Utopian.

Holbach accepted Locke's theory that the right to property was originally derived from the intermixing of a man's labour

with the produce of nature.[29] 'Property', he wrote, 'has as its
basis a necessary relation established between a man and the fruit
of his labour. The field watered with the sweat of his brow
becomes, as it were, a part of himself. The fruits it brings forth
belong to him . . . because were it not for his labour these fruits
would either not exist at all or at least in a different form'.[30]

Where Holbach differs from Locke is that he does not modify
the labour theory by adding a doctrine of tacit consent to the use
of money, which serves in the end for Locke to justify property
based on rent and inheritance as distinct from labour; Holbach
sticks to labour as the one source of entitlement,[31] adding to it
only a utilitarian justification of differences in wealth: 'society
reduces men to mutual dependence; the great have need of the
small and the small of the great'.[32] Elsewhere he suggests: 'An
enlightened policy ought to work in such a way that the greatest
number of citizens may possess some property of their own . . .
when a small number of men absorb all the property and wealth
of a state, they become its masters, and thereafter it is only with
the very greatest difficulty that it can take from them the fortune
they have amassed.'[33]

Holbach singled out two sorts of large fortune for condemnation; first there were those, like that of Helvétius, derived from
tax-farming, a form of revenue-raising which Holbach described
as suited only to a despot, since it led to taxes paid by the king's
subjects being doubled, one part serving to finance the state and
the other going to enrich extortioners. Secondly, Holbach condemned fortunes derived from rent or interest by idle landowners, who were corrupted by their own exemption from
labour; 'every man who does not work becomes a bad citizen, a
vicious libertine'.[34] Holbach himself could never be accused of
idleness. He wrote books which brought him no income; and the
unearned income he derived from rents and investments gave him
the freedom to do so. Hence his strictures on 'idle landowners'
could not apply to himself, since he was the most industrious of
men.

As for fortunes derived from commerce, Holbach's attitude
was much more critical. He was mistrustful of trade. He believed
that the happiest nation was one with a predominantly pastoral
economy. He was not at all in favour of industrialization. In this
respect he was far closer to Rousseau, whom he disliked, than to

Diderot, whom he loved. 'A nation . . . will be sufficiently rich', said Holbach, 'when, without excessive labour, its soil provides the products necessary to its existence.'[35] An unbridled passion for trade had, he suggested, been the chief cause of the corruption of England.[36] And far from sharing the progressive opinion that commerce was conducive to peace, he suggested that most of the wars which afflicted Europe in his time were essentially commercial wars. The age of dynastic wars was over. The only reason why the French and the English were still fighting each other in the eighteenth century was that the two kingdoms had collided in their colonial and commercial adventures in the New World and in India.[37]

As an early critic of what is now called 'imperialism' Holbach was really closer to Lenin than was Diderot, who is often claimed as a forerunner of Lenin. For Holbach ascribes the empire-building of his time to specifically capitalist motives, contrasting it with the Roman endeavour to build an empire for the sake of power and the Spanish endeavour to build an empire in order to propagate religion. The new imperialists—French, English, Dutch—he alleged were scrambling for markets, profits, and gold, to such an extent that rivalry between them was the greatest single cause of war. He seems to have considered the English the most culpable in this activity. In one of his more purple passages, he implores the people of England—'O Albion' is the form of address—to turn away from their worship of money and rediscover virtue in the cultivation of their own soil.[38]

To some extent Holbach was simply reflecting a changed attitude in French public opinion towards the English after the defeat of French armies in Canada; but his chief objections to the English were peculiarly his own. Indeed, he disliked and disapproved of the English for features of their character which other French intellectuals admired, and his hostility to English politics and English philosophy extended to English economics. He had no belief in Adam Smith and his theory of an invisible hand reconciling the individual's pursuit of his own good with the realization of the common good. Holbach said that the common good could be realized only if everyone sought directly to promote the common good; hence the necessity of virtue, understood by Holbach, as by Montesquieu, as the disposition in the citizen always to put the public interest before his private interest.

And yet there is a kind of 'invisible hand' in Holbach's own scheme, and that is the hand exercised by nature—in the sense of Mother Nature. The workings of this force help to explain how Holbach could be at the same time a puritan and a utilitarian. The end he points out to man is happiness. Nature impels everyone to seek happiness, but it does not instruct everyone how to achieve happiness. The wise man alone knows that the happiness of each is only to be found in the happiness of all, since Mother Nature has arranged things so that unselfish actions are rewarded and selfish actions punished, with the result that the individual whose actions are directed towards the realization of universal happiness will experience enduring personal happiness, while the individual who pursues only personal gratification is doomed to disappointment. Admittedly brutish nature impels many men to seek such short-term satisfaction, but in the long run Mother Nature will deny them real happiness.

Since the word 'pleasure' is commonly associated with the kind of instant gratification that Holbach warns against, 'pleasure' cannot serve in his type of utilitarian ethics, as it does in that of Helvétius and Jeremy Bentham, as a measure of the good. Happiness, as Holbach understands it, is often achieved only at the expense of pleasure. Happiness is the reward of virtue; and virtue is as often as not a matter of self-denial. Theorists like Adam Smith and Voltaire seemed to Holbach to be suggesting that one could have one's cake and eat it; think of yourself and the invisible hand will ensure that everyone is thought of. Holbach's Mother Nature is altogether less indulgent to her children. She will reward efforts and abstinence; but she has nothing but misery to offer the self-indulgent, the lazy, and the licentious.

On the subject of luxury, so much debated in the Enlightenment, Holbach is with Diderot and Rousseau and against Voltaire and Hume.[39] He argues that there is no substance in the claim that luxury benefits the poor by providing employment for their skills as artisans.[40] He maintains that luxury is injurious to the working classes in diverting their skills from the production of useful to the production of useless goods. As for the middle and upper classes, they derive no real advantages from luxury; for the middle classes are forced to spend more than they can afford in order to make themselves look richer than they really are, while the upper classes are led to seek satisfaction in the empty pleasures and frivolous refinements of life instead of pursuing true happiness by doing their duty and cultivating pure joys, which are the most intense that human beings can experience. In a society where luxury dominates, Holbach concludes, wealth itself comes to be thought of as honourable and poverty disgraceful.[41]

Such is the reasoning behind Holbach's pleas for the abolition of conspicuous consumption. He suggests that this should be accomplished partly by means of sumptuary laws, and partly by heavy taxation on palaces, carriages, liveried servants, ornamental gardens, jewellery, and finery. Gambling and prostitution he would have suppressed by law. He quotes Hesiod's remark that 'The gods gave men work in order to preserve virtue'; and these words hold the key to Holbach's scheme.[42] Work is productive from the point of view of the economy, and redemptive from that of morals. The 'work ethic' is yet another feature of his thinking which he shares with Calvin. Indeed Holbach's whole programme of social reform recalls that devised by Calvin for Geneva in the sixteenth century. Holbach never mentions Geneva. His references are always to the more glamorous republics of Sparta and Rome, although he singles out for praise those institutions of the ancient world which Calvin copied. Holbach evokes, for example, the censorial tribunals of Rome, which served 'as a powerful barrier against luxury and vice'. By the surveillance of private morals they helped individuals to resist temptation. 'Men, all too often lacking in experience and reason, are nothing but children perpetually driven by vices, passions, and tastes that a solicitous government should carefully correct.'[43] In practice this means that the state, in doing its duty to overcome 'brutish nature', must put a stop to all activities on which brutish nature feeds: not only gambling and prostitution, but balls, public festivities, feasts, entertainments, comedies, operas, and indeed all drama except serious tragedies which convey a moral. The state, as Holbach saw it, would not be diminishing happiness by taking away so many pleasures: it would simply be removing impediments to a life of virtue, which is the path of true happiness.

Since Holbach advocates such radical changes in the organization of society, the question is bound to be asked: is Holbach a revolutionary? In a certain sense he is. In another sense he is not. His situation has much in common with that of Rousseau, another theorist close to Calvin, and understandably so as a native of Calvin's Geneva. When Rousseau considered what a society would be like in which men were both free and ruled, he outlined the republic we find in his *Social Contract*, an idealized fusion of Geneva and Sparta. When Holbach came to describe a society in which men could recover both happiness and morality, he envisaged an ideal kingdom where a virtuous monarch ruled over virtuous subjects, with much the same laws as those of Rousseau's city-state. There is, however, one great difference between Rousseau's model republic and Holbach's model kingdom; Rousseau demands absolute and undivided sovereignty for the people; Holbach refuses to allow absolute and undivided sovereignty to the king. Here we meet another side of Holbach's thinking, one which has echoes of Locke and Montesquieu.

The sovereignty which reposes in the king, Holbach argues, must derive from the consent of the people;[44] and he adds that constitutional or fundamental laws are needed to prevent a monarch from slipping into despotism.[45] Even an enlightened monarch is intolerable if he becomes despotic: 'No man can acquire the right to rule a nation against its will. The most legitimate, wise, and virtuous of sovereigns would be no better than a tyrant if he governed in the teeth of his people's wishes.'[46] A nation therefore has the right 'to force its monarchs to be just and reasonable, and failing that to depose them from the throne'.[47] In another context Holbach wrote: 'It is impossible to repeat too often that the rights of nations are prior to those of the kings they have chosen to put at their head. They have never lost the right to limit, alter, circumscribe, and revoke the powers they have given, whenever they recognize that they have been abused.'[48] The word 'nation' is crucial here, because Holbach does not confer on the population in general the right to rebel against their king. Revolutions which are manifestations of popular rage are likely to lead to anarchy. Tyrannicide is wrong; persecuted minorities should simply emigrate. The people must never take the law into their own hands: 'it is only the nation as a whole, through its representatives, that has the right to resist, to enforce obligations and to punish its oppressors'.[49]

When Holbach asserted the right of a society to overthrow its sovereign by force,[50] he may have been thinking of the kind of revolution which happened in England in 1689 when the national magistrates had placed a new king on the throne of a monarch who had fled; but when he spoke of society acting through a 'corps of representatives', he did not have in mind an elected assembly on the lines of the English Parliament; he refers to that body of citizens who are 'the most upright, the most enlightened and the most devoted to the public interest'.[51] In a word, an aristocracy is here envisaged as the authentic representative body of the nation.[52] Furthermore, Holbach suggested that this corps should be institutionalized, with a right to meet without being convoked by the monarch.[53] Hence, although he speaks approvingly in dedicating his book *Éthocratie* to Louis XVI of that king's 'absolute power', the constitution he sketches out in the text is plainly one where the monarch's sovereignty is *not* absolute, but limited by the right of the 'corps of representatives' to have a share in that sovereignty, and to function as an autonomous institution in the state.

If there are similarities between Holbach's 'ethocracy' and Calvin's 'theocracy', one must not overlook one great difference. Calvin's theory made provision for its translation from the world of intellectual speculation to that of practical politics, as indeed it needed to, since Calvin was called upon by the burghers of Geneva to redraft the constitution for their city-state. No one gave such a commission to Holbach, and his *Éthocratie* offers little indication of how its programme might be actualized in the France of the 1770s.[54] His book calls for a king who is educated from infancy in the paths of austere virtue. But Louis XVI was 60 years old in 1770, and far removed from any Spartan ethic; his heir was already 16. France would have to wait a long time for a prince who could be educated on entirely new lines. Holbach also calls for the institution of a 'censorial tribunal' to preserve the people's virtue by means of surveillance and sanctions. Calvin provided such a body, under the control of his Church, and it proved to be very active for several generations in upholding puritan morality in Geneva. But Holbach, as an atheist, could have no church from which to recruit a similar censorial tribunal. Then again, Holbach calls for the institution of a *corps of representatives*, composed of the most virtuous and enlightened persons in the kingdom. But how was such an aristocracy of morals to be recognized?

In the event, as Holbach lifted his eyes from his books to survey the real world of French politics outside, he saw no corps of 'the most virtuous and most enlightened men in the kingdom', but only a body which fancied itself to be composed of such men, namely the *noblesse de robe* as assembled in the *parlements*. Thus he found himself in a position where, to the horror of Voltaire, he felt it necessary to accept the self-image of the *parlements*; and to come out in the 1770s as a champion of those *parlements* when they were suppressed by the King. Finding no other point of contact between his abstract schemes of reform and the concrete exigencies of his situation, he passed from his argument that an aristocracy of virtue was necessary to a good monarchy to the conclusion that the restoration of the powers of the *noblesse de robe* was necessary to the regeneration of France.

It would be a vulgar error to suggest that Holbach came down from the clouds of revolutionary speculation to end up as yet another ideologue of his class; a *baron* at last, alarmed at the suppression of a privileged order. He was not, after all, a member, like Montesquieu, of the *noblesse de robe*; he derived his nobility from the regime of Louis XIV, who made a point of giving titles to tradesmen. Holbach owed his rank to unencumbered royal absolutism, which made it all the harder for Voltaire to understand how Holbach could go over to the other side.

But it seems that Holbach felt forced into this position by the lack of any alternatives; better a defective corps of representatives than no corps of representatives at all. Besides, he could not fail to listen to the arguments of Diderot, who had come to be more than ever opposed to royal absolutism after his experience with the Empress Catherine.[55] Diderot helped to persuade him that the *parlements* were essential to maintain what little was left of liberty.

Holbach and Diderot had stood together before against Voltaire and the *voltairiens*. They had been for atheism against deism; for the state management of the economy against *laissez-faire*; for the poor against the rich. In 1770 they found themselves together once more.

From the perspective of Voltaire, the *parlements* were the judicial murderers of Calas and Lally and la Barre, the burners of books, the defenders of feudal privilege; so that when Louis XV banished them and replaced them with royal salaried magistrates

Voltaire felt that his cry of 'écrasez l'infâme!' had at last been heard at Versailles. He saw the suppression of the *noblesse de robe* as the removal of the chief obstacle to reform in France. But Holbach shared with Diderot the fear that what was being removed was rather the last obstacle to tyranny in France.[56] So Holbach pleaded for the restoration of the *parlements*, and attacked the centralizing policy of Versailles.[57] He did not want enlightened government if royal despotism was the price of it. He preferred the haphazard oppression of familiar, confused, and divided authorities, a situation in which a clever man could find freedom in the interstices, and make blueprints of a better world.

# 6

# Condorcet

Jean-Antoine-Nicolas Caritat, Marquis de Condorcet, was the youngest of the leading *encyclopédistes*, and the only prominent member of that group who lived to play an active part in the French Revolution. Born into a family of the *noblesse de race* in 1743, Condorcet was fifty years younger than Voltaire, thirty years younger than Diderot, and twenty years younger than Holbach. He distinguished himself at an early age as a mathematician, winning the friendship and support of d'Alembert, who arranged for him to write articles on mathematical subjects for the *Encyclopédie*. In spite of his noble blood, Condorcet did not deign to exploit all means of climbing to the top of the cultural institutions of the kingdom, and he succeeded in becoming at the age of 25 a member of the Academy of Sciences; at 33 he was its Perpetual Secretary; and five years later he was elected to the Académie Française. Although generally considered cold and unattractive, he married one of the most beautiful and intelligent women in France, Sophie de Grouchy, in whose *salon* hospitality was extended to Condorcet's influential friends.

After he had conquered the world of science as d'Alembert's protégé, Condorcet sought the patronage of Turgot in pursuing political ambitions. His earlier writings of the time expound ideas very close to those of Turgot: freedom for commerce together with centralized monarchical government. Then when the Revolution came, Condorcet emerged as one of the most radical participants, both as a theorist and as a member, then president, of the legislative assembly. He became an increasingly eager champion of popular government and universal suffrage until faced with the democratic policies of revolutionaries more extreme than himself; he died, aged 50, a victim of the Terror.

Condorcet's biographer, Léon Cahen, claims that the storming of the Bastille 'produced in his mind a veritable revolution',[1] turning Condorcet overnight from a royalist into a republican, but there is really more continuity in Condorcet's political thinking than this romantic story would have us believe. Research on his published and unpublished writings[2] suggests that he was neither a true royalist before 14 July 1789 nor a true democrat afterwards. Condorcet always believed in what he called the sovereignty of reason. Before the flight of Louis XVI to Varennes, he thought the king had a place in the scheme of rational government in France; afterwards, although he did not vote for the execution of the King (believing that capital punishment was always wrong) he voted for his deposition, and devised a constitution for republican government. Ever since the 1770s Condorcet had been excited by the possibilities of republican government in America, and had corresponded with various American friends about the forms of a republican constitution; he was even elected an honorary citizen of New Haven in Connecticut.[3] The date 14 July was not a decisive one in the evolution of Condorcet's political thought, and there are no good grounds for thinking that his 'ideas changed abruptly'.[4]

In spite of his relatively early death Condorcet produced a great deal of published work, and was one of the founders, in direct succession to Francis Bacon, of what are now called the 'social sciences'. All modern endeavours to solve social problems, including political and public policy problems, with the aid of empirical research, statistical investigation, sampling, and so forth, all attempts to apply mathematics to the organization of elections and decision procedures, owe something to the inspiration of Condorcet. When Bacon first 'rang the bell', as he put it, to 'call the wits together' to improve the lot of man on earth he envisaged practical scientists finding ways to grow more food, make better medicines, and so forth, under the orders of the king. For Condorcet the rule of science meant the rule of enlightened minds coupled with a complicated set of constitutional procedures to ensure that such government by experts was combined with the sovereignty of the people. He first worked out his formula for the fusion of minority government with majority rule in advising his American friends how to organize their republic; later he offered his system to the French.

In his metaphysics, Condorcet accepted the argument of David Hume that no knowledge could be certain; but instead of using this as the basis for a general scepticism, he went on to suggest that since all sciences rested on nothing more than probability, the social sciences—economics, psychology, anthropology, even moral and political science—had no worse credentials than astronomy or physics. While he admitted that the laws discovered by the social sciences might have a weaker probability than those of the natural sciences, Condorcet claimed that 'the probability of all statements of experience can be expressed and evaluated mathematically within probability theory'.[5] The meteorologist cannot be certain that it will rain tomorrow, but on the basis of observations he can calculate the probability of rain. 'Similarly, the economist, who cannot be certain that the standard of living will continue to rise, can in theory arrive at a mathematical estimate of the probability of its doing so.'[6]

Many of Condorcet's publications are highly technical, addressed to readers with a specialized knowledge of mathematics, but an essay he wrote for a popular audience in 1783 entitled *A General Picture of Science, which has for its Object the Application of Arithmetic to the Moral and Political Sciences* sets out his ideas in a readily intelligible form. He depicts man as acting always as a gambler. Since no one has certain knowledge of the future, everyone has to balance the likelihood of one option against another, to weigh the probable outcome of one course of action against the probable outcome of an alternative. Condorcet's 'social arithmetic' was designed to enable men to make those calculations more systematically instead of relying on habit, custom, and tradition in their decisions. Social arithmetic, he claimed, 'would free man from instinct and passion and restore the empire of reason in human affairs'.[7]

Condorcet had a conception of liberty which has certain affinities with that of Rousseau. Rousseau's argument that a people would be free, and could only be free, if it ruled itself, Condorcet agreed. He did not subscribe to the Hobbesian idea that liberty was the 'silence of the law', but rather to Rousseau's idea that the law could make men free provided that the law was self-imposed. In the *Quatre lettres* he wrote as a citizen of New Haven, Condorcet asserted: 'The law does not demand any sacrifice of reason or of liberty—even from those who do not approve it. The law only becomes a threat to liberty when it extends beyond those objects which, by their nature, must be subject to a general rule.'[8]

The main difference between Condorcet and Rousseau is that Condorcet believed that the sovereignty of the people would be expressed not in the rule of the general will but in that of the 'public reason', a concept which clearly requires some explanation. Originally Condorcet took it from Turgot, who had spoken of the 'public reason' in such works as his *Mémoire sur les municipalités*. It was part of the armoury of Turgot's lifelong attack on the theory of representative government which was being used to justify the pretensions of the *parlements*—the theory that those *parlements* derived their authority from the 'will of the nation'. Against this doctrine of will Turgot, and Condorcet after him, proclaimed the doctrine of reason. Both of them pleaded for political institutions which would represent reason rather than will on the grounds that reason rather than will was the faculty in man that was open to the light of truth.

Condorcet's heroes were those men who, as he put it, 'made it their life-work to destroy errors rather than to drive back the frontiers of human knowledge'.[9] All his endeavours to devise new political institutions were prompted by the belief that they could be made to reach *true* decisions, as distinct from those which simply reflected popular opinion. Truth, for Condorcet, was inseparable from goodness on the grounds that 'nature has linked together in an unbreakable chain, truth, happiness, and virtue'.[10] This belief, so alien to modern positivism, Condorcet shared with Holbach and most of his fellow *encyclopédistes*. It is a measure of their confidence that the triumph of knowledge over ignorance would ensure the triumph of virtue over vice.

Applied to politics, this doctrine would seem to require the monopoly of power by the most knowledgeable of men. In such terms Turgot always reasoned and it was the basis of his monarchism. A unified administration could more readily be made a rational administration than one where sovereignty was divided. Turgot was also an optimist. As a young clergyman of 23 he gave a celebrated address at the Sorbonne depicting the history of the human race as a continuous development from ignorance and misery towards knowledge and emancipation. Again Turgot provided Condorcet with a theme he was to take up and elaborate in his last and most famous book, the *Sketch for an Historical Picture of the Human Mind*. But it was a doctrine too much at odds with Christian orthodoxy for Turgot to remain a priest. He became instead an economist, a contributor to the *Encyclopédie*, and, for a time, a remarkably efficient administrator. In the

1760s he enjoyed a great success as intendant of the province of Limousin, but his policies—based on a physiocratic fusion of economic liberalism and political *dirigisme*—did not work well in other provinces; and they were bitterly opposed by those *philosophes* who argued that free trade injured the poor.

When Louis XVI came to the throne Turgot was appointed to the government at Versailles, first as Minister of the Navy, then as Minister of Finance. In turn, Turgot made Condorcet governor of the Mint, making him in effect his assistant in devising policies of economic reform for a kingdom on the verge of bankruptcy. The reforms they proposed included the abolition of restrictions on trade, of fiscal anomalies, and of feudal privileges. They could address the King as philosophers, for philosophy had become fashionable in France in the 1770s; but unfortunately philosophy did not speak with a single voice. The disciples of Voltaire urged the King to give more power to Turgot; the disciples of Montesquieu urged him to recall the *parlements* and restore the 'ancient liberties' of France.

It has often been argued that Turgot's reforms could have rebuilt the French economy and saved the monarchy; but the monarch himself did not think so. Yielding to aristocratic pressure he recalled the *parlements* and dismissed Turgot, who took leave of Louis XVI with words as prophetic as they were impertinent: 'Do not forget, Sire, that it was weakness which put the head of Charles I of England on the block.'[11]

Neither Turgot nor Condorcet had proposed that the King should become an 'enlightened despot'. They believed that he derived his authority from the people and was entitled, as their representative, to exercise it. They also believed that the *parlements* represented only a sectional interest, and one which was at variance with the public interest, which lay in decisions being reached that were comfortable to reason. But how could this be achieved? Condorcet addressed the problem in a whole series of writings.

In the absence of a philosopher-king who might in some sense represent the public reason, he suggested that representative assemblies would be needed, provided that they were constituted and conducted in such a way as to ensure the correctness and reliability of their decisions. Condorcet invoked mathematical techniques as a means to this end. He was not so foolish as to suggest that mere numbers could guarantee that the correct choice was made; on the contrary, he pointed out that if mistaken opinions were held by many people, then the more people who were involved in a collective choice, the more probable it was that the majority decision would be a wrong one. If finding the truth was to be largely a matter of calculation, it would seem that those persons most skilled at reckoning should be recruited to act in the interests of all. Condorcet saw a need for élites, but like Rousseau, he was conscious of the danger of any élite turning itself into a dominant vested interest, and it was for this reason that he proposed that all élite groups should be answerable to popular assemblies.

On the other hand, Condorcet did not advocate democracy. 'It is clear', he wrote,

that it can be dangerous to give a democratic constitution to an unenlightened people. A pure democracy, indeed, would only be appropriate to a people much more enlightened, much more free from prejudices than any known to history . . . For every other nation such assemblies become harmful unless they are limited to making decisions relating to the maintenance of security, liberty and property—objects upon which a direct personal interest can adequately enlighten all minds.[12]

Elsewhere Condorcet wrote that 'a republic with tyrannical laws can fall far short of a monarchy'.[13] For this reason he considered it not only important to educate electors but equally important to set up procedures whereby elections could be made to yield 'truths'.

There is a certain parallel between Condorcet's attitude to democracy and that of Rousseau. Rousseau also considers democracy impracticable, and he proposes in *The Social Contract* that popular assemblies shall vote only on a legislative code drawn up by a superior lawgiver and on laws drafted by magistrates of superior virtue. One big difference is that whereas Rousseau tries to banish the idea of representation entirely, Condorcet seeks to perfect it. Condorcet tries to make the rules and procedures of electoral institutions so sophisticated that they will compensate for defects in substance. 'The truth of the decisions of an assembly', he wrote, 'depends on the forms according to which they are reached as much, perhaps, as on the enlightenment of those who make up the assembly.'[14]

Ideas on representative government which Condorcet had first adumbrated in his writings on the American republic he began to apply to the situation in France in the months leading up to the Revolution, when there was an increasing clamour for the recall of the Estates-General. Condorcet's objections to the Estates-General were much the same as his objections to the *parlements*; namely that that body was representative only of interests—the Church, the nobility, and the Third Estate—each of which was sectional, and none of which was national. He argued that the recall of such a body would simply revive the civil strife of the feudal past.

Instead, Condorcet proposed the institution of provincial assemblies of citizens, leading to the formation of a national assembly in which the 'public reason' might at last find expression. Such assemblies—unlike Rousseau's *corps legislatif* in which every citizen would participate in person—would be composed of a moderate number of elected deputies; he stipulated that there should not be so many as to lend themselves to demagogy or so few as to be subject to the private passions and interests of individuals. The duties of these assemblies would, moreover, be strictly limited: to little beyond electing national deputies who would in turn elect national administrators.

Such a brief agenda could be completed by the provincial assemblies in a single day, which Condorcet considered highly advantageous since there would then be no time for the formation of parties or factions. He even went so far as to suggest that the assemblies should not actually hold meetings, but communicate their votes by postal ballot. The aim, after all, was to enthrone truth, and Condorcet did not think that the truth about candidates for the *députation nationale* was likely to emerge in public debate.

To those who understand politics as an exercise in open dialogue and discussion, Condorcet's proposals must necessarily seem peculiar. For while he calls for frequent voting, and the citizen's preferences to be measured and weighed by all sorts of mathematical devices, he does not want too much *talk*—on the grounds that talk, among the unenlightened, can only excite passions and do harm. Politics for Condorcet is reduced to an exercise in collective choice, and the essential thing, for him, is that this choice shall be rational.

In his later writings, when he is frankly republican, and assigns not only the suffrage to citizens, but the whole sovereignty of the nation to the people, it is more than ever important for Condorcet to bring about the fusion of knowledge, which is possessed only by a fully enlightened minority, and consent, which can only be given by the people as a whole. The outcome is something akin to what came to be known to later generations as bureaucracy: administration by a universal class dedicated to the national interest, a professional élite, having for its mission the formulation of a scientific policy in the areas of defence, the economy, the building of roads and bridges, sanitation, health, and welfare; for Condorcet had a wide-ranging, almost twentieth-century conception of the extent of the business of the state.

Even so, he was not a 'centralizer'. On the basis of the success of Turgot as administrator of the province of Limousin, he concluded that it would be desirable to divide the state into quasi-autonomous regions, in order to allow for the government of each to be adapted to regional needs. The 'public mind' was not simply a national mind; it was also a provincial and local mind which should be given means of expression through its own assemblies and bureaucracies. To the extent that there could be more intimate contact between the citizen and his local or provincial government, those institutions might give more concrete expression to the citizen's freedom.

Although Condorcet criticized the democracies of the ancient world on the grounds that 'the language of liberty and utility was more important to them than that of truth and justice',[15] he believed that all men had a natural right to liberty as well as to life and property. Moreover he believed, with Locke, that the authenticity of such rights was visible to the eye of reason. Everybody should be able to understand what natural rights are and everybody ought to respect them. For this reason, Condorcet was highly critical of Helvétius and other utilitarian moralists who argued that the worth of any policy could be measured by the amount of pleasure it generated or the amount of pain it diminished. If the greatest happiness of the greatest number was all that mattered, the rights of a single individual could readily be sacrificed to enlarge the pleasure of many. Condorcet rejected Helvétius' claim that men's conduct was governed by impulsions of pleasure and pain, asserting instead that a sense of justice developed in everyone as a result of the interaction of sensation and reflection. Again he came close to Rousseau in suggesting that men's moral feelings arose from a sense of participation in the sufferings and joys of others, from sympathy and compassion. It was this natural sense of justice, he argued, which enabled the eye of reason to discern the validity of human rights and the duties which those rights imposed.

As the events of the French Revolution unfolded, Condorcet turned increasingly from philosophy to pamphleteering. Although he deplored the decision of the King to convoke the Estates-General, he tried—unsuccessfully—to secure a seat in that body: he was more successful afterwards in getting elected to the Paris commune and the Legislative Assembly. There were, of course, no political parties at the time, but there were clubs, and Condorcet became a leading member of the Society of 1789, with the Marquis de Lafayette, the Duc de la Rochefoucauld, the Duc de Liancourt, and Dupont de Nemours. Looking at these names, one can well understand why Louis XVI first believed that the French Revolution was a conspiracy of noblemen. The Society of 1789 considered itself, however, to be representative rather of scientific opinion in France. Condorcet invoked his authority as Perpetual Secretary of the Academy of Science when he said: 'We regarded the social art as a true science, founded like all the others on facts, experiment, reasoning and calculation; susceptible, like all the others, of indefinite advance and development, and becoming progressively more useful as its true principles are spread.'[16]

Politically, however, the most important member of the Society of 1789 was no scientist but the soldier Lafayette, and Condorcet was more than willing for a time to act with him. Lafayette had returned from his service in the American War of Independence with a zeal for American-style affirmations of the rights of man, and Condorcet, as a theorist of natural rights, collaborated with him in drafting that *Déclaration des droits de l'homme et du citoyen* which proved to be such a spectacular feature of the rhetoric of the French Revolution. The Society of 1789, however, began to lose favour as the public became more hostile to all forms of élitism. Lafayette distanced himself from the other members, and in May 1791 Condorcet himself went over in the dubious company of Talleyrand to the Jacobin Club, on the grounds that it 'was the party of the people'. This move enabled Condorcet—no longer a *marquis* but a *citoyen*—to have a certain influence on the development of the Revolution. Although he was not especially effective as an orator, he was a fluent writer, and contributed articles almost daily to the Revolutionary newspapers.

Undoubtedly he moved to the left. In the summer of 1791, after the flight of Louis XVI to Varennes and the massacre of fifty people demonstrating against the King on the Champ de Mars, for which Lafayette was held responsible, Condorcet turned violently against his old ally, voted for the deposition of the King, and set to work on the formulation of a constitution for the newly proclaimed French Republic. He also joined Thomas Paine in planning the publication of a republican journal. In July 1791 there appeared his *Lettre d'un jeune mécanicien* which reached almost Voltairean standards of mockery on the subject of a constitutional monarch. In its pages Condorcet describes the invention of a robot monarch who will sign decrees, attend Mass, take the salute at military parades, and even appoint ministers. The inventor admits he cannot make his clockwork king hereditary, but claims that with careful maintenance, the royal automation can be made to last almost for ever.

It is all very amusing; but the age of satire was over, and the French Revolution had entered a phase of grim earnestness and intense ideological fervour. Condorcet could no longer depend on the prestige of science. His support for universal suffrage might sound radical enough, but there were those who suspected that his pleas for the rule of reason were nothing more than a veiled argument for the rule by a caste of intellectuals. One deputy indeed accused Condorcet of seeking 'to create a state within a state, an aristocratic corporation in the heart of a republic, an immoral and impolitic monstrosity that would hand over science—and hence public opinion and liberty—to a privileged class, an ostensibly philosophical priesthood'.[17]

It was a well-aimed attack, and a portent of more to come. Condorcet had more success with his arguments for a system of universal education.[18] For despite his faith in the powers of constitutional arrangements to counteract the force of ignorance, he still believed in enlightening the electorate to the greatest possible extent. He set forth these proposals in five essays entitled

*Mémoirs sur l'instruction publique.* By *instruction* he meant
what others preferred to call *éducation*, that is to say not merely
the introjection of knowledge into the pupils, but the formation of character—the upbringing of good patriots. Even so, he
rejected the proposal of Holbach—and Talleyrand—that some
kind of 'social catechism' should be taught in schools to direct
children in the path of virtue. He believed it was enough to teach
them the use of reason.

Like most men of the Revolution, Condorcet wanted all
careers to be open to talent without regard to social class. At the
same time he argued that public education should take account of
the inequalities of natural talent in order to develop the intelligence of the more gifted. Schools should adapt their teaching to
the abilities of each child. If the result was to create an intellectual
hierarchy, Condorcet saw no reason to lament: 'It would indeed
be a fatal love of equality', he wrote, 'that feared to extend the
class of enlightened men and to increase their enlightenment.'[19]

Nevertheless Condorcet considered himself an egalitarian, and
with reason. He was ahead of most egalitarians of his time in
advocating equal rights to vote for men and women. He had
disagreed with Lafayette over the formulation of the *Déclaration
des droits de l'homme et du citoyen* because he wanted to spell
out the rights of women at the same time as those of men; but had
been overruled by Lafayette's sense of the politically possible. In
the *Quatre lettres* he wrote as a citizen of New Haven before the
Revolution, Condorcet had argued that women ought to be
admitted equally with men to the *droit de cité*.[20] He made no
apology for dwelling at length on the equal rights of women since
it was a matter of 'the rights of half the human race'.[21]

Where Condorcet fell short of the egalitarianism of many of
his colleagues in the Legislative Assembly was in his resistance to
the principle of one man, one vote. The right to vote, he argued,
should be tied to ownership of property. A property owner was
entitled to a vote of his own; while those with less than a certain
minimum should have only a share in a vote. The reasoning
behind this was that the property-owners had a greater stake in
the nation, and more to lose from irrational legislation. At the
same time, Condorcet suggested that there was a national interest
which was of concern to non-owners as well as owners, so that
non-owners ought not to be entirely excluded from the suffrage.

In his *Lettres* to his American friends, Condorcet urged them not to allow bad laws to promote too great differences of wealth between individuals: 'republican equality', he reminded them, 'cannot exist in a country where the laws make possible the long duration of vast fortunes'. He was aware of the danger of exaggerating the natural right to property to a point where the rich could feel entitled to have anything they could buy. He did not wish to see plutocracy replace aristocracy, but rather to see a new aristocracy of the mind arise to replace the old aristocracy of blood.

His election in October 1792 to the national Convention and his nomination to the Committee on the Constitution gave Condorcet the opportunity to pass from philosophizing to drafting positive legislation. The so-called 'Girondin Constitution' which emerged from that committee was largely his work. This does not mean that Condorcet had joined the Girondins, although his opinions were generally far closer to theirs than to those of the Jacobins; it was rather the case that the Girondins made his *projet de constitution* theirs, as an alternative to the more radically democratic proposals of the Jacobins. For although Condorcet's draft constitution was extremely complicated, the Girondins could see that in aiming at 'the sovereignty of reason' it introduced universal suffrage without conferring any substantial power on the electorate,[22] that it would uphold order and property and the rule of the educated classes, and furthermore that it would provide a safety-valve for protest without giving the discontented elements any facilities for undermining the tranquillity of the state.

The Jacobins, who judged that the effect of Condorcet's draft constitution would be to emasculate the Paris mob which gave them so much support, replied to the challenge by hurriedly drawing up an alternative constitution. Condorcet in turn produced a pamphlet, *Aux citoyens français sur la nouvelle constitution*, in which he invited his readers to compare this newly fabricated Jacobin document with the earlier draft, which had been the result of much reflection and deliberation. Whereas the former could be relied on to ensure the accurate expression of the public reason, the latter, he argued, would maximize the probability of erroneous decisions and provoke an endless conflict of wills.

The pamphlet appeared anonymously, but Condorcet realized that his authorship would be recognized, and since it had become mortally dangerous for any Frenchman to publish opinions displeasing to the regime in power, he decided to go into hiding.[23] He spent the next nine months shut up in the house of Madame Vernet, near the Palais de Luxembourg, writing his *Sketch for an Historical Picture of the Progress of the Human Mind*. The book gives no hint of the circumstances under which it was written, or any indication that the turn of events in the French Revolution had diminished its author's optimism.

Indeed Condorcet seems have been concerned only to develop a more scientific case for optimism than that of Turgot. In his celebrated Sorbonne lecture, Turgot had represented progress as a continuous development towards the perfection of man that was both necessary and inevitable. While he admitted the existence of error, he asserted that error was a wholly positive element in the enlargement of human understanding. Since science operated through a process of trial and error, error was necessary to the discovery of knowledge.

Christianity also figured in Turgot's view of history as a progressive force which had replaced the earlier pagan cults and given Europe a sound moral doctrine which paganism had lacked. Providence also had a role, if not an obtrusive one, in the unfolding of progress; a role rather like that of the invisible hand in the economics of Adam Smith. In a sense, Turgot provided a secular equivalent of the Christian optimism of Alexander Pope. As has been said, 'there was a kind of cosmic Toryism about Turgot's philosophy of history. Nothing in history was wasted; nothing that did not turn out in the end to have promoted human happiness.'[24]

Condorcet's theory of progress was more 'dialectical'. He believed no less than did Turgot in the perfectibility of man, and by the word *perfectibilité* he did not mean, as Rousseau meant, merely man's capacity for self-improvement; he believed that man really was capable of perfection, and that man's history was the history of his ascent to perfection. Only Condorcet did not see that ascent, as Turgot had seen it, as one of continuous and steady betterment, discreetly helped forward by Providence. For Condorcet had no belief in Providence. He was an atheist. He visualized the history of man on earth as a constant struggle between the forces of light and the forces of darkness which the former were destined in the end to win. Every form of religion, including Christianity, Condorcet placed among the forces of darkness. The forces of reason triumphed over those forces of superstition and falsehood only by a series of revolutions. He distinguished as many as nine epochs in man's past, each of them ended by a revolutionary change. The tenth was the epoch to come, and Condorcet felt able to predict that 'the present state of knowledge assures us that the future will be happy but it is upon condition that we know how to assist it, with all our strength.'[25]

Each of Condorcet's ten epochs is distinguished in terms of the particular problems which confronted it, and its story is told in terms of the solution it found to those problems. In a certain sense, Condorcet's theory can be read as a doctrine of the rise and fall of cultures, each upward movement being followed by periods of decline which have to be reversed before the next step forward can be taken. He dwells at length on one long period of 'decadence'—the thousand years of European experience which followed the eclipse of Roman glory[26]—and he clearly takes great pleasure in ascribing responsibility to the Christian religion for all the defects of the Middle Ages, or what he calls the 'sixth stage' of human history. The earlier stages were these: first, the association of primitive men in tribes; second, the transition from pastoral life to agricultural communities; third, the introduction of social groups based on military domination; fourth, the emergence of political societies based on consent; and fifth, the age of Classical Antiquity, which marked the high point of science and philosophy before the Roman Empire was undermined by those forces of darkness which dominated the thousand years of priestcraft and ignorance. The seventh to ninth stages were those where light emerged once again to do battle with darkness, the heroes of that struggle being Galileo and the humanists at the time of the Italian Renaissance, Descartes and Bacon and Newton and Locke in the seventeenth-century Age of Reason, and then in Condorcet's own time, the philosophers of the Enlightenment and the makers of the American Revolution.

Why had all these people to fight to secure the movement of history to a superior stage? Condorcet suggests three reasons. First, that there was a form of inertia at work in every period which made men cling to familiar ideas and resist innovation;

secondly, that the vested interests of the professions which lived off existing superstitions opposed change; thirdly, that there was sheer prejudice among the uneducated classes in favour of false beliefs. And yet, despite his sense of the continued presence of these forces, Condorcet ends his *Sketch for an Historical Picture of the Progress of the Human Mind* with a confident prediction of the triumph of reason. He depicts the next, or tenth stage, of human history as the period of man's self-perfection. Errors will still occur, but they will be less destructive, and there will be no danger of a relapse into the old ignorance. Inequalities between individuals and between nations will diminish; international peace will be established; enlightened commerce and a universal language will set the seal on the fraternity between people. 'Co-operative scholarship will promote, and education will disseminate, enlightenment, while the advance of the mechanical arts will bring new comfort and happiness to the mass of mankind.'[27]

The trouble with Condorcet's *Sketch* is that the account he gives of the first nine periods of human history offers no basis whatever for his extraordinarily optimistic predictions for the tenth stage. As Auguste Comte once pointed out: 'In examining successively these different ages, Condorcet presents them almost always as having been, in the last analysis, eras of retrogression. He has on his hands, consequently, a perpetual miracle, and the advance of civilisation becomes an effect without a cause.'[28]

Looking out into the world from his place of hiding in the ominously named 'street of the gravediggers' (Rue des Fossoyeurs) at the height of the Terror in 1794, Condorcet can have seen little to confirm his view that the powers of light were about to prevail over the powers of darkness. When he slipped out of Paris to seek refuge with his old friends, the Suards, only to be turned from their door, his faith in progress must again have been sorely tested. After this rebuff, he looked to no other friend for help, but put up at a country inn incognito; it is said that his table manners betrayed his identity as an aristocrat; he was arrested, and died in prison before he could be taken to the guillotine—it is possible that he committed suicide.

His *Sketch for an Historical Picture of the Progress of the Human Mind*, translated into many languages, has remained Condorcet's best-known book. His predictions have not turned out to be entirely fanciful. In the two centuries that have passed since he wrote it, inequalities between social classes have diminished in many places, colonies have been given their independence, literacy has become almost universal in the Western world, science and industry have made continuous advances, welfare states have been instituted, and medicine has overcome many diseases; on the other hand, the world seems no nearer to being a place where 'the sun will shine only on free men',[29] with 'poverty eradicated';[30] all experience refutes Condorcet's prediction that the fine arts and philosophy will 'increase in perfection';[31] and there is no sign yet of a 'universal language' that will unite nations in a bond of peace.[32]

It would be a vulgar error to judge Condorcet on the accuracy of his predictions, or to regard him simply as the author of this one book. His importance derives from his endeavour to formulate solutions to one of the central problems posed by the political theory of the Enlightenment: that of reconciling the enthronement of reason with the rule of freedom, the enthronement of reason demanding government by an intellectual class of experts, and the rule of freedom demanding the sovereignty of the people.

His introduction of the concept of 'public reason' in place of the more familiar concept of the 'general will' could perhaps be dismissed as a rhetorical device designed to eliminate rather than resolve this problem, but for the fact that he devoted so much time and thought to the constitutional and electoral devices which he proposed to reconcile popular participation with élitist management. Later generations, faced with increasingly universal demands for democracy while dreading, as he did, the dominion of an ignorant majority, have lived with much the same problem; and political science since Condorcet's time has built extensively on foundations laid by him.

In some respects, Condorcet strikes the modern reader as curiously naïve: in his insistence on the infinite perfectibility of man and of science; in his belief that to enlarge men's knowledge was necessarily to improve their morals; and in his belief that there could be a social or moral science capable of settling disputes with the finality of mathematics.

On the other hand, he was one of the most practically minded of the French *encyclopédistes*. Not only was he the one—the only one—to engage in practical politics; but after the fall of Robespierre, the regime of the *Directoire* took up a number of his ideas, and his followers became influential in the state. The most obvious impact was in the field of education. In line with Condorcet's proposals, the *écoles centrales* and the *École normale supérieure* were set up together with the Polytechnique and the Institut de France. Among Condorcet's friends, Daubenton took up the chair of natural science at the *École normale supérieure* and Desmarest that of natural history at the École normale de la Seine, while Deleyre was put in charge of the schools. The pattern of French public education was established for generations.

Condorcet's family kept his ideas before the public. His widow entertained the younger generation of intellectuals at a salon which recovered, and kept, its brilliance; she edited his *Collected Works* for publication in twenty-one volumes under the Napoleonic Empire in 1804; then his son-in-law produced a second and more extensive collection in the reign of Louis-Philippe. Condorcet was very widely read in the nineteenth century, even when the philosophy of the Enlightenment in general was most unfashionable; the '*last of the philosophes*', as Michelet called him, was also the first of the new politically-motivated social scientists; the standard bearer of a line that stretches from St. Simon and Bentham to Marx and Mrs. Webb; he was also the prophet of twentieth-century statistical method and empirical political research and the first theorist of what has come to be known as plebiscitary, as opposed to participatory or parliamentary, democracy.

# Notes

## Chapter 1: Montesquieu

ABBREVIATIONS

OC            Montesquieu *Œuvres complètes*, ed. Daniel Oster, Paris, 1964

Shackleton, 1961      Robert Shackleton, *Montesquieu: a Critical Biography*, Oxford, 1961

Shackleton, 1977      Robert Shackleton, 'Allies and Enemies: Voltaire and Montesquieu' in J. Press (ed.), *Essays by Divers Hands*, London, 1977

Starobinski      Jean Starobinski, *Montesquieu*, Paris, 1953

1. See Jean Starobinski, *Montaigne en mouvement*, Paris, 1982.
2. 'Montesquieu belonged to the provincial nobility and could trace his ancestry through his mother to St. Louis, King of France, through his father to the Plantagenets . . .' (Shackleton, 1977, p. 128).
3. He was called *président à mortier* because he wore a mortar board; he was the effective chairman of the bench, the *président* being a royal nominee who seldom participated.
4. *OC* p. 111.
5. Montesquieu was no more than a gifted amateur in science: his Classical education had provided an inadequate basis for him to reach professional standards. As Starobinski writes, 'Montesquieu n'est pas mathématicien. Il est appliqué aux sciences exactes sans avoir jamais appris à mesurer les faits observés', (Starobinski, pp. 18-19). In this respect Montesquieu was in no worse a condition than most of the *philosophes* of the Enlightenment: they were enthusiasts for science without any real education in science. Holbach and d'Alembert were exceptional in being trained scientists as well as philosophers.
6. Louis Althusser, *Montesquieu, la politique et l'histoire*, Paris, 1959.
7. Franklin L. Ford, *Robe and Sword*, London, 1965.
8. Montesquieu was essentially a prose writer; he had no talent for poetry, and in *Les Lettres persanes* he mocks poets 'as authors whose trade is to put barriers in the way of common sense, as the grotesques of the human race' (Shackleton, 1977, p. 131). This was very much Locke's opinion: but Voltaire was shocked, and said

Montesquieu wanted 'to overthrow a throne he could not sit on' (ibid.).

9. 'Helvétius reports that Montesquieu once said that he was "favourably received in French society as a man of wit, until the *Lettres persanes* showed that perhaps he was in fact such, thereafter he suffered a thousand ills" ' (Shackleton, 1961, p. 85).

10. Montesquieu's erotic tale *Le Temple de Gnide* dates from this period of his life. It is said to have been inspired by Mlle de Clermont, a princess of the blood, to whom he paid court. It did not repeat the commercial success of *Les Lettres persanes*, but sold only 600 copies of the 2,000 printed of the first edition. Starobinski speaks of it as 'sa plus mauvaise œuvre' (p. 18). It is a relic of the time when Montesquieu devoted himself to pleasure. Unlike Voltaire, he did not go in for long-lasting affairs; he once wrote 'Il faut rompre brusquement avec les femmes: rien n'est si insupportable qu'une vieille affaire éreintée' (Starobinski, p. 40).

11. The Abbé de Saint-Pierre was also the author of a *Projet de paix perpetuelle*, of which Rousseau was both editor and critic.

12. The importance of the Abbé de Saint-Pierre in relation to Montesquieu's political thought is that he was a champion of divided sovereignty. In 1718 he published his *Discours sur la polysynodie*, a plea for the plurality of councils, in which he argued that 'un concert unanimine, pour régler les affaires, est préférable à la voie de l'autorité'. He set out the advantages of plurality—that it would make facts better known, enable difficulties to be more easily resolved, and the public interest better protected against private interests; it would also give the nobility a greater share in government. Saint-Pierre's proposals were criticized at the time as impracticable (see George Pélissier, *Les Écrivains politiques en France*, Paris, 1884).

13. *OC* p. 115.

14. *OC* p. 85.

15. *OC* p. 91.

16. *OC* p. 119.

17. *OC* p. 69.

18. *OC* p. 70.

19. Ibid.

20. For a discussion of Montesquieu's concept of virtue see L. M. Levin, *The Political Doctrine of Montesquieu's Esprit des Lois*, New York, 1937, pp. 69–73.

21. See H. J. Merry, *Montesquieu's System of Natural Government*, West Lafayette, 1970, p. 27.

22. *OC* p. 127.

23. Montesquieu made copious notes at every city he visited, many of

them to do with the fine arts (indifferent to poetry, the author of *L'Essai sur le goût* responded eagerly to painting and sculpture) and those are most prominent in his records of such places as Rome and Florence where there was no political life to observe. He endeavoured everywhere to obtain the widest view of things: 'quand j'arrive dans une ville, je vais toujours sur le plus haut clocher ou la plus haute tour, pour voir le tout ensemble' (Starobinski, p. 37). Shackleton writes: 'The most striking fact about the President's interests in Rome is the absence of any close attention to the remains of the ancient world. He displays no serious archaeological enthusiasm at all' (Shackleton, 1961, p. 95).

24. *OC* p. 216.
25. Ibid.
26. *OC* p. 1036.
27. *OC* p. 244.
28. Ibid.
29. Ibid.
30. *OC* p. 327.
31. Ibid.
32. Ibid.
33. *OC* p. 328.
34. *OC* p. 327.
35. *OC* p. 330.
36. *OC* p. 1006.
37. *OC* p. 332.
38. For an account of Montesquieu's relation with leading English politicians during his stay in England, 1729–31, see Shackleton, 1961, pp. 117–45.
39. *OC* p. 333.
40. Ibid.
41. *OC* p. 332.
42. *OC* p. 331.
43. *OC* p. 334.
44. *OC* p. 1004.
45. *OC* p. 1005.
46. Ibid.
47. Ibid.
48. *OC* p. 334.
49. Montesquieu kept a journal during his stay in England, but as that was destroyed by his grandson, we have less detailed knowledge of his impressions of England and the English than we could wish.
50. *OC* p. 586.
51. Daniel Oster (*OC*, p. 331). See also Joseph Dedieu, *Montesquieu et la tradition politique anglaise*, Paris, 1909.

52. Starobinski, p. 15.
53. The dowry was no more than 10,000 livres. See Shackleton, 1961, p. 199.
54. After he had finished writing *L'Esprit des lois*, Montesquieu said: 'Je puis dire que j'y ai travaillé toute ma vie: au sortir du collège on me mit dans les mains des livres de droit; j'en cherchai l'esprit, je travaillai, je ne faisais rien qui vaille. Il y a vingt ans je découvris mes principes; ils sont très simples; un autre qui aurait autant travaillé que moi aurait fait mieux que moi. Mais j'avoue que cet ouvrage a pensé me tuer' (quoted in Starobinski, p. 24).
55. Montesquieu was a naturally happy man. As he himself wrote, 'Ma machine est si heureusement construite'; and in the words of Starobinski, 'ce bonheur est au centre de son caractère' (Starobinski, p. 26).
56. 'It must be judged now that in the nervous oppressive atmosphere of the mid century Montesquieu was lucky to avoid condemnation by the government or the legal authorities, notwithstanding the prestige of his name in parliamentary circles. But clerical censure was inevitable. He was attacked both by the Jesuits and the Jansenists; the Sorbonne and the General Assembly of the French Clergy prepared to pronounce their ban; the Holy See, against the Pope's own wishes, added his work to the Index of Prohibited Books. Montesquieu had acquired a new role: he was the victim of oppression' (Shackleton, 1977, p. 140).
57. *OC* p. 538.
58. Ibid.
59. Ibid.
60. On Montesquieu's debt to Mandeville see Melvin Richter, *The Political Theory of Montesquieu*, Cambridge, 1977, pp. 43–5; and on Adam Smith's debt to Montesquieu see F. T. H. Fletcher, *Montesquieu and English Politics*, London, 1939, pp. 46–67.
61. 'La modération, telle que Montesquieu la pratique, n'est pas une vertu de rétrécissement. C'est tout au contraire l'attitude qui rend possible la plus vaste ouverture sur le monde et le plus large accueil' (Starobinski, p. 26).
62. *OC* pp. 552–3.
63. Montesquieu is not, however, consistent in his use of the expression *les gouvernements modérés*. Sometimes it seems to mean any government except a despotism; sometimes nothing other than a constitutional monarchy. See Shackleton, 1961, pp. 272–7.
64. *OC* p. 563.
65. Ibid.
66. See Shackleton, 1961, pp. 237–8.

67. For an appraisal of Montesquieu's 'personal faith' see Shackleton, 1961, pp. 349–355.

68. *OC* p. 613.

69. *OC* p. 630.

70. Shackleton writes: 'His handling of historical evidence is naive. In each chapter he selects one authority and clings faithfully to it, through thick and thin. As an archaeologist he is unsure: he uses one inscription only, from the Rubicon, but it was a forgery of modern times and he ought to have known it. But he shows wisdom and originality in his study of historical causation, and his political judgement is sound and liberal' (Shackleton, 1977, p. 137).

71. It is only fair to add that Gibbon's whole historical enterprise owed much to the suggestions of Montesquieu. As Professor Hugh Trevor-Roper (Lord Dacre) writes: 'In 1748 Montesquieu published his great work *De l'esprit des lois*. In 1750 Turgot, in his *Discours* to the Sorbonne, traced the concept of progress in history. Thereafter the great work of "philosophical history" appeared, precipitated if not originally inspired by these two ideas: Hume's *History of England*, Voltaire's *Essai sur les mœurs*, Robertson's *Charles V* and the *History of America* and greatest of all, Gibbon's *Decline and Fall of the Roman Empire* . . . Thus, in the third quarter of the 18th century, the revolution in historical studies was completed. Montesquieu had declared the principles on which historians should work, Turgot had suggested the thread they should pursue. History was no longer to be 'a dull chronicle of speeches and battles'; it was to be . . . a history of society' (*Studies on Voltaire and the Eighteenth Century*, Vol. 27 (1963), pp. 1671 and 1675.

72. Voltaire, however, was not impressed by the *Considérations*: 'This book is full of hints, is less a book than an ingenious *table des matières* writ in an odd style' (Shackleton, 1961, p. 157).

73. *OC* p. 122.

74. Starobinski writes: 'La causalité ne se déroule pas sous ses yeux comme un enchaînement linéaire de causes et d'effets, l'histoire ne s'avance pas sur une seule voie; Montesquieu rejette l'explication naïve qui ramène la succession des faits historiques au problème mécanique de la simple communication du mouvement. L'histoire, selon lui, n'est pas "unicausale" ' (Starobinski, p. 81).

75. *OC* p. 489.

76. *OC* p. 615.

77. R. Aron, *Main Currents in Sociological Thought*, New York, 1965, Vol. I, p. 43.

78. 'This conception of an *esprit général* is basic to Montesquieu's

thought. All laws and institutions are relative to it. The *esprit général* is the resultant of a multitude of conditioning factors, but since some of these—such as religious beliefs and the economic organisation of a society—are the products of human volition, Montesquieu had arrived at Vico's concept of human nature as at least partially a social product . . . Moreover, the *esprit général* was both the effect of environmental conditioning in the widest sense and also the cause of reactions to that environment. As an active force it implied that different societies would respond differently to similar material pressures. There is far more than a crude theory of climate behind Montesquieu's penetrating observation that "The customs of an enslaved people are part of its servitude, those of a free people are part of its liberty" ' (Norman Hampson, *The Enlightenment*, New York and Harmondsworth, 1968, p. 238).

79. *OC* p. 111.
80. Montesquieu rejected the theory of a *pacte d'association* but accepted the idea of a *pacte de soumission*.
81. *OC* p. 530.
82. See Richter, pp. 21–30.
83. See S. Cotta, *Montesquieu e la scienza della società*, Turin, 1953, pp. 326–30.
84. *OC* p. 260.
85. *OC* p. 618.
86. Ibid.
87. *OC* p. 622.
88. Ibid.
89. *OC* p. 623.
90. Ibid.
91. *OC* p. 624.
92. *OC* p. 622.
93. *OC* p. 624.
94. Shackleton, 1961, p. 279.
95. *OC* p. 535.
96. *OC* p. 698.
97. *OC* p. 705.
98. *OC* p. 702.
99. *OC* p. 536.
100. 'la grande originalité de Montesquieu, ce sera . . . d'avoir été le théoricien de la liberté politique' (Dedieu, p. 138). For other appraisals of Montesquieu's political theory, see in addition to works already cited in these notes: Élie Carcassonne, *Montesquieu et le problème de la constitution française*, Paris, 1927; Albert Sorel, *Montesquieu*, Paris, 1887; Gustave Lanson, *Montesquieu*,

Paris, 1932; Norman Hampson, *Will and Circumstance: Montesquieu and Rousseau*, London, 1983; J. Ehrard, *La Politique de Montesquieu*, Paris, 1965; and E. Durkheim, *Montesquieu and Rousseau*, Ann Arbor, 1960.

101. 'La liberté est le droit de faire tout ce que les lois permettent; et si un citoyen pouvait faire ce qu'elles défendent, il n'aurait plus de liberté, parce que les autres auraient tout de même ce pouvoir' (Starobinski, p. 91).

102. Locke, *Second Treatise of Government*, § 57.

103. There were so many different sorts of Whigs in eighteenth–century England that it may be worth noting that Montesquieu's friends (or his acquaintances if it is true that he 'made no friends') when he stayed in London were either Tories or dissident Whigs. There was something of Tory paternalism in his argument that the state 'owes to every citizen an assured subsistence, food, decent clothing, and a standard of living which is not inimical to health' (see Starobinski, p. 16). The English statesman who taught him most was Bolingbroke, as Shackleton explains: 'With the great anti-Minister Bolingbroke, the power behind the opposition to Walpole, Montesquieu was already acquainted and it was through his eyes that Montesquieu saw English politics' (Shackleton, 1961, p. 126). See also J. G. A. Pocock, *Politics, Language and Time*, London, 1972, pp. 104–47.

104. *OC* p. 23.

105. *OC* p. 28.

## Chapter 2: Voltaire

ABBREVIATIONS

| | |
|---|---|
| D. | T. Besterman (ed.), *Complete Works of Voltaire*, Vols. 85–135 ('D' numbered citations) |
| *Dic. phil.* | *Dictionnaire philosophique*, ed. J. Benda, two vols., Paris, 1968 |
| Gay, 1959 | Peter Gay, *Voltaire's Politics*, Princeton, 1959 |
| *Let. phil.* | *Lettres philosophiques* |
| Mason | Haydn Mason, *Voltaire: A Biography*, London, 1981 |
| Morley | John Morley, *Voltaire*, London, 1886 |
| *OCV* | *Œuvres complètes de Voltaire*, ed. Louis Moland, Paris, 1877–85 |
| Sée | H. Sée, *Idées politiques en France au XVIIIe siècle*, Paris, 1920 |

SVEC    *Studies on Voltaire and the Eighteenth Century*, Geneva and Oxford, 1955–

Wade, 1947   Ira O. Wade, *Studies on Voltaire*, Princeton, 1947

Wade, 1969   Ira O. Wade, *The Intellectual Development of Voltaire*, Princeton, 1969

Wade, 1977   Ira O. Wade, *The Structure and Form of the French Enlightenment*, 2 vols., Princeton, 1977

1. T. Carlyle, *Critical and Miscellaneous Essays*, Vol. I, London, 1899, p. 411.
2. H. Taine, *The Ancien Régime*, trans. J. Durand, London, 1876, p. 262.
3. Byron, *Childe Harold*, canto III.
4. See R. Shackleton, 'Allies and Enemies: Voltaire and Montesquieu', in J. Press (ed.), *Essays by Divers Hands*, London, 1977.
5. *Encyclopédie*, Vol. III, art. *'Gens de lettres'*.
6. Voltaire was not banished to England; he was only required to leave Paris. He chose England because, as the British Ambassador, Horace Walpole, explained, he wanted 'to print by subscription an excellent poem called *Henry IV*, which, on account of some bold strokes in it against presentation and the priests, cannot be printed here' (D.295). Voltaire made a great commercial success of his *Henriade* in England; he was one of the few authors who knew how to publish his own works profitably. Professor Haydn Mason writes that 'he recouped a large profit, probably in the region of 30,000 francs (if one includes George I's generous present of 2,000 crowns). If he had arrived in England "without a penny, a stranger, alone, helpless" he would leave it comfortably well off' (Mason, p. 19).
7. To Nicolas Thieriot, 26 October 1726 (D. 303).
8. There are, however, passages where Voltaire seems to subscribe to the same view of freedom as Locke and Montesquieu. He writes, for example: 'Freedom consists in depending on the laws alone. On this basis, every man is free today in Sweden, Holland, Switzerland, Geneva, Hamburg . . . A citizen of Amsterdam is a man; a citizen several degrees of longitude from there is a beast of burden' (*Pensées sur le gouvernement*, *OCV* Vol. XXIII, p. 526).
9. *OCV* Vol. XIX, pp. 295–6. See also Sée, p. 87.
10. *OCV* Vol. XXVIII, p. 421. See also Sée, p. 85.
11. *Let. phil.*, Vol. I, pp. 89–90. See also Sée, p. 86.
12. *OCV* Vol. XXIII, p. 331. See also Sée, p. 89.
13. *Pensées sur le gouvernement*, *OCV* Vol. XXIII.
14. *Let. phil.*, Vol. I, pp. 61 and 74.

15. Ibid. p. 74.

16. Ibid. p. 120.

17. Ibid. p. 106.

18. The letter continues: 'You, as a perfect Briton, should cross the Channel and come to us. I assure you that a man of your temper would not dislike a country where one obeys to the laws only and to one's whims' (D. 330. 11 April 1728).

19. Wade, 1969, p. 151.

20. *OCV* Vol. LXII, pp. 140–9. See also Morley, p. 60.

21. On Voltaire's literary friendships in England see Wade, 1969, pp. 153–72.

22. *OCV* Vol. XXVII, pp. 399–400.

23. 'Voltaire had genuine, deep religious convictions; he was an emotional, even a mystical deist' (Gay, 1959, p. 240).

24. *Socrate*, 1759, III (i).

25. Voltaire's *Poeme sur le désastre de Lisbonne* ends with the hope: 'un jour tout sera bien'. And yet, as Professor Lively has written, 'There is no reason given why this hope should be fulfilled, no programme pointed out by which means its realisation could be ensured' (J. F. Lively, *The Enlightenment*, London, 1966, p. 51).

26. *OCV* Vol. XLIV, p. 47. See also Morley, p. 87.

27. *OCV* Vol. XIX, p. 296. See also Sée, p. 83.

28. 'The *Lettres philosophiques* is the defence of an open middle-class England and an attack on caste-ridden, aristocratic France' (Gay, 1959, p. 55).

29. See J. van den Heuvel (ed.), *L'Affaire Calas*, Paris, 1965.

30. Catholic intolerance of Protestants was especially virulent in the Toulouse area. 'In September 1761 a Protestant minister, François Rochette, was arrested in a village near Montauban and found guilty of having carried on his pastoral duties within the Huguenot assemblies; he was publicly hanged in Toulouse on 19 February 1762. Voltaire, appealed to for assistance by a local Protestant, intervened with his friend the Duc de Richelieu, who was then governor of the neighbouring province of Guyenne, but nothing could be done to save Rochette. It was, however, a significant curtain-raiser to Voltaire's activities when he learned of the execution of Jean Calas' (Mason, p. 98).

31. *Correspondance avec les Tronchin*, ed. André Delattre, Paris, 1950, p. 569.

32. *Dic. phil.*, Vol. II, pp. 277–8.

33. Morley, p. 229.

34. Mason, p. 99.

35. On Voltaire's attitude to homosexuality see Mason, p. 53; and A. O. Aldridge, *Voltaire and the Century of Light*, pp. 66–7. Voltaire

once told Alexander Pope's mother: 'those d . . . d Jesuits, when I was a boy, b . . . d me to such a degree that I shall never get over it as long as I live' (*SVEC* 124 (1974), 113. Voltaire described Frederick to Maupertuis as a 'respectable, singular and lovable prostitute' (D. 2377).

36. *Dic. phil.*, Vol. II, pp. 23–6.

37. *OCV* Vol. XXVII, pp. 347–8.

38. Unlike most of the younger *philosophes*, Voltaire did not even favour universal literacy. In a letter to Damilaville written in 1766, Voltaire said it was not the labourer who should be educated, but the *bon bourgeois* who lived in the town (D. 13232).

39. In Geneva in 1758 Voltaire heard that Madame de Pompadour had declared him *persona non grata* at court: 'it is from this moment', writes Besterman, 'that can be dated his severance from his fatherland' (D.7836, editorial note). Voltaire moved from Geneva to Tournay, just outside the frontier, in time to spend Christmas 1758 in his own 'rather nice kingdom' (D.7988); he moved within a year to the nearby château at Ferney, which remained his home from 1759 until his return to Paris in 1778. Ferney was an ideal situation for Voltaire's estate; he was on French soil, but close enough to Swiss territory to escape quietly if the need arose, and also in an area of France which enjoyed fiscal privileges.

40. Quoted by Peter Gay, *The Party of Humanity*, London, 1970, p. 90.

41. See Wade, 1977, Vol. I, pp. 366–78 and Gay, 1959, pp. 185–238.

42. P. Chaponnière, *Voltaire chez les Calvinistes*, Paris, 1936, p. 210.

43. 'We burned this book. The act of burning it was perhaps as odious as that of writing it' *OCV* Vol. XXIV, p. 424.

44. We must be careful not to exaggerate Voltaire's hedonism. Professor Mason writes 'In keeping with his times, it is not enjoyment that he is defending so much as action; hedonism has its place when the pleasure principle can be made compatible with social utility' (Mason, p. 33).

45. See G. R. Havens (ed.), *Voltaire's Marginalia on the Pages of Rousseau*, Columbus, 1933, p. 15. Voltaire goes on to say: 'Behold the philosophy of a beggar who would like the rich to be robbed by the poor.'

46. See M. Cranston, *Political Dialogues*, London, 1968, p. 69.

47. See Wade, 1947, pp. 48–9.

48. See Wade, 1947, pp. 21–48.

49. Voltaire's *Commentaire sur le livre des délits et des peines* was published at Geneva in 1766. In a letter he wrote to Damilaville in March of that year, Voltaire exclaimed: 'Oh, how I love this philosophy of action and goodwill!' (D.13212).

50. *Œuvres complètes de Voltaire*, Paris, 1785, Vol. 29, p. 213.
51. Voltaire returned to Paris in triumph in 1778; he was 'crowned' at the Comédie-Française on 30 March, only to die on 30 May. The Church authorities went to extraordinary lengths to deny him a decent burial. The Chief of Police allowed his body to be removed from Paris for interment at Ferney. 'After a hasty embalming the body was clad in a nightgown and nightcap, placed in a coach and smuggled out of the capital. In the event, the decision to go to Ferney was cancelled; it was feared that resistance from the Bishop of Annecy might prove insuperable. The abbé Mignot took the corpse to the abbey of Scellières, in Champagne . . . and there he prevailed upon the prior to bury it with due ceremony in the church, pending an eventual transfer to Ferney. As it was, the interment took place only just in time. The Archbishop of Paris . . . wrote with all speed to the Bishop of Troyes urging him to prevent such a burial within the latter's diocese. When this proved to be too late, the abbey prior was made the scapegoat and removed from office' (Mason, p. 150).

## Chapter 3: Rousseau

ABBREVIATIONS

| | |
|---|---|
| *Annales* | *Annales de la Société Jean-Jacques Rousseau*, Geneva, 1905– |
| *CC* | *Correspondance complète de J. J. Rousseau*, ed. R. A. Leigh, Geneva and Oxford, 1965–1984 |
| *DI* | *A Discourse on Inequality*, trans. M. Cranston, New York and Harmondsworth 1984 |
| *JJ* | M. Cranston, *Jean-Jacques: The Early Life and Work of Jean-Jacques Rousseau*, New York and London, 1983 |
| *OC* | *Œuvres complètes de J. J. Rousseau*, ed. B. Gagnebin *et al.*, Paris, 1959– |
| *Reappraisals* | *Reappraisals of Rousseau*, ed. S. Harvey *et al.*, Manchester, 1980 |
| *SC* | *The Social Contract*, trans. M. Cranston, Baltimore and Harmondsworth, 1968 |

1. Most political and legal theorists of the seventeenth and eighteenth centuries subscribed to one form or another of the social contract theory. It fell out of favour with philosophers of the nineteenth century, but has been revived in recent years by theorists as diverse as Jean-Paul Sartre, John Rawls, and Robert Nozick. For a modern criticism of the idea of a social contract see Mortimer

J. Adler, *Ten Philosophical Mistakes*, New York and London, 1985, chapter 9.

2. The full title of this work is *Discours sur l'origine et les fondements de l'inégalité parmi les hommes*, and it was first published in 1755 by Marc-Michel Rey, a Genevan bookseller operating in exile in Amsterdam, where the Press was free, in marked contrast to the strict censorship which prevailed in Geneva. The manuscript of this discourse has disappeared, but some fragments have been traced. See R. A. Leigh, 'Manuscrits disparus de Jean-Jacques Rousseau', *Annales*, XXXIV (1956–8) and the commentary by Jean Starobinski in *OC* Vol. III, pp. 1286–1389.

3. Rousseau's *Essai sur l'origine des langues* was not published in his lifetime and it is not clear when he wrote it. There are, however, good reasons for believing that he began it in the 1750s, when he was concentrating on the theory of music, and returned to it in the 1760s. See Charles Porset, 'L'Inquiétante Étrangeté de l'essai', and Robert Wokler, 'L'Essai en tant que fragment du *Discours sur l'inégalité*', in M. Launay, ed., *Rousseau et Voltaire en 1978*, Geneva, 1981, pp. 145–69. An English translation is available in *On the Origin of Language: Two Essays by J. J. Rousseau and J. G. Herder*, translated by John H. Moran and Alexander Gode, New York, 1966. The best edition of Rousseau's original text is that of Charles Porset, published in Bordeaux and Paris, 1970.

4. *Du Contrat social ou Principes du droit politique par J. J. Rousseau* was first published by Marc-Michel Rey in Amsterdam in 1762. The whereabouts of the manuscript used by Rey is unknown. In the Public and University Library in Geneva there is the manuscript of an earlier draft of the work, and other fragments can be seen in the Municipal Library, Neuchâtel. See Albert Schinz, *Jean-Jacques Rousseau et le libraire-imprimeur Marc-Michel Rey*, Geneva, 1916, and *CC* Vol. III, pp. 49–136.

5. *OC* Vol. I, p. 388.

6. *OC* Vol. I, p. 389.

7. See B. Glass, ed. *Forerunners of Darwin*, Baltimore, 1968; E. Guyénot, *Les Sciences de la vie au XVIIᵉ et XVIIIᵉ siècles*, Paris, 1941.

8. See C. Lévi-Strauss, 'J. J. Rousseau, *fondateur* des sciences de l'homme', in *J. J. Rousseau*, Neuchâtel, 1962, pp. 240 ff; J. Derrida, *De la grammatologie*, Paris, 1967, pp. 149–202; M. Duchet, *Anthropologie et histoire au siècle des lumières*, Paris, 1971; R. Wokler, '*Le Discours sur les sciences et les arts* and its offspring', in *Reappraisals*, pp. 250–78.

9. See Roger Masters, *The Political Philosophy of Rousseau*, Princeton, 1968; Jean Starobinski, *J. J. Rousseau: La Transparence et l'obstacle*, Paris, 1971; John Charvet, *The Social*

*Problem in the Philosophy of Rousseau*, Cambridge, 1974; R. Polin, *La Politique de la solitude*, Paris, 1971; and the special number of *Daedalus* magazine, Vol. 107, No. 3 (Summer, 1978), 'Rousseau for Our Time'.

10. The most thoroughgoing supporter of Rousseau's theory about the relationship between man and the orang-utan was Lord Monboddo. See his *Of the Origin and Progress of Language*, Edinburgh, 1774. See also A. O. Lovejoy, 'Monboddo and Rousseau', in his *Essays on the History of Ideas*, Baltimore, 1948, and R. Wokler, 'The Ape Debates in Enlightenment Anthropology', in *Studies in Voltaire and the Eighteenth Century*, Vol. CXCII (1980), pp. 1164–75.

11. *OC* Vol. III, p. 132; *DI*, p. 78.

12. Thomas Hobbes, *Leviathan* I.13.§11.

13. *OC* Vol. III, pp. 134–5; *DI*, p. 81.

14. Ibid.

15. Rousseau drew on the authority of such explorers and travellers as Peter Kolben, Father du Tetre, Olferet Dapper, Jerome Merolla, Andrew Battel, and others whose reports were published in *Samuel Purchas, his Pilgrimage*, 4 vols., London, 1625, and A. F. Prévost, *Histoire générale des voyages*, 20 vols., Paris, 1746. These writers were largely responsible for promoting the idea of the 'noble savage', which is often associated exclusively with Rousseau's name. But which was widely entertained in the eighteenth century. Rousseau never used the expression 'noble savage', but his close friend Diderot provided a notably idealized picture of what he called the 'noble, sacred character' of the savage in his *Supplément au voyage de Bougainville*. (See *Œuvres complètes de Diderot*, ed J. Assezat and M. Tourneux, Vol, II, Paris, 1875, p. 203).

16. *OC* Vol. III, p. 134; *DI*, p. 82.

17. A veneration for the republics of antiquity was as common among the philosophers of the Enlightenment as it was among those of the Renaissance. On Rousseau's particular attachment to Sparta, see Denise Leduc-Fayette, *J. J. Rousseau et le mythe de l'Antiquité*, Paris, 1974. The more disagreeable features of the Spartan regime—its oppression of subject peoples, for example, and the systematic extermination of helots, to which modern historians draw our attention—were unknown to Rousseau, who as a self-educated man had, in any case, a very imperfect knowledge of ancient history, even by eighteenth-century standards.

18. See Norman Hampson, *The Enlightenment*, Harmondsworth and New York, 1968, pp. 73–96.

19. *OC* Vol. III, p. 141; *DI*, p. 87.

20. *OC* Vol. III, p. 161; *DI*, p. 106.
21. Other philosophers of the French Enlightenment were eager adherents of the doctrine that man was destined to progress from a dark past towards a golden future, a progress which had only been hindered by the superstitions of the Middle Ages. See Robert Nisbet, *History of the Idea of Progress*, New York, 1980.
22. *OC* Vol. III, p. 214; *DI*, p. 161.
23. *OC* Vol. III, p. 147; *DI*, p. 93.
24. Rousseau refers here to Locke's *Two Treatises of Government*, Book III, chapter vii. He read the book in David Mazel's French translation, published in Amsterdam in 1691 and again in Geneva in 1724 as *Du Gouvernement civil*. Rousseau probably derived a more extensive knowledge of Locke's philosophy from his friend, the Abbé de Condillac, who was Locke's chief French disciple. See *JJ*, pp. 217–19.
25. *OC* Vol. III, p. 217; *DI*, p. 165.
26. *OC* Vol. III, p. 216; *DI*, p. 163.
27. 'The oldest of all societies, and the only natural one, is that of the family' (*OC* Vol. III, p. 325; *SC*, p. 50).
28. *OC* Vol. III, p. 151: *DI*, p. 96.
29. *OC* Vol. III, p. 154; *DI*, p. 99. In this passage Rousseau seeks to refute an assertion he ascribes to Hobbes that man is naturally wicked. He is presumably thinking here of *De Cive*, chapter X, §1, where Hobbes argues that in the state of nature brigandage is continual, passions reign, and barbarism, ignorance, and brutality deprive men of the sweetness of life. Rousseau could have read *De Cive* in the French translation of S. Sorbière, first published in 1649 in Amsterdam. But he seems to have owed much of his knowledge of Hobbes's philosophy to conversation with Diderot, who read English. See R. Wokler, *Studies in Voltaire and the Eighteenth Century*, CXXXII (1975), pp. 52–112, and Arthur Wilson, *Diderot*, New York, 1972.
30. *OC* Vol. III, p. 154; *DI*, p. 99.
31. *OC* Vol. III, pp. 155–6; *DI*, p. 101.
32. *OC* Vol. III, p. 156; *DI*, p. 101. In his *Confessions* (*OC* Vol. I, p. 389) he says in a footnote that he took from Diderot this remark about the philosopher putting his hands over his ears to harden his heart against the cries of a man being murdered. But Rousseau himself had written something very similar several years earlier in the preface to his play *Narcisse*: 'The taste for philosophy slackens all bonds of sympathy and goodwill which join a man to society' (*OC* Vol. II, p. 967).
33. *OC* Vol. III, p. 167; *DI*, p. 112.

Notes to Chapter 3

34. Ibid.
35. On Rousseau's vision of an earthly paradise see Ronald Grimsley, *Rousseau and the Religious Quest*, Oxford, 1968, pp. 87–107.
36. *OC* Vol. III, p. 167; *DI*, p. 112.
37. *OC* Vol. III, p. 170; *DI*, p. 115
38. *OC* Vol. III, p. 171; *DI*, p. 115.
39. *Essai sur l'origine des langues*, ed. C. Porset, Bordeaux and Paris, 1970, p. 113. See also R. Polin, *La Politique de la solitude*, Paris, 1971, pp. 1–34.
40. *OC* Vol. III, p. 168; *DI*, p. 113.
41. *OC* Vol. III, p. 170; *DI*, p. 114.
42. *OC* Vol. III, p. 169; *DI*, p. 114.
43. *OC* Vol. III, p. 170; *DI*, p. 114.
44. *OC* Vol. III, p. 219; *DI*, p. 167.
45. See Joel Schwartz, *The Sexual Politics of Jean-Jacques Rousseau*, Chicago and London, 1984, pp. 10–40.
46. *OC* Vol. III, p. 169; *DI*, p. 114.
47. Schwartz, p. 27.
48. *OC* Vol. III, p. 158; *DI*, p. 103.
49. *OC* Vol. III, p. 171; *DI*, p. 116.
50. Ibid.
51. *OC* Vol. III, p. 174; *DI*, p. 118.
52. *OC* Vol. III, p. 176; *DI*, p. 120.
53. Ibid.
54. On the temporal aspects of Rousseau's evolutionary theory see William Pickles, 'The Notion of Time in Rousseau's Political Thought', in M. Cranston and R. S. Peters, eds., *Hobbes and Rousseau*, New York, 1972, pp. 366–400.
55. *OC* Vol. III, p. 177; *DI*, p. 121.
56. *OC* Vol. III, p. 178; *DI*, p. 122.
57. *OC* Vol. III, p. 164; *DI*, p. 109.
58. For the argument that Rousseau is a forerunner of Marx, see Galvano della Volpe, *Rousseau and Marx*, trans. John Fraser, London, 1978. Another commentator who sees Rousseau as a man of the left is Michel Launay, *Jean-Jacques Rousseau, écrivain politique*, Cannes, 1971. For commentaries which draw attention to Rousseau's conservatism see C. E. Vaughan, *Rousseau's Political Writings*, London, 1915, Vol. I, J. Starobinski's notes in *OC* Vol. III, pp. 1285–1389 and the contributions of Bertrand de Jouvenel, John McManners and William Pickles to Cranston and Peters.
59. *OC* Vol. III, p. 203; *DI*, p. 148.
60. Ibid.
61. *OC* Vol. III, p. 203; *DI*, p. 149.

62. *OC* Vol. III, p. 202; *DI*, p. 147.
63. *OC* Vol. III, pp. 188–9; *DI*, p. 132–3.
64. *OC* Vol. III, pp. 193; *DI*, p. 136.
65. *Discours sur cette question: si le rétablissement des Sciences et des Arts a contribué à épurer les mœurs* (*OC*, Vol. III, pp. 1–107, with notes by François Bouchardy, pp. 1237–84). For the circumstances in which Rousseau wrote this prize-winning essay see *JJ*, pp. 230–70. The best English translation is by R. and D. Masters in *J. J. Rousseau: First and Second Discourses*, New York, 1964.
66. Voltaire to Rousseau, 30 August, 1755 (*OC* Vol. III, pp. 1379–81).
67. *OC* Vol. III, p. 111; *DI*, p. 57.
68. Ibid.
69. In *The Social Contract* Rousseau speaks of Calvin as a lawgiver like Lycurgus, but in a fragmentary *History of Geneva* which he wrote soon afterwards, he speaks of Geneva having a constitution whose origin was 'lost in the night of time' and he names an earlier Genevan 'lawgiver' than Calvin, one Bishop Adémarus Fabri, who in 1387 gave the city 'the charter of its rights and liberties' (M. Launay, ed., *Œuvres complètes de J. J. Rousseau*, Paris, 1971, Vol. III, p. 384).
70. See *JJ*, pp. 21–9.
71. *OC* Vol. V, p. 242.
72. *OC* Vol. I, p. 17.
73. *OC* Vol. III, p. 810.
74. T. Hobbes, *Leviathan*, chapter 21.
75. Ibid.
76. *OC* Vol. III, p. 406; *SC*, p. 114.
77. *OC* Vol. III, p. 114; *DI*, p. 60.
78. Ibid.
79. *OC* Vol. III, p. 406; *SC*, p. 115.
80. Ibid.
81. *OC* Vol. III, p. 421; *SC*, p. 131.
82. For up-to-date accounts of Genevan history see Lousi Binz, *Brève histoire de Genève*, Geneva, 1981; R. Guerdan, *Histoire de Genève*, Paris, 1981; and the collective work, *Histoire de Genève des origines à 1798*, published by the Société d'histoire et d'archéologie de Genève, 1951.
83. *Lettre à M. d'Alembert*, ed. Fuchs, Lille, 1948, pp. 181–2; *JJ* p. 26.
84. *OC* Vol. III, p. 1661.
85. *OC* Vol. V, p. 242.
86. *OC* Vol. III, p. 430; *SC*, p. 141.
87. *OC* Vol. III, p. 120; *DI*, p. 65.
88. Schwartz, pp. 10–65.

89. *JJ*, pp. 205-7.
90. *Émile*, trans. A. Bloom, New York, 1979, p. 358.
91. *OC* Vol. III, p. 351; *SC*, p. 49.
92. *OC* Vol. III, p. 364; *SC*, p. 65.
93. *OC* Vol. III, p. 365; *SC*, p. 65.
94. *OC* Vol. III, p. 360; *SC*, p. 60.
95. *OC* Vol. III, p. 364; *SC*, p. 64.
96. *OC* Vol. III, p. 440; *SC*, p. 153.
97. *Émile*, Paris, 1924, p. 270.
98. *OC* Vol. III, p. 371; *SC*, p. 72. Rousseau goes on to say: 'We always want what is advantageous to us, but we do not always discern it.'
99. *OC* Vol. III, p. 381; *SC*, p. 84.
100. See n. 69 above.
101. See B. Baczko, *'Moïse, législateur'*, in *Reappraisals*, pp. 111-31.
102. The quotation comes from Machiavelli's *Discorsi*, I.11.§4
103. *OC* Vol. III, p. 384; *SC*, p. 87.
104. *Lettre à M. d'Alembert*, Amsterdam, 1758, p. 143.
105. Ibid.
106. *OC* Vol. III, p. 466; *SC*, pp. 183-4.
107. *OC* Vol. III, p. 467; *SC*, p. 184.
108. See B. Constant, *Cours de politique constitutionelle*, ed. E. Laboulaye, 2 vols, Paris, 1872.
109. See Stephen Holmes, *Benjamin Constant and the Making of Modern Liberalism*, New Haven, 1984, pp. 28-103.
110. Constant, Vol. II, p. 554.
111. Ibid. p. 541.
112. Ibid. p. 556.
113. Ibid. p. 558.

## Chapter 4: Diderot

ABBREVIATIONS

A-T — J. Assézat et M. Tourneux (eds.), *Œuvres complètes de Diderot*, 20 vols. Paris, 1875-7

*Correspondance* — G. Roth at J. Varloot, (eds.), *Correspondance de Diderot*, 16 vols., Paris, 1955-1970

France — Peter France, *Diderot*, Oxford, 1983

Gay, 1969 — Peter Gay, *The Enlightenment: An Interpretation*, Vol. II, London, 1969

JHM — John Hope Mason, *The Irresistible Diderot*, London, 1982

Jean-Jacques — Maurice Cranston, *Jean-Jacques: The Early Life and Work of Jean-Jacques Rousseau*, London, 1983

| Lewinter | Roger Lewinter (ed.), *D. Diderot: Œuvres complètes*, 15 vols, Paris, 1971 |
| Lough | John Lough (ed.), *Diderot: Selected Philosophical Writings*, Cambridge, 1953 |
| *O. phil.* | *Œuvres philosophiques*, ed. P. Vernière, Paris, 1956 |
| *O. pol.* | *Œuvres politiques*, ed. P. Vernière, Paris, 1963 |
| Proust | Jacques Proust, *Diderot et l'Encyclopédie*, Paris, 1962 |
| Strugnell | A. Strugnell, *Diderot's Politics*, The Hague, 1973 |
| Wade, 1977 | Ira O. Wade, *The Structure and Form of the French Enlightenment*, 2 vols., Princeton, 1977 |
| Wilson | Arthur M. Wilson, *Diderot*, New York, 1972 |

1. Wade, 1977, Vol. II, p. 68.
2. Wilson, pp. 47–58.
3. *Jean-Jacques*, pp. 307–8.
4. Diderot's strong feelings about man's sociability led in the end to his personal break with Rousseau. As Cassirer writes, Diderot 'regarded Rousseau's untameable urge for solitude as a singular quirk. For Diderot needed social intercourse not only as the essential medium for his activity, but also as the spiritual fluid in which alone he was capable of thinking. The will to solitude accordingly appeared to him as nothing less than spiritual and moral aberration. It is well known that Diderot's phrase in the postscript to the *Fils naturel*, that only the evil man loves solitude—a phrase that Rousseau immediately applied to himself and for which he took Diderot to task—gave the first impetus to their break. After this break Diderot's feeling of something uncanny in Rousseau's nature rose until it became almost intolerable. "[He] makes me uneasy" Diderot wrote on the evening of their last meeting, "and I feel as if a damned soul stood beside me . . . I never want to see that man again" ' (E. Cassirer, *The Question of J.-J. Rousseau*, trans. P. Gay, Bloomington, 1963, p. 91).
5. Proust, pp. 371–2.
6. This book was written when Diderot was 59, in 1772, immediately after the publication of Bougainville's *Voyage autour du monde*. Diderot circulated copies of his text, but the book was not published until 1796.
7. A–T Vol. VI, p. 439.
8. F. Bacon, *The Great Instauration*, preface. On Bacon's influence on Diderot's idea of an encyclopaedia see Mortimer Adler, *A Guidebook to Learning*. New York and London, 1986, pp. 52–63.
9. *Correspondance*, 29 September 1762
10. The various publishers of the *Encyclopédie* had produced about

24,000 copies before 1789. See Robert Darton, *L'Aventure de l'Encyclopédie*, Paris, 1982, p. 47.

11. *O. phil.*, p. 112 (JHM, p. 7).
12. *Correspondance*, No. 1213; France, p. 59.
13. To Paul Landois, 1756; France, p. 80.
14. Diderot, *Salons*, ed. J. Seznec and J. Adhémar, 3 vols, Oxford, 1957–67, Vol. II, p. 147.
15. *Encyclopédie*, Vol. V (1755), p. 212.
16. Ibid. p. 281.
17. A–T Vol. II, p. 430.
18. See Proust, p. 482.
19. A–T Vol. II, pp. 427 ff.
20. Strugnell, p. 67.
21. *O. pol.*, p. 85.
22. 'Le droit de propriété est sacré de particulier à particulier . . . C'est le contraire de ce droit de particulier relativement à la société. Car si c'était quelque chose de sacré, il ne se ferait rien de grand, d'utile dans cette société' (*Apologie de l'Abbé Galiani*, A–T, Vol. VIII, p. 778).
23. 'Facts, of whatever kind, constitute the philosopher's true wealth' (*O. phil.*, p. 191).
24. *Pensées*, § XXX (Lough, p. 45 and JHM, p. 58).
25. *O. phil.*, p. 218 (JHM, p. 58).
26. *Pensées* §XII (Lough, p. 38 and JHM, p. 64).
27. *Correspondance*, Vol. V, p. 27 (Strugnell, p. 108).
28. *Correspondance*, Vol. VII, p. 87.
29. *O. pol.*, p. 18.
30. Lewinter, Vol. X, p. 103 (JHM, p. 333).
31. Ibid. p. 529 (JHM, p. 331).
32. Ibid. p. 550 (JHM, p. 331).
33. Ibid. p. 558 (JHM, p. 331). As late as the year 1769 Diderot had welcomed Voltaire's attack on the Paris *parlement* and argued only that it was not far-reaching enough, since that *parlement* was the greatest enemy in France 'of all liberty, be it civil or religious' (Gay, 1969, p. 480). But when the government of Maupeou banished the Paris *parlement* to Voltaire's great joy in 1771, Diderot protested vehemently; the *parlements*, he now declared, were a bastion of freedom, a 'corrective principle preventing monarchy from degenerating into despotism' (JHM, p. 482).
34. *Observations*, §I (JHM, p. 335).
35. *Observations*, §XIII (JHM, p. 337).
36. *Observations*, §VIII (JHM, p. 337).
37. *Observations*, §III (JHM, p. 336).
38. Wilson, p. 636.

39. Louis-Philippe Ségur, *Mémoires* (Vol. III, pp. 34–5 English edition), quoted by Vernière in *O. pol.*, p. 219.
40. Ibid.
41. Diderot told Madame Necker 'Our *philosophes*, who give the impression of having known what despotism is, have seen it only through the neck of a bottle. What a difference there is between a tiger painted by Oudry and a tiger in the forest' (France, p. 13).
42. A–T Vol. VI, p. 448 (Strugnell, p. 140).
43. *Histoire philosophique et politique des deux Indes*, Paris, 10 vols, 1795–96, Vol. IX, p. 239 (Strugnell, p. 213).
44. Diderot was not well known to American readers. According to Paul Merrill Spurlin his writings 'did not enjoy any wide dissemination here. The diffusion of his books could not compare with the spread of those of Voltaire, Rousseau and Montesquieu' (*The French Enlightenment in America*, Athens, Georgia, 1984, p. 112).
45. The *Histoire philosophique et politique des deux Indes* was a work which enjoyed at the end of the eighteenth century a success which, if now forgotten, was comparable at the time to that of the *Encyclopédie* itself. See J.-C. Bonnet, *Diderot*, Paris, 1984, pp. 306–45. Diderot revised the second edition of this work and rewrote the third. See Michèle Duchet, *Diderot et l'Histoire des deux Indes*, Paris, 1978.
46. JHM, p. 357.
47. See Yves Benot, *Diderot, de l'athéisme à l'anticolonialisme*, Paris, 1970, p. 196.
48. *Œuvres complètes de J. J. Rousseau*, ed. B. Gagnebin *et al.*, Vol. III, Paris, 1964, p. 200.
49. *Histoire des deux Indes*, 1781 edn., Vol. I, pp. 178 and 180 (see also Benot, pp. 176–7).
50. *Histoire des deux Indes*, 1783 edn., Vol. IX, p. 116 (JHM, p. 355).

## Chapter 5: Holbach

ABBREVIATIONS

| | |
|---|---|
| *Éléments* | *Éléments de la morale universelle*, Paris, 1790 |
| *Éth.* | *Éthocratie*, Amsterdam, 1776 |
| *Mor. univ.* | *La Morale universelle*, 3 vols., Amsterdam, 1776 |
| Naville | Pierre Naville, *D'Holbach et la philosophie scientifique au XVIII<sup>e</sup> siècle*, Paris, 1967 |
| *Pol. nat.* | *Politique naturelle*, 3 vols., London, 1773 |
| *S. nat.* | *Système de la nature*, 2 vols., London, 1781 |
| *S. soc.* | *Système social*, 2 vols., Paris, 1822 |

Topazio    Virgil W. Topazio, *D'Holbach's Moral Philosophy*, Geneva, 1956

Wickwar    W. H. Wickwar, *Baron d'Holbach*, London, 1935

1. Diderot, *Correspondance inédite*, 2 vols, Paris, 1883, Vol II, p. 94.

2. See John Lough, *Essay on the Encyclopédie*, London, 1968, pp. 111–229.

3. *Œuvres complètes de J. J. Rousseau*, ed. B. Gagnebin *et al.*, Paris, 1959–, Vol. I, p. 371. For evidence of Holbach's nobility see Naville, pp. 24–5.

4. André Babelon (ed.), *Lettres à Sophie Volland*, 3 vols, Paris, 1930, Vol. I, p. 92.

5. Cited by Naville, p. 61.

6. See Topazio, pp. 117–32.

7. *Pol. nat.* Book II, pp. 78–9.

8. *S. nat.* Vol. I, p. 142.

9. Ibid. p. 82.

10. Ibid. p. 179.

11. Cited in Edgar Faure, *Le disgrâce de Turgot*, Paris, 1961, p. 499.

12. Cited in Yves Benot, *Diderot, de l'athéisme à l'anticolonialisme*, Paris, 1970, pp. 44–6.

13. *S. nat.* Vol. I, p. 217.

14. 'A perpetually open mind became a perpetually vacant mind and therefore useless. Achievements are the results of positive actions, and scepticism by its very nature disastrously paralysed man in a state of inaction, and led to a society of indifferent spectators' (Topazio, p. 160).

15. *S. nat.* Vol. II, pp. 342–3.

16. See J. Lough, *Revue d'histoire littéraire*, Vol. XLI, No. 222, 143.

17. *S. soc.* Vol. I, pp. 66–7. See also Topazio, pp. 143–8.

18. 'Liberty is . . . the power to do for one's happiness all that is allowed by the nature of man in society . . . The good of society as a whole ought therefore to be the measure of the liberty of its members' (Wickwar, p. 184).

19. *S. soc.* Vol. II, pp. 29–43.

20. *Éth.* pp. 12–13.

21. *Éth.* pp. 168.

22. 'The purpose of government is to make men practise virtue. An ethical code can only invite people to do good; the government can, however, either compel them by law or encourage them with rewards and benefits' (*S. soc.* Vol. I, p. x. See also *Éléments*, p. 64).

23. *Éth*. p. 22.
24. *Éth*. p. 28.
25. Ibid.
26. Ibid. p. 46.
27. Ibid. p. 113.
28. 'The chimera of equality, so adored in democratic states, is totally incompatible with our nature' (*S. soc*. Vol. I, p. 355).
29. *Pol. nat*. Book I, p. 38 ('Since men's strength is unequal, their labour will be unequal; hence their property will also be unequal').
30. Wickwar, p. 176.
31. *Éléments*, p. 162.
32. *Mor. univ*. Book IV, chap. viii.
33. Wickwar, p. 180.
34. Ibid. p. 212.
35. Ibid. p. 204.
36. 'Here, ye Britons, is the cause of your misfortunes' (Wickwar, p. 211).
37. *S. soc*. Vol. II, pp. 278–98.
38. *Mor. univ*. Book IV, xi.
39. *Pol. nat*. Book II, pp. 242–62.
40. *Éth*. p. 126.
41. Ibid. pp. 127–43.
42. Ibid. p. 143.
43. Ibid. p. 253.
44. See Wickwar, p. 192.
45. *Pol. nat*. Book V, xxvii.
46. Ibid. Book IV, vii.
47. Ibid. Book V, xxx.
48. Wickwar, p. 193.
49. *Pol. nat*. Book III, xix.
50. 'The citizen cannot judge the sovereign: only society has the right' (*Éléments*, p. 78).
51. *Éth*. p. 16.
52. For Holbach's conception of a purified nobility see *Éth*. pp. 43–57.
53. *S. soc*. Vol. II, p. 32.
54. See Naville, pp. 399–403.
55. On Diderot's influence on Holbach, see Topazio, pp. 87–116.
56. See Naville, p. 387.
57. See Wickwar, p. 199.

## Chapter 6: Condorcet

ABBREVIATIONS

| | |
|---|---|
| Baker | K. M. Baker, *Condorcet: From Natural Philosophy to Social Mathematics*, Chicago, 1975 |
| SW | *Selected Writings of Condorcet*, ed. K. M. Baker, New York, 1975 |
| Gourevitch | Victor Gourevitch, 'Condorcet', in *International Studies in Philosophy*, Vol. XI, 1979, 157–64 |
| RHP | *Recherches historiques et politiques sur les États-Unis*, 4 vols., Colle, 1788 |
| Sketch | *Sketch for an Historical Picture of the Human Mind*, trans. J. Barraclough, London, 1953 |

1. L. Cahen, *Condorcet et la révolution française*, Paris, 1904, pp. 137–8.
2. The main sources of manuscript material are the library of the Institut de France and the Bibliothèque Nationale in Paris; the Palais des Arts in Lyons; the Academy of Bordeaux; the Boston Public Library; and the American Philosophical Society. The *Œuvres de Condorcet*, edited by Arago and O'Connor, remains the 'standard' edition, but it is far from complete, and many of Condorcet's writings on political and social theory are available only in their original editions.
3. This honour prompted Condorcet to write 'Quatre lettres d'un bourgeois de New Heaven [sic] sur l'unité de la legislation', published in *Recherches historiques et politiques sur les États-Unis* by a 'Citoyen de Virginie' (identified as Filippo Mazzei (1730–1816) in the copy preserved at the Beinecke Library, Yale).
4. Cahen, pp. 137–8.
5. K. M. Baker, 'Condorcet', in P. Edwards (ed.), *Encyclopaedia of Philosophy*, 8 volumes, New York, 1967, Vol. II, p. 183.
6. Ibid.
7. Ibid. p. 184.
8. *RHP* Vol. I, p. 268 (in French).
9. *Sketch*, p. 136.
10. As Gourevitch remarks, *truth* 'is the common theme of his projects for the reorganisation of the Academy of Sciences and for the reform of the Provincial Assemblies of the *ancien régime*, of his more formal studies of voting, of his 1793 draft of a Constitution, as well as of the *Sketch for an Historical Picture of the Human Mind*. It is also the basis of his repeated proposals for detailed quantitative records to monitor all aspects of the nation's social and economic life' (Gourevitch, p. 157).

11. *Sketch*, p. 193.
12. Baker, p. 236.
13. *SW*, p. 74.
14. *Essai sur la constitution*, 1788, Vol. I, p. 3. 'Condorcet's analysis of the probabilities with which electorates of different degrees of enlightenment will elect "true" representatives, and of the probabilities that these representatives will vote for "true" policies or decisions, is widely regarded as his most important contribution to positive knowledge' (Gourevitch, p. 158).
15. *SW*, p. 34.
16. Baker, p. 274.
17. Masuyer, quoted in Roger Hahn, *The Anatomy of a Scientific Institution: Paris Academy of Sciences*, Berkeley, 1971, p. 222.
18. Condorcet vigorously rejected the argument of Voltaire and others that education ought to be confined to the property-owning classes. He wanted elementary education to be available without charge to anyone who wanted it, so that ordinary people should learn what it meant to be a citizen and to have rights, and thus be given a start on the ladder towards a superior culture.
19. Baker, p. 294.
20. *RHP*, p. 282.
21. Ibid. p. 286.
22. See Gourevitch, p. 159. Despite the feminist arguments of his theoretical writings, Condorcet's *projet de constitution* did not even extend the vote to women.
23. See Alexandre Koyré, 'Condorcet', *Journal of the History of Ideas*, Vol. IX (1948), p. 151.
24. Charles Frankel, *The Faith of Reason*, New York, 1947, p. 122.
25. Quoted in Frankel, p. 128.
26. See H. Vyverberg, *Historical Pessimism in the French Enlightenment*, Cambridge, Mass., 1958, p. 69.
27. Quoted in Vyverberg, p. 70.
28. Quoted in Frankel, p. 143. Despite this criticism of Condorcet, Comte himself depicted human history as a progressive movement from one stage to another—from the theological to the metaphysical, and on to the positivistic.
29. *Sketch*, p. 179.
30. Ibid. p. 188.
31. Ibid. p. 195.
32. Ibid. p. 197.

# Further Reading

GENERAL

The best introduction to the history of the Enlightenment is Norman Hampson, *The Enlightenment*, New York and Harmondsworth, 1968. The best introduction to the thought of the period is J. H. Brumfitt, *The French Enlightenment*, London, 1972. There is no general work in English on the political theory of the Enlightenment, but important elements of it are dealt with by Peter Gay in *The Party of Humanity*, London, 1970, and the second volume of the same author's *The Enlightenment: An Interpretation*, 2 vols, London, 1969. The latter also contains an extensive bibliography. Ronald Grimsley (ed.), *The Age of Enlightenment*, Harmondsworth, 1979, contains some excellent critical chapters on individual *philosophes*, and J. F. Lively, *The Enlightenment*, London, 1966, contains excerpts in translation from some of their works.

Charles Frankel, *The Faith of Reason*, New York, 1947, and G. R. Havens, *The Age of Ideas*, New York, 1955, both provide a fairly sympathetic account of Enlightenment thought from an American perspective, and Ernst Cassirer's *The Philosophy of the Enlightenment*, Princeton, 1951, a liberal Kantian German view, not dissimilar in its general approach to that of Cassirer's pupil Peter Gay. Among the numerous publications on the Enlightenment by Ira O. Wade, his *Intellectual Origins of the French Enlightenment*, Princeton, 1971, is of particular importance. Alfred Cobban, *In Search of Humanity*, London, 1960, provides a spirited defence of the ethos of the Enlightenment, as does Kingsley Martin's outdated, but readable, *French Liberal Thought in the Eighteenth Century*, London, 1929.

MONTESQUIEU

Most of Montesquieu's books have been translated into English, and the best biography of Montesquieu in any language is Robert Shackleton, *Montesquieu*, Oxford, 1961. Translations that can be recommended include: *The Spirit of the Laws*, London, 1750; *The Persian Letters*, Harmondsworth, 1973; *Reflections on the Causes of the Grandeur and the Declension of the Romans*, London, 1748. A well-informed critical commentary is provided by Thomas L. Pangle, *Montesquieu's Philosophy of Liberalism*, New York, 1974. Mark Hulliung, *Montesquieu and the Old Regime*, New York, 1976, seeks to place Montesquieu in the context of the political experience of his own time. Norman Hampson,

*Will and Circumstance: Montesquieu and Rousseau*, London, 1983, discusses Montesquieu (with Rousseau) in relation to the ideology of the French Revolution. John A. Baum, *Montesquieu and Social Theory*, New York, 1979, introduces Montesquieu as a founder of sociology.

## VOLTAIRE

An admirably lucid analysis of Voltaire's political theory is given in Peter Gay, *Voltaire's Politics*, Princeton, 1959, and a brilliant account of his life and ideas in general by Haydn Mason in *Voltaire: A Biography*, London, 1981. A more detailed and more ponderous study is Ira O. Wade, *The Intellectual Development of Voltaire*, Princeton, 1969. Virgil W. Topazio, *Voltaire: A Critical Study of his Major Works*, can be recommended as a commentary on Voltaire's writings as a whole, and J. H. Brumfitt, *Voltaire, Historian*, London, 1970, as an appraisal of the historical writings. David D. Bien, *The Calas Affair*, Princeton, 1960, discusses Voltaire's activities as a champion of toleration.

Many, but by no means all, of Voltaire's books have been translated into English. The most important for the student of his political ideas are: *Philosophical Dictionary*, London, 1945; *Philosophical Letters*, London, 1738; *Philosophy of History*, London, 1965; *The Century of Louis XIV*, London, 1966; *Notebooks*, ed. T. Besterman, Oxford, 1958. *Studies in Voltaire and the Eighteenth Century*, published by the Voltaire Foundation, Oxford at irregular intervals since 1955, contains important material for the student of Voltaire and Enlightenment thought in general.

## ROUSSEAU

Rousseau's political writings have been translated into English on several occasions since their publication in French. The most up-to-date translations are: *The Social Contract*, Baltimore and Harmondsworth, 1968; *A Discourse on Inequality*, Harmondsworth and New York, 1984; *The Reveries of a Solitary Walker*, Harmondsworth and New York, 1985; *The First and Second Discourses*, New York, 1964; *The Government of Poland*, New York, 1972; *Politics and the Arts*, Glencoe, 1960; *Émile*, New York, 1979; *The Origin of Languages*, New York, 1966; *Confessions*, Harmondsworth, 1953. *The Indispensable Rousseau*, ed. J. H. Mason, London, 1979, contains translations from Rousseau's less accessible works.

James Miller, *Rousseau; Dreamer of Democracy*, New Haven, 1984, is a useful introductory work which takes full account of recent scholarship. John Charvet, *The Social Problem in the Philosophy of Rousseau*, Cambridge, 1974, offers a penetrating critique of Rousseau's social and political theory. Roger Masters, *The Political Philosophy of Rousseau*,

Princeton, 1968, is a carefully argued analysis of the text. C. W. Hendel, *Jean-Jacques Rousseau, Moralist*, London, 1934, is still useful as a general survey of Rousseau's thought. Joel Schwartz, *The Sexual Politics of Jean-Jacques Rousseau*, Chicago and London, 1984, is a pioneering study of a neglected aspect of Rousseau's social theory. R. Grimsley, *The Philosophy of Rousseau*, Oxford, 1973, is an excellent exposition of Rousseau's moral and religious ideas; Maurice Cranston, *Jean-Jacques: The Early Life and Work of Jean-Jacques Rousseau*, London, 1983, is the most up-to-date biography.

DIDEROT

Diderot has been more fortunate than most *encyclopédistes* in his translators, especially in view of the unsatisfactory nature of the original editions of his works. John Hope Mason, *The Irresistible Diderot*, London, 1982, contains excerpts in English from most of the writings of interest to students of Diderot's politics. *Selected Writings*, ed. L. G. Croker, New York, 1966, is also useful. Other translations that can be recommended are: *Rameau's Nephew and Other Works*, Indianapolis, 1964; *The Nun*, Harmondsworth, 1974; *Jacques the Fatalist*, New York, 1959; *Early Philosophical Works*, Chicago, 1916; *Letters to Sophie Volland*, London, 1972. John Lough, *The Encyclopaedia of Diderot and d'Alembert*, Cambridge, 1954, contains a good sample of Diderot's work for the *Encyclopédie*.

Peter France, *Diderot*, Oxford, 1983, is an exemplary introductory essay, and the same author has more to say about Diderot in his *Rhetoric and Truth in France*, Oxford, 1972. Arthur M. Wilson, *Diderot*, New York, 1972, is the best available biography. A. Vartanian, *Diderot and Descartes*, Princeton, 1953, is an important study of Diderot's rationalism, and A. Strugnell, *Diderot's Politics*, The Hague, 1973, the most thorough treatment in English of Diderot's political ideas. The reader should also consult the chapter on Diderot in R. Niklaus, *A Literary History of France*, London, 1970. The periodical *Diderot Studies* has since 1949 carried occasional articles in English.

HOLBACH

Holbach's works have never been published in collected form, but several of the most important were translated into English soon after they were first published in French. These include: *The System of Nature*, London, 1796; *Common Sense*, New York, 1795; *Christianity Unveiled*, London, 1795. Later reprints of these translations are almost as difficult to find as are the first editions.

Two modern commentaries on Holbach that can be recommended are W. H. Wickwar, *Baron d'Holbach*, London, 1935, and Virgil

W. Topazio, *D'Holbach's Moral Philosophy*, Geneva, 1956. Alan C. Kors, *D'Holbach's Coterie*, Princeton, 1976, is a well-researched study of Holbach's relations with other *encyclopédistes*. Max P. Cushing, *Baron d'Holbach*, New York, 1914, is still useful. Students of Holbach's thought will find much that is of interest in John McManners, *Death and the Enlightenment*, Oxford, 1981, and Robert Darnton, *The Literary Underground of the Old Regime*, Cambridge, Mass., 1982.

## CONDORCET

Very few of Condorcet's writings have been translated into English, but the *Esquisse* has been translated more than once, most recently as *Sketch for an Historical Picture of the Human Mind*, London, 1953, with an introduction by Stuart Hampshire. *Selected Writings of Condorcet*, ed. K. M. Baker, New York, 1975, contains much that is relevant to the study of his political theory.

An excellent commentary in English is K. M. Baker, *Condorcet: From Natural Philosophy to Social Mathematics*, Chicago, 1975. J. S. Schapiro, *Condorcet and the Rise of Liberalism*, New York, 1934, provides an instructive appraisal of Condorcet's place in the history of liberal thought. There is a good section on Condorcet in Frank E. Manuel, *The Prophets of Paris*, Cambridge, Mass., 1962, and H. Vyverberg, *Historical Pessimism in the French Enlightenment*, Cambridge, Mass., 1959, throws a curious light on Condorcet's theory of progress. L. C. Rosenfeld (ed.), *Condorcet Studies*, Atlantic Highlands, NJ, 1984, is the first of what promises to be a series of essays on Condorcet's thought.

# Index

OXFORD

## MORE OXFORD PAPERBACKS

Details of a selection of other books follow. A complete list of Oxford Paperbacks, including The World's Classics, Twentieth-Century Classics, OPUS, Past Masters, Oxford Authors, Oxford Shakespeare, and Oxford Paperback Reference, is available in the UK from the General Publicity Department, Oxford University Press (JH), Walton Street, Oxford OX2 6DP.

In the USA, complete lists are available from the Paperbacks Marketing Manager, Oxford University Press, 200 Madison Avenue, New York, NY 10016.

Oxford Paperbacks are available from all good bookshops. In case of difficulty, customers in the UK can order direct from Oxford University Press Bookshop, 116 High Street, Oxford, Freepost, OX1 4BR, enclosing full payment. Please add 10 per cent of published price for postage and packing.

# DEATH AND THE ENLIGHTENMENT
## Changing Attitudes to Death in Eighteenth-Century France

### *John McManners*

In eighteenth-century France death was at the centre of life as the graveyard was at the centre of the village. Most died before middle age, falling victim to disease, accident, or malnutrition, if not to riot or public execution. How did people assess their chances of survival? Professor McManners brilliantly describes how both Christians and unbelievers faced the tragedy 'that comes to us all and makes us all equal when it comes'.

'a fascinating vade-mecum into archives of eighteenth-century France' Isabel Butterfield, *The Times*

'a magisterial and very moving history' Sean French, *Sunday Times*

'a learned and scholarly book with not a page in it that is arid' Owen Chadwick, *Times Literary Supplement*

## FRANCE 1848–1945

### *Theodore Zeldin*

'One of the major historical works of our collective lifetime . . . brilliantly stimulating.' *Listener*

'The most enjoyable book of its kind in nearly forty years.' *New Statesman*

'Masterpieces of the historian's art are rare in any generation. Zeldin's *France* belongs in that category. It is a stunning achievement, a monument of scholarship.' *Times Literary Supplement*

These are just a few of the tributes critics have paid to Theodore Zeldin and his magnificent study *France 1848–1945*. The original two-volume hardback edition is available in five paperback volumes:

Ambition and Love
Anxiety and Hypocrisy
Intellect and Pride
Politics and Anger
Taste and Corruption

# REVOLUTION AND REVOLUTIONARIES

## A. J. P. Taylor

Violent political upheavals have occurred as long as there have been political communities. But, in Europe, only since the French Revolution have they sought not merely to change the rulers but to transform the entire social and political system. One of A. J. P. Taylor's themes in this generously illustrated book, is that revolutions and revolutionaries do not always coincide: those who start them often do so unintentionally, while revolutionaries tend to be most active in periods of counter-revolution. He traces the line of development of the revolutionary tradition from 1789 through Chartism, the social and national upheavals of 1848, the 'revolutionaries without a revolution' of the following sixty years—Marx, Engels, Bakunin, and others—to the Bolshevik seizure of power in 1917.

# THE FRENCH REVOLUTION

## J. M. Roberts

Dr Roberts studies the puzzling nature of what came to be called the French Revolution, with its Janus-like aspect, looking to past and future at the same time. The five main sections of the book deal with the beginnings of the Revolution; the Revolution in France seen as a great disruption; the Revolution in France as the vehicle of continuity; the Revolution abroad; and the Revolution as history and as myth. There is also a review of recent scholarship in the field.

This lively and authoritative book, which will appeal to the general reader and student of history alike, makes a significant original contribution to our understanding of the French Revolution.

'Dr Roberts has packed a great deal into a short space and his great knowledge and lucid style make this into an excellent introduction to a complex subject.' *British Book News*

'deserves to become a classic' *Journal of European Studies*

An OPUS book

# THE POLICE AND THE PEOPLE

French Popular Protest 1789–1820

*Richard Cobb*

'One has come to expect from Mr Cobb's work a combination of erudition, verve, originality and eminent readability and those who approach this volume with these expectations will be in no way disappointed. It falls into three parts, each an entity in itself: the first a critical and humorous discussion of the sources at the disposal of the popular historian, the second a study of the manifold expressions of popular protest, and the last a moving analysis of popular response to 'dearth' meaning, in its eighteenth-century context, extreme scarcity of food often resulting in famine, plague, and other such horrors. . . The result is a work teeming in humanity and with the infinite variety of a Breughel canvas.' *English Historical Review*

# EARLY MODERN FRANCE

## 1560–1715

*Robin Briggs*

This book provides an overall interpretation of a decisive period in French history, from the chaos of the Wars of Religion to the death of Louis XIV. A clear but economical narrative of the major political events is combined with an analysis of the long-term factors which decisively moulded the evolution of both state and society.

'A very fine, thorough and conscientious study of a formative period of French History . . . his account of the French provinces in the age of Richelieu and Louis XIV . . . is one of the best things of its kind in English.' *Sunday Telegraph*

'this vigorously-written book deserves wide use as an introduction to absolutist France' *History*

An OPUS book

## KARL MARX: HIS LIFE AND ENVIRONMENT

*Isaiah Berlin*

### Fourth edition

Isaiah Berlin's brilliant account of the life and doctrines of the author of *Das Kapital* has long been established as a classic of intellectual biography. It provides a lucid, comprehensive introduction to the traditional Marx—his personality and ideas as they were understood by those who, in his name and guided by his ideas, made the revolutions which transformed the world. For this new edition the author has written a new preface, revised the text throughout, and added a number of fresh passages.

'As a portrait of the man and the intellectual climate of the mid-nineteenth century it is, perhaps, the finest we have in any European language.' Chimen Abramsky

An OPUS book

## RECOLLECTIONS OF WITTGENSTEIN

*Edited by Rush Rhees*

### Introduction by Norman Malcolm

Ludwig Wittgenstein's works argue his status as one of the greatest philosophers ever. He was also a man of exceptional personal qualities who both disturbed and inspired those with whom he came into contact. In this book five people who knew him well—his sister Hermine, fellow don F. R. Leavis, his teacher Fania Pascal, and two of his pupils—give their recollections of a fascinating and often baffling man.

'Rush Rhees has put together a wonderful book.' Norman Malcolm; *London Review of Books*

## LUDWIG WITTGENSTEIN—A Memoir

*Norman Malcolm with a biographical sketch by G. H. Von Wright*

Norman Malcolm, a close friend of Wittgenstein, wrote this personal memoir of a gifted, difficult man in 1958. Although Wittgenstein is widely acknowledged as a powerful influence on contemporary philosophy, he shunned publicity and was essentially a private man. The fifty-seven letters, written by Wittgenstein to Malcolm, contained in this new edition reveal Wittgenstein as a warm, affectionate, and caring man.

'A reader does not need to care about philosophy to be excited by Mr Malcolm's book; it is about Wittgenstein as a man, and its interest is human interest.' *Guardian*

## THE AGE OF ENLIGHTENMENT

### The Eighteenth-Century Philosophers

*Edited by Isaiah Berlin*

'The intellectual power, honesty, lucidity, courage, and disinterested love of the truth of the most gifted thinkers of the eighteenth century remain to this day without parallel. Their age is one of the best and most helpful episodes in the life of mankind.' These are the closing words of Isaiah Berlin's introduction to his selection from and commentary on the basic writings of Locke, Berkeley, Hume, and other eighteenth-century philosophers.

# CONCEPTS AND CATEGORIES

*Isaiah Berlin*

## With an introduction by Bernard Williams

This second volume of Isaiah Berlin's four-volume *Selected Writings* contains most of his philosophical essays, apart from those already reissued in *Four Essays on Liberty*. It includes his early arguments against logical positivism, and later essays which more evidently reflect his lifelong interest in political theory, the history of ideas, and the philosophy of history. And in two related pieces he gives his view of the nature of philosophy's task, best summed up in his own words: 'The goal of philosophy is always the same, to assist men to understand themselves and thus operate in the open, and not wildly, in the dark.'

'No one writes about large and abstract matters in a more richly nutritive and idiosyncratic way.' Anthony Quinton

'Isaiah Berlin's many admirers and readers will be glad to have this book; and those too young to have had the chance to listen to his lectures might well begin their acquaintance by reading it.' *British Book News*

# PLATO

*R. M. Hare*

Even after twenty-three centuries, Plato's work remains the starting-point for the study of logic, metaphysics, and moral and political philosophy. But though his dialogues retain their freshness and immediacy, they can be difficult to follow. R. M. Hare has provided a short introduction to Plato's work that makes their meaning clear.

'in less then ninety pages [R. M. Hare] makes [this] monumental subject real, intelligible, and interesting' *Times Literary Supplement*

Past Masters

# VICO

### Peter Burke

Vico was one of the most original thinkers of the eighteenth century. In his book, Peter Burke seeks to unravel Vico's ideas and to explain their appeal to posterity. Whereas most books about Vico tend to present him as a forerunner in the evolution of modern attitudes, this book places him in his cultural and social context and shows that he was attempting, in his distinctive way, to solve the main intellectual problems of his own time.

Past Masters

# JOHN LOCKE

### Maurice Cranston

This masterly work, winner of the James Tait Black Memorial Prize, is the definitive biography of John Locke, the world's foremost philosopher of liberalism and toleration.

'a magnificent biography of a man of the greatest importance to Western civilization' E. S. de Beer, *Daily Telegraph*

'a model of discriminating scholarship, detached, critical, urbane and civilized' *Times Literary Supplement*

Past Masters

# DIDEROT

## Peter France

Denis Diderot was one of the most brilliant minds of the French Enlightenment, on which his editorship of the *Encyclopedia* gave him a unique vantage-point. In no man were the currents of eighteenth-century thought more intensely present.

This book takes account of the full range of Diderot's writing, from politics to the theatre, from physiology to painting. It stresses the critical impulse which lies at the heart of his work, and pays particular attention to the complexity of his writing, with its manifold and often contradictory voices, and to the nature of his demands on his readers.

'*Diderot* is a provocative study which makes a genuine attempt to give a rapid appraisal of Diderot's breadth. The book never fails to interest.' *Journal of European Studies*

Past Masters

# MARX

## Peter Singer

Peter Singer identifies the central vision that unifies Marx's thought, enabling us to grasp Marx's views as a whole. He views him as a philosopher primarily concerned with human freedom, rather than as an economist or social scientist. He explains alienation, historical materialism, the economic theory of *Capital,* and Marx's idea of communism, in plain English, and concludes with a balanced assessment of Marx's achievement.

'an admirably balanced portrait of the man and his achievement' *Observer*

Past Masters

# MACHIAVELLI

## Quentin Skinner

Niccolò Machiavelli taught that political leaders must be prepared to do evil that good may come of it, and his name has been a byword ever since for duplicity and immorality. Is his sinister reputation really deserved? In answering this question Quentin Skinner focuses on three major works, *The Prince*, the *Discourses*, and *The History of Florence*, and distils from them an introduction to Machiavelli's doctrines of exemplary clarity.

'without doubt the best short account of the author of "The Prince" that we are likely to see for some time: a model of clarity and good judgement' *Sunday Times*

'compulsive reading' *New Society*

Past Masters

# LOCKE

## John Dunn

Although John Locke's *Essay concerning Human Understanding*, in which he set out his theory that men's knowledge reaches them exclusively through their senses, is his best-known and most admired work, it is still curiously misunderstood. By restoring Locke's theory of knowledge to its proper context, John Dunn explains how Locke came to the conclusions he did, and why his views on this fundamental question have so profoundly influenced later generations of philosophers and natural scientists. He also explores Locke's exposition of the liberal values of tolerance and responsible government which was to become the backbone of enlightened European thought in the eighteenth century.

'In eighty lucid and lively pages Dunn has stripped the myths and given us a new key to Locke.' *New Society*

Past Masters